FULL CONTACT

new interchange

English for international communication

Jack C. Richards

with Jonathan Hull, Susan Proctor, & Charles Shields

student's

1

book

CAMBRIDGE
UNIVERSITY PRESS

PUBLISHED BY THE PRESS SYNDICATE OF THE UNIVERSITY OF CAMBRIDGE
The Pitt Building, Trumpington Street, Cambridge, United Kingdom

CAMBRIDGE UNIVERSITY PRESS
The Edinburgh Building, Cambridge CB2 2RU, UK
40 West 20th Street, New York, NY 10011–4211, USA
477 Williamstown Road, Port Melbourne, VIC 3207, Australia
Ruiz de Alarcón 13, 28014 Madrid, Spain
Dock House, The Waterfront, Cape Town 8001, South Africa

http://www.cambridge.org

Student's Book 1 first published 1997
Video Activity Book 1 first published 1997
Workbook 1 first published 1997
CD-ROM first published 1998

Full Contact edition first published 2003
3rd printing 2003

New Interchange Level 1 has been developed from Interchange Level 1,
first published by Cambridge University Press in 1990.

Printed in Hong Kong, China

Typeface New Century Schoolbook   System QuarkXPress®   [AH]

ISBN 0 521 53573 5 Full Contact Edition 1
ISBN 0 521 62875 X Teacher's Edition 1
ISBN 0 521 62874 1 Teacher's Manual 1
ISBN 0 521 62873 3 Class Audio Cassettes 1
ISBN 0 521 62871 7 Student's Audio Cassette 1A
ISBN 0 521 62869 5 Student's Audio Cassette 1B
ISBN 0 521 62872 5 Class Audio CDs 1
ISBN 0 521 62870 9 Student's Audio CD 1A
ISBN 0 521 62868 7 Student's Audio CD 1B
ISBN 0 521 65913 2 Intro–3 Audio Sampler
ISBN 0 521 62867 9 Video 1 (NTSC)
ISBN 0 521 62866 0 Video 1 (PAL)
ISBN 0 521 62865 2 Video 1 (SECAM)
ISBN 0 521 62863 6 Video Teacher's Guide 1
ISBN 0 521 91481 7 Video Sampler Intro–3

Also available
ISBN 0 521 77381 4 Lab Guide 1
ISBN 0 521 77380 6 Lab Cassettes 1
ISBN 0 521 62882 2 New Interchange/Passages
                   Placement and Evaluation Package
ISBN 0 521 80575 9 Teacher-Training Video with
                   Video Manual

Book design, art direction, and layout services: Adventure House, NYC
Illustrators: Adventure House, Barbara Griffel, Randy Jones, Mark Kaufman, Kevin Spaulding, Sam Viviano
Photo researchers: Sylvia P. Bloch

Introduction

THE NEW EDITION

New Interchange is a revision of *Interchange*, one of the world's most successful and popular English courses. *New Interchange* incorporates many improvements suggested by teachers and students from around the world. Some major changes include many new Conversations, Snapshots, and Readings; more extensive Grammar Focus models and activities; a greater variety and amount of listening materials; extensive changes to the **Teacher's Edition** and **Workbook**; and additions to the **Video.**

New Interchange is a multi-level course in English as a second or foreign language for young adults and adults. The course covers the four skills of listening, speaking, reading, and writing, as well as improving pronunciation and building vocabulary. Particular emphasis is placed on listening and speaking. The primary goal of the course is to teach communicative competence, that is, the ability to communicate in English according to the situation, purpose, and roles of the participants. The language used in *New Interchange* is American English; however, the course reflects the fact that English is the major language of international communication and is not limited to any one country, region, or culture. This level is for beginners and takes students from the beginning to low-intermediate level.

This level builds on the foundations for accurate and fluent communication already established in the prior level by extending grammatical, lexical, and functional skills. Because the syllabus covered in this Student's Book reviews language features taught at the prior level, students who have not previously used *New Interchange* can successfully study at this level.

COURSE LENGTH

Each full level of *New Interchange* contains between 70 and 120 hours of class instruction time. For classes where more time is available, the Teacher's Edition gives detailed suggestions for Optional Activities to extend each unit.

Where less time is available, the amount of time spent on Interchange Activities, Reading, Writing, Optional Activities, and the Workbook can be reduced.

Each split edition contains approximately 35 to 60 hours of classroom material. The Student's Book, Workbook, and Student's Audio Cassettes or CDs are available in split editions.

COURSE COMPONENTS

The **Student's Book** contains 16 six-page units, each divided into two topical/functional "cycles," as well as four review units. At the back of the book are 16 communication tasks, called "Interchange Activities," and summaries of grammar and vocabulary taught in each unit.

the full-color Teacher's edition features

The full-color **Teacher's Edition** features detailed teaching instructions directly across from the Student's Book pages, along with audio scripts, cultural notes, answer keys, and optional activities. At the back of the Teacher's Edition are instructions for Interchange Activities, an Optional Activities Index, a Workbook Answer Key, and four photocopiable Achievement Tests with audio scripts and answer keys.

The **Workbook** provides a variety of reading, writing, and spelling exercises to reinforce the grammar and vocabulary taught in the Student's Book. Each six-page unit follows the same teaching sequence as the Student's Book; some exercises recycle teaching points from previous units in the context of the new topic. The Workbook can be used for classwork or homework.

The **Class Audio Program**, available on cassette or CD, is intended for classroom use. The Conversations, Grammar Focus models, Pronunciation exercises, and Listening activities in the Student's Book are all recorded naturally with a variety of native and some nonnative accents. Recorded exercises are indicated with the symbol.

The **Student's Audio Program** provides opportunities for self-study. It contains recordings of all Student's Book exercises marked with the symbol ☞, except for the Listening tasks, which are intended only for classroom use. These tasks appear exclusively on the Class Audio Program and are indicated by the symbol CLASS AUDIO ONLY ▶.

The **Video** offers entertaining dramatic or documentary sequences that review and extend language learned in each unit of the Student's Book. The **Video Activity Book** contains comprehension, conversation, and language practice activities, and the **Video Teacher's Guide** provides instructional support, answer keys, and photocopiable transcripts of the video sequences.

The **CD-ROM**, appropriate for home or laboratory use, offers a wealth of additional practice. Each of the 16 units is based on a sequence from the Video. Four tests help students monitor their progress.

The **Placement Test** helps determine the most appropriate level of *New Interchange* for incoming students. A booklet contains the four-skills test on photocopiable pages, as well as instructions for test administration and scoring. A cassette accompanies the listening section of the test.

The **Lab Cassettes** provide self-study activities in the areas of grammar, vocabulary, pronunciation, listening, and functional use of English. The **Lab Guide** contains photocopiable pages that guide students through the activities.

The **Teacher-Training Video** offers clear guidance for teaching each section of the Student's Book and professional development activities appropriate for individual or group use.

■ APPROACH AND METHODOLOGY

New Interchange teaches students to use English for everyday situations and purposes related to school, social life, work, and leisure. The underlying philosophy is that learning a second or foreign language is more rewarding, meaningful, and effective when the language is used for authentic communication. Throughout *New Interchange*, students are presented with natural and useful language. In addition, students have the opportunity to personalize the language they learn, make use of their own knowledge and experiences, and express their ideas and opinions.

■ KEY FEATURES

Adult and International Content *New Interchange* deals with contemporary topics that are of high interest and relevant to both students and teachers. The topics have been selected for their interest to both homogeneous and heterogeneous classes.

Integrated Syllabus *New Interchange* has an integrated, multi-skills syllabus that links topics, communicative functions, and grammar. Grammar – seen as an essential component of second and foreign language proficiency and competence – is always presented communicatively, with controlled accuracy-based activities leading to fluency-based communicative practice. In this way, there is a link between grammatical form and communicative function. The syllabus is carefully graded, with a gradual progression of teaching items.

Enjoyable and Useful Learning Activities A variety of interesting and enjoyable activities provides thorough individual student practice and enables learners to apply the language they learn. The course also makes extensive use of information-gap tasks; role plays; and pair, group, and whole class activities. Task-based and information-sharing activities provide a maximum amount of student-generated communication.

■ WHAT EACH UNIT CONTAINS

Snapshot The Snapshots graphically present interesting real-world information that introduces the topic of a unit or cycle, and also develop vocabulary. Follow-up questions encourage discussion of the Snapshot material and personalize the topic.

Conversation The Conversations introduce the new grammar of each cycle in a communicative context and present functional and conversational expressions.

Grammar Focus The new grammar of each unit is presented in color boxes and is followed by controlled and freer communicative practice activities. These freer activities often have students use the grammar in a personal context.

Fluency Exercise These pair, group, whole class, or role-play activities provide more personal practice of the new teaching points and increase the opportunity for individual student practice.

Pronunciation These exercises focus on important features of spoken English, including stress, rhythm, intonation, reductions, and blending.

Listening The Listening activities develop a wide variety of listening skills, including listening for gist, listening for details, and inferring meaning from context. Charts or graphics often accompany these task-based exercises to lend support to students.

Word Power The Word Power activities develop students' vocabulary through a variety of interesting tasks, such as word maps and collocation exercises. Word Power activities are usually followed by oral or written practice that helps students understand how to use the vocabulary in context.

Writing The Writing exercises include practical writing tasks that extend and reinforce the teaching points in the unit and help develop student's compositional skills. The Teacher's Edition demonstrates how to use the models and exercises to focus on the process of writing.

Reading The reading passages use various types of texts adapted from authentic sources. The Readings develop a variety of reading skills, including reading for details, skimming, scanning, and making inferences. Also included are pre-reading and post-reading questions that use the topic of the reading as a springboard to discussion.

Interchange Activities The Interchange Activities are pair work, group work, or whole class activities involving information sharing and role playing to encourage real communication. These exercises are a central part of the course and allow students to extend and personalize what they have practiced and learned in each unit.

Unit Summaries Unit Summaries are located at the back of the Student's Book. They contain lists of the key vocabulary and functional expressions, as well as grammar extensions for each unit.

■ FROM THE AUTHORS

We hope that you will like using *New Interchange* and find it useful, interesting, and fun. Our goal has been to provide teachers and students with activities that make the English class a time to look forward to and, at the same time, provide students with the skills they need to use English outside the classroom. Please let us know how you enjoy it and good luck!

Jack C. Richards
Jonathan Hull
Susan Proctor

Authors' Acknowledgments

A great number of people contributed to the development of *New Interchange*. Particular thanks are owed to the following:

The **reviewers** using the first edition of *Interchange* in the following schools and institutes – the insights and suggestions of these teachers and their students have helped define the content and format of the new edition: Jorge Haber Resque, **Centro Cultural Brasil-Estados Unidos (CCBEU),** Belém, Brazil; Lynne Roecklein, **Gifu University,** Japan; Mary Oliveira and Montserrat M. Djmal, **Instituto Brasil-Esatdos Unidos (IBEU),** Rio de Janeiro, Brazil; Liliana Baltra, **Instituto Chileno Norte-Americano,** Santiago de Chile; Blanca Arazi and the teachers at **Instituto Cultural Argentino Norteamericano (ICANA),** Buenos Aires, Argentina; Mike Millin and Kelley Seymour, **James English School,** Japan; Matilde Legorreta, **Kratos, S.A. de C.V.,** Mexico D.F.; Peg Donner, Ricia Doren, and Andrew Sachar, **Rancho Santiago College Centennial Education Center,** Santa Ana, California, USA; James Hale, **Sundai ELS,** Japan; Christopher Lynch, **Sunshine College,** Tokyo,

Japan; Valerie Benson, **Suzugamine Women's College,** Hiroshima, Japan; Michael Barnes, **Tokyu Be Seminar,** Japan; Claude Arnaud and Paul Chris McVay, **Toyo Women's College,** Tokyo, Japan; Maria Emilia Rey Silva, **UCBEU,** São Paulo, Brazil; Lilia Ortega Sepulveda, **Unidad Lomoa Hermosa,** Mexico D.F.; Eric Bray, **Kyoto YMCA English School,** Kyoto, Japan; John Pak, **Yokohama YMCA English School,** Yokohama, Japan; and the many teachers around the world who responded to the *Interchange* questionnaire.

The **editorial** and **production** team: Suzette André, Sylvia P. Bloch, John Borrelli, Mary Carson, Natalie Nordby Chen, Karen Davy, Randee Falk, Andrew Gitzy, Pauline Ireland, Penny Laporte, Kathy Niemczyk, Kathleen Schultz, Rosie Stamp, and Mary Vaughn.

And Cambridge University Press **staff** and **advisors**: Carlos Barbisan, Kate Cory-Wright, Riitta da Costa, Peter Davison, Peter Donovan, Cecilia Gómez, Colin Hayes, Thares Keeree, Jinsook Kim, Koen Van Landeghem, Carine Mitchell, Sabina Sahni, Helen Sandiford, Dan Schulte, Ian Sutherland, Chris White, and Ellen Zlotnick.

Plan of the Book

Title/Topics	Functions	Grammar

Listening/Pronunciation	Writing/Reading	Interchange Activity
		PAGE IC-2 **UNIT 1**
Recognizing formal and informal names; listening for personal information Intonation of clarification questions	Writing questions requesting personal information "Meeting and Greeting Customs": Reading about greeting customs	"Getting to know you": Collecting personal information from classmates
		PAGE IC-3 **UNIT 2**
Listening to descriptions of jobs and daily schedules Unstressed words	Writing a description of an occupation "The Daily Grind": Reading about students with part-time work	"Common ground": Finding similarities in classmates' daily schedules
		PAGE IC-4 and IC-5 **UNIT 3**
Listening to people shopping; listening for items, prices, and opinions Linked sounds	Writing a comparison of prices in different countries "Shop Till You Drop": Reading about different kinds of shopping	"Swap meet": Buying and selling things
		PAGE IC-6 **UNIT 4**
Identifying musical styles; listening for likes and dislikes; listening to invitations Question intonation	Writing invitations and excuses "The Sound of Music": Reading about musicians from around the world	"What an invitation! What an excuse!": Making up unusual invitations and excuses
		REVIEW OF UNITS 1–4
		PAGE IC-7 **UNIT 5**
Listening for family relationships; listening to information about families and family life Blending with *does*	Writing a description of family life "The Changing Family": Reading about an American family	"Family facts": Finding out information about classmates' families and family members
		PAGE IC-8 **UNIT 6**
Listening to people talk about free-time activities; listening to routines; listening to descriptions of sports participation Sentence stress	Writing a description of favorite activities "Smart Moves": Reading about fitness for the brain	"Fitness quiz": Interviewing about fitness habits
		PAGE IC-9 and IC-10 **UNIT 7**
Listening to descriptions and opinions of past events and vacations Reduced forms of *did you*	Writing a postcard "Vacation Postcards": Reading about different kinds of vacations	"Vacation photos": Telling a story using pictures
		PAGE IC-11 **UNIT 8**
Listening for locations of places; listening to descriptions of places in neighborhoods Reduced forms of *there is* and *there are*	Writing a description of a home "City Scenes": Reading about neighborhood life in cities around the world	"Neighborhood survey": Comparing two neighborhoods
		REVIEW OF UNITS 5–8

1 Please call me Chuck.

1 CONVERSATION *Introducing yourself*

🔊 Listen and practice.

Elizabeth: Hello, I'm Elizabeth Mandel.
Chuck: Hi! My name is Charles Chang.
But please call me Chuck.
Elizabeth: Nice to meet you, Chuck.
You can call me Liz.
Chuck: OK. And what's your last name again?
Elizabeth: Mandel.

2 CHECKING INFORMATION

A 🔊 Match the questions in column A with the responses in column B.
Listen and check. Then practice with a partner. Give your own information.

A

1. How do you pronounce your last name? ..b...
2. Excuse me, what's your first name again? ..d....
3. How do you spell your last name? ...a...
4. What do people call you? ...c....

B

a. C-H-A-N-G.
b. It's Mandel, with the accent on "del."
c. Well, everyone calls me Chuck.
d. Oh, it's Amy.

B *Group work* Make a list of names and nicknames for your group.
Introduce yourself with your full name. Use the expressions above.

A: Hi! I'm Joseph Block. Please call me Joe.
B: OK, Joe. And what's your last name again?
A: It's Block.

2

3 NAMES AND TITLES

A Use a title with a last name to address someone formally.

Amy, this is my father.

Hello, Mr. Mandel.

tairols

	Titles	Single	Married
males:	Mr.	✓	✓
females:	Ms.	✓	✓
	Miss	✓	
	Mrs.		✓

Use a first name or nickname without a title to address someone informally.

This is Chuck.

Hi, Chuck.

CLASS AUDIO ONLY

B Listen to people talk to Chuck Chang, Elizabeth Mandel, and Amy Kim. Do they address them formally (**F**) or informally (**I**)?

1. F   2. I   3. F   4. ......   5. ......   6. ......

4 CONVERSATION *Introducing someone*

A Listen and practice.

Tom: Paulo, who is that over there?
Paulo: Oh, that's my father! And that's my mother with him.
Tom: I'd like to meet them.

Paulo: Mom and Dad, this is Tom Hayes. Tom, these are my parents.
Tom: Pleased to meet you, Mr. and Mrs. Tavares.
Mrs. Tavares: Nice to meet you, Tom.
Paulo: My parents are here from Brazil. They're on vacation.
Tom: Oh, where are you from in Brazil?
Mr. Tavares: We're from Rio.

B Group work Take turns introducing a partner to others.

A: Juan, this is Maria. She's from Argentina.
B: Hi, Maria.

5 GRAMMAR FOCUS

Wh-questions and statements with be

		Contractions		Subject pronouns	Possessive adjectives
What's your name?	My name **is** Chuck.	I am = I'm		I	my
Where are you from?	**I'm** from Taiwan.	You are = You're		you	your
		He is = He's		he	his
Who is that?	His name **is** Tom. _am_	She is = She's		she	her
What's her name?	Her name **is** Amy.	It is = It's		it	its
Where is she from?	**She's** from Korea. _correa_	We are = We're		we	our
Where are you from?	**We're** from the United States.	They are = They're		you	your
Who are they?	**They're** Amy's parents.			they	their
What are their names?	Their names **are** Mr. and Mrs. Kim.	What is = What's			
Where are they from?	**They're** from Korea.				

For a list of countries and nationalities, see the appendix at the back of the book.

A Complete this conversation. Then compare with a partner.

Yoko: Rich, who are the two women over there?
Rich: Oh, _their_ names are Lisa and Kate.

Rich: Hi, Kate. This _is_ Yoko. _She's_ from Japan.
Yoko: Hello. Nice to meet you.
Kate: Good to meet you, Yoko.
Lisa: And _my_ name _is_ Lisa.
Yoko: Hi, Lisa.
Rich: Lisa and Kate _are_ from Canada.
Yoko: Oh? Where _are_ you from in Canada?
Kate: _I'm_ from Toronto.

B Complete these questions.
Then practice with a partner.

1. A: _Who is_ that?
   B: That's Rich.
2. A: _Where is_ he from?
   B: He's from Los Angeles.
3. A: _What's_ his last name?
   B: It's Brown.
4. A: _Who are_ the two students over there?
   B: Their names are Lisa and Kate.
5. A: _Where are_ they from?
   B: They're from Canada.

C Group work Write five questions about your classmates.
Then take turns asking and answering your questions.

Who is she?
Where is Su Hee from?

4

6 SNAPSHOT

Greetings from Around the World

a handshake a bow a kiss on the cheek

a hug a pat on the back

Source: Brigham Young University,
Center for International Studies

Talk about these questions.

Which greetings are typical in your country?
Can you name a country for each greeting?

7 CONVERSATION *Asking about someone*

A 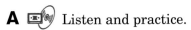 Listen and practice.

Sarah: Hi, Tom. How's everything?
 Tom: Not bad. How are you?
Sarah: Pretty good, thanks.

 Tom: Sarah, this is Paulo. He's from Brazil.
Sarah: Hello, Paulo. Are you on vacation?
Paulo: No, I'm not. I'm a student here.
Sarah: Oh, are you studying English?
Paulo: Well, yes, I am. And engineering, too.
Sarah: Are you and Tom in the same class?
Paulo: No, we aren't. But we're on the same
   volleyball team.

CLASS AUDIO ONLY ▶ **B** 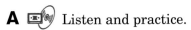 Listen to the rest of the conversation.

Where is Sarah from?

5

8 GRAMMAR FOCUS

Yes/No questions and short answers with be

Are you on vacation?	No, I'**m not**. I'**m** a student.
Are you a student?	Yes, I **am**.
Is Sarah from the United States?	No, she **isn't**. (No, she'**s not**.) She'**s** from Australia.
Is Sarah from Australia?	Yes, she **is**.
Are you and Tom in the same class?	No, we **aren't**. (No, we'**re not**.) We'**re** on the same volleyball team.
Are you and Tom on the volleyball team?	Yes, we **are**.
Are Mr. and Mrs. Tavares American?	No, they **aren't**. (No, they'**re not**.) They'**re** Brazilian.
Are Mr. and Mrs. Tavares Brazilian?	Yes, they **are**.

~eim   telm

A Complete these conversations. Then practice with a partner.

1. A: ....Are.... you from the United States?
   B: Yes, I ..'m... . ..I'm... from Chicago.

2. A: ...Is.... Rosa in English 101?
   B: No, she ..isn't.. ..she's.. in English 102.

3. A: ..Are... you and Monique from France?
   B: Yes, we ..are.. . ..We're.. from Paris.   *(Paarris)*

B *Pair work* Read the conversations in Exercises 4 and 7 again. Then answer
these questions. For questions you answer "no," give the correct information.

1. Are Tom and Paulo on the baseball team? ...Yes, they are...
2. Are Mr. and Mrs. Tavares on vacation? ...Yes, they are...
3. Are Mr. and Mrs. Tavares from Mexico? ...No, they aren't. they're Brazilian...
4. Is Paulo from Brazil? ...Yes, he is...   *(mises)*
5. Is Paulo on vacation? ...No, he isn't , he's a student...

C *Group work* Write five questions about your classmates.
Then take turns asking and answering your questions.

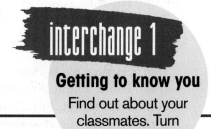

interchange 1

Getting to know you
Find out about your classmates. Turn to page IC-2.

Are Maria and Su Hee friends?

9 LISTENING

CLASS
AUDIO
ONLY ▶   Listen to these conversations and complete the information about each person.

	First name	Last name	Where from?	Studying?
1.	Joe	Mill	the United States	Xchemistry
2.	Elena	Vera	México	engineering
3.	Min Ho	Kim	Korea	English

6   *Homework*

10 *READING*

Meeting and Greeting Customs

How do you think the people in these countries greet each other?

There are many different greeting customs around the world. Here are some.

saludos

Costumbres

Chile

People usually shake hands when they meet for the first time. When two women first meet, they sometimes give one kiss on the cheek. (They actually "kiss the air.") Women also greet both male and female friends with a kiss. Chilean men give their friends warm *abrazos* (hugs) or sometimes kiss women on the cheek.

acchdy

(hugs)

mejills

inclinacs?

Finland

firme

Finns greet each other with a firm handshake. Hugs and kisses are only for close friends and family.

Nacional

The Philippines

The everyday greeting for friends is a handshake for both men and women. Men sometimes pat each other on the back.

(guimen)

golpetear   *espalda*

Korea

Men bow slightly and shake hands to greet each other. Women do not usually shake hands. To address someone with his or her full name, the family name comes first, then the first name.

(óchually)

family fé'mili

The United States

People shake hands when they are first introduced. Friends and family members often hug or kiss on the cheek when they see each other. In these situations, men often kiss women but not other men.

A According to the article, in which country or countries are the following true? Check (✓) the correct boxes.

(Korria)

	Chile	Finland	the Philippines	Korea	the U.S.
1. People shake hands every time they meet.	☐	✓	✓	☐	☑
2. Women do not shake hands.	☐	☐	☐	✓	☐
3. Women kiss at the first meeting.	✓	☐	☐	☐	☐
4. Men hug or pat each other on the back.	✓	✓	✓	☐	✓
5. Women kiss male friends.	✓	✓	☐	☐	✓
6. The family name comes first.	☐	☐	☐	✓	☐

B *Pair work* How do these people greet each other in your country?

1. two male friends
2. a male and female friend
3. two strangers
4. two female friends

2 How do you spend your day?

1 SNAPSHOT

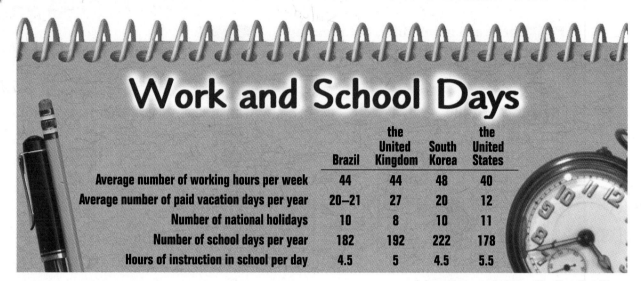

Work and School Days

	Brazil	the United Kingdom	South Korea	the United States
Average number of working hours per week	44	44	48	40
Average number of paid vacation days per year	20–21	27	20	12
Number of national holidays	10	8	10	11
Number of school days per year	182	192	222	178
Hours of instruction in school per day	4.5	5	4.5	5.5

Information compiled from *The New York Times, Digest of Educational Statistics,* and interviews.

Talk about these questions.

Which country would you like to work in? Why?
Where would you like to be a student? Why?

2 WORD POWER Jobs

(pleis) = Lugar = place

A Complete the word map with jobs from the list.

- architect
- receptionist
- company director
- flight attendant
- supervisor
- engineer
- salesperson
- secretary
- professor
- sales manager
- security guard
- word processor

Professionals
architect
engineer
flight attendant
Professor

Service occupations
flight attendant
Salesperson
security guard

Jobs

Management positions
company director
Supervisor   Sepervaisor
Sales Manager
seils manager

Office work
receptionist
secretary
word processor

B Add two more jobs to each category. Then compare with a partner.

8

3 WORK AND WORKPLACES

A Look at the pictures. Match the information in columns A, B, and C.

A	B	C
a salesperson	for an airline	builds houses
a chef	in a restaurant	cares for patients
a flight attendant	for a construction company	answers the phone
a carpenter	in a hospital	cooks food
a receptionist	in a department store	serves passengers
a nurse	in an office	sells clothes

B *Pair work* Take turns describing each person's job.

"She's a salesperson. She works in a department store. She sells clothes."

4 CONVERSATION *Describing work*

A 🔊 Listen and practice.

Jason: Where do you work, Andrea?
Andrea: I work for Thomas Cook Travel.
Jason: Oh, really? What do you do there?
Andrea: I'm a guide. I take people on tours to countries in South America, like Peru.
Jason: That sounds interesting!
Andrea: Yes, it's a great job. I love it. And what do you do?
Jason: I'm a student, and I have a part-time job, too.
Andrea: Oh? Where do you work?
Jason: In a fast-food restaurant.
Andrea: Which restaurant?
Jason: Hamburger Heaven.

HAMBURGER HEAVEN

B 🔊 Listen to the rest of the conversation.

1. What does Jason do, exactly?
2. How does he like his job?

5 GRAMMAR FOCUS

oraciones enunciadas

Simple present Wh-questions and statements 🔊

			I/You	He/She	
What do you **do**?	I'm a student, and I **have** a part-time job.		work	works	
Where do you **work**?	I **work** at/in a restaurant.		take	takes	
Where do you **go** to school?	I **go** to the University of Texas.		study	studies	
How do you **like** your school?	I **like** it very much.		teach	teaches	*tiches*
			do	does *dar*	
Where does Andrea **work**?	She **works** for Thomas Cook Travel.		go	goes *gowz*	
What does she **do**?	She's a guide. She **takes** people on tours.		have	has *Jas*	
Where does Jason **go** to school?	He **goes** to New York University.				
How does he **like** it?	He **loves** it.				

Go to / goru →

A Complete these conversations. Then practice with a partner.

1. A: What ___do___ you ___do___? *bisnes*
   B: I'm a student. I study business.
   A: And ___where___ do you ___go___ to school?
   B: I ___go___ to Jefferson College.
   A: ___How___ do you like your classes?
   B: I ___like___ them a lot. *I laysem a lot*

2. A: What ___does___ Kanya do?
   B: She's a teacher. She ___teaches___ mathematics
   at a school in Bangkok.
   A: And what about Somsak? Where ___does___ he work?
   B: He ___works___ for an electronics company.
   A: ___what___ does he do, exactly?
   B: He's a salesman. He ___sells___ computer equipment.

B Pair work What do you know about these jobs? Complete the chart.
Then write sentences describing each job, using *he* or *she*.

A doctor	A travel agent	A police officer
▪ works in a hospital	▪ works for an airline	▪
▪ has an office	▪ serves passengers	▪
▪ works long hours	▪ works for days	▪
▪ cares for patients	▪	▪

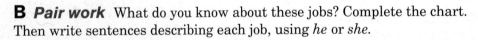

A doctor works in a hospital. She has an office, too. . . .

C Group work Ask your classmates questions about work and school.

A: What do you do, Aki?
B: I'm a student.
C: Where do you go to school?
B: . . .

6 *WRITING*

A Write a description of what you do. Don't write your name on the paper.

> *I'm a student. I go to McGill University in Canada.*
> *I'm a freshman. I study computer science. I work*
> *part time at a radio station, too. I'm a disc jockey.*
> *I play music. I love my job!*

B *Group work* Pass your descriptions around the group. Can you guess who wrote each description?

7 **CONVERSATION** *Daily schedules*

A Listen and practice.

Daniel: How do you spend your day, Helen?
Helen: Well, on weekdays I get up around ten. Then I read the paper for an hour and have lunch at about noon.
Daniel: Really? What time do you go to work?
Helen: I start work at three.
Daniel: And when do you get home at night?
Helen: I get home pretty late, around midnight.
Daniel: So what do you do, exactly?
Helen: I'm a TV announcer. Don't you recognize me? I do the weather report on KNTV!
Daniel: Gee, I'm sorry. I don't watch TV.

CLASS AUDIO ONLY ▶ **B** Listen to Daniel describe how he spends his day.

1. What time does he get up? start work? study until?
2. What does he do?

8 **PRONUNCIATION** *Unstressed words*

A Listen and practice. The prepositions in these sentences (*around, for,* and *at*) are not stressed.

I get **úp** around **tén.**
I read the **pá**per for an **hóur**.
I have **lúnch** at about **nóon**.

B *Pair work* Practice the conversation in Exercise 7 again. Be careful not to stress prepositions.

9 GRAMMAR FOCUS

Time expressions

I get up	**at** 7:00	**in** the morning	**on** weekdays.
I go to bed	**around** ten	**in** the evening	**on** weeknights.
I leave work	**early**	**in** the afternoon	**on** weekends.
I get home	**late** *or maid*	**at** night	**on** Fridays.
I stay up	**until** midnight	**on** Saturdays.	
I wake up	**before/after** noon	**on** Sundays.	

| *Ways to express clock time* |
| 7:00 |
| seven o'clock |
| seven |
| 7:00 in the morning = 7:00 A.M. |
| 7:00 in the evening = 7:00 P.M. |

A Complete these sentences with time expressions.

1. I get up ....at.... six ..in.. the morning
   ..on.. weekdays.
2. I go to bed ...around midnight ..on.. weeknights.
3. I start work ....at.... 11:30 ..at.. night.
4. I arrive at work ....on......... Mondays,
   ....at.. 7:00 A.M.
5. I have lunch ......at... three ..in... the afternoon
   ..on.. weekdays.
6. I stay up ....on....... weekends.
7. I have a little snack ....at.. 9:00 ...in.. the evening.
8. I sleep ..after.. noon ..on.. Sundays.

B Rewrite the sentences above so that they are true for you.
Then compare with a partner.

C *Pair work* Take turns asking and answering these questions.

1. What days do you get up early? late?
2. What are two things you do before 8:00 in the morning?
3. What are three things you do on Saturday mornings?
4. How late do you stay up on Saturday nights?
5. What is something you do only on Sundays?

interchange 2

Common ground

Take a survey. Compare
your schedule with your
classmates' schedules.
Turn to page IC-3.

10 LISTENING

 CLASS AUDIO ONLY

A Listen to Rodney, Tina, and Ellen talk about
their daily schedules. Complete the chart.

	Job	Gets up at . . .	Gets home at . . .	Goes to bed at . . .
Rodney	....	....	....	....
Tina	....	....	....	....
Ellen	....	....	....	....

B *Class activity* Who do you think has the best daily schedule? Why?

11 *READING*

The Daily Grind

Is it a good idea for a student to have a job? Why or why not?

Brandon Smith

I'm a junior in high school, and I have a part-time job in a restaurant. I bus dishes on Saturdays and Sundays from 8:00 until 4:00. I earn $5.50 an hour. It isn't much money, but I save almost every penny! I want to go to a good university, and the cost goes up every year. Of course, I spend some money when I go out on Saturday nights.

Lauren Russell

I'm a senior in high school. I have a job as a cashier in a grocery store. The job pays well – about $6.75 an hour. I work every weeknight after school from 4:00 until 8:00. I don't have time for homework, and my grades aren't very good this year. But I have to work, or I can't buy nice clothes and I can't go out on Saturday nights. Also, a car costs a lot of money.

Erica Davis

I'm a freshman in college. College is very expensive, so I work in a law office for three hours every weekday afternoon. I make photocopies, file papers, and sort mail for $8.25 an hour. The job gives me good experience because I want to be a lawyer someday. But I don't want to work every semester. I need time to study.

A Read the article. Why do these students work? Check (✓) the correct boxes.

	Brandon	Lauren	Erica
1. To earn money for college	☐	☐	☑
2. To buy nice clothes	☐	☑	☐
3. To go out on the weekend	☐	☑	☐
4. To pay for a car	☐	☑	☐
5. To get job experience	☐	☐	☑

B *Pair work* Talk about these questions.

1. Look at the reasons why each student works. Who has good reasons to work? Who doesn't, in your opinion?
2. How many hours a week does each student work?
3. How much money does each student earn per week?
4. What are the advantages and disadvantages of part-time work for students?

3 How much is it?

1 SNAPSHOT

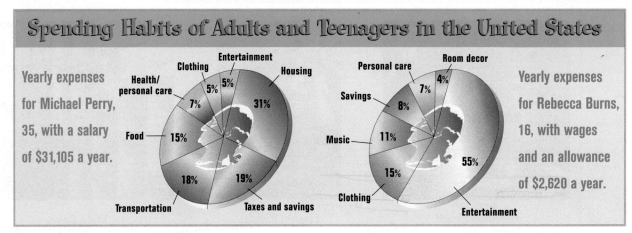

Spending Habits of Adults and Teenagers in the United States

Yearly expenses for Michael Perry, 35, with a salary of $31,105 a year.

- Health/personal care 7%
- Clothing 5%
- Entertainment 5%
- Housing 31%
- Food 15%
- Transportation 18%
- Taxes and savings 19%

Yearly expenses for Rebecca Burns, 16, with wages and an allowance of $2,620 a year.

- Personal care 7%
- Room decor 4%
- Savings 8%
- Music 11%
- Clothing 15%
- Entertainment 55%

Portraits based on information from the *Statistical Abstract of the U.S.* and the Rand Youth Poll.

Talk about these questions.

How does Michael Perry spend most of his money?
How does Rebecca Burns spend most of her money?
How do their spending habits compare?
How do you spend your money? Make two lists: things you have to buy and things you like to buy.

2 CONVERSATION Prices

A Listen and practice.

Steve: Oh, look at those earrings, Maria. They're perfect for you.
Maria: These red ones? I'm not sure.
Steve: No, the yellow ones.
Maria: Oh, these? Hmm. Yellow isn't a good color for me.
Steve: Well, that necklace isn't bad.
Maria: Which one?
Steve: That blue one right there. How much is it?
Maria: It's $42! That's expensive!
Steve: Hey, let me get it for you. It's your birthday present.

CLASS AUDIO ONLY **B** 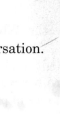 Listen to the rest of the conversation.

1. What else do they buy?
2. Who pays for it?

14

3 GRAMMAR FOCUS

Demonstratives; one, ones

How much is **this** necklace? **this one**?	How much is **that** necklace? **that one**?	Which **one**? The blue **one**. It's $42.
How much are **these** earrings? **these**?	How much are **those** earrings? **those**?	Which **ones**? The yellow **ones**. They're $18.

Prices
$42 = forty-two dollars
$59.95 = fifty-nine ninety-five
or fifty-nine dollars and
ninety-five cents

Colors

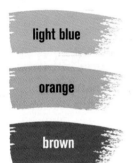
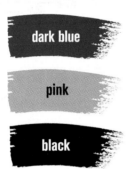
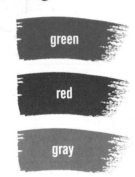
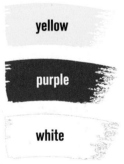

light blue | dark blue | green | yellow
orange | pink | red | purple
brown | black | gray | white

Look at the pictures and complete these conversations.
Then practice with a partner.

1. A: Excuse me. How much
   ...these... jeans?
   B: Which ...ones...? Do you mean ...these...?
   A: No, the light blue ...ones...
   B: Oh, ...they're... $59.95.
   A: Almost sixty dollars! Are you kidding?

2. A: I like ...that... backpack over there.
   How much ...is... it?
   B: Which ...one...? Each backpack has a different price.
   A: ...that... red ...one...
   B: It's $98.50. But ...this... green
   ...it... is only $45.
   A: OK. Let me look at it.

4 THAT'S EXPENSIVE!

Pair work Ask and answer questions about these products.
For help with numbers, see the appendix at the back of the book.

| Computers | Jeans | Athletic Shoes | Watches |

$5,456
$1,696
$16.99
$54.39
$21.89
$79.95
$6.99
$124.50

A: How much is the computer?
B: Which one?
A: The small one./This one.
B: It's $5,456.
A: That's expensive!

useful expressions
That's cheap.
That's reasonable.
That's OK/not bad.
That's expensive.

5 LISTENING

CLASS
AUDIO
ONLY

 Listen to Tim and Sandra shopping, and complete the chart.

Item	Price	Do they buy it?		Reason
		Yes	**No**	
1. Rollerblades	....	☐	☐	....
2. cap	....	☐	☐	....
3. sunglasses	....	☐	☐	....

6 PRONUNCIATION *Linked sounds*

A  Listen and practice. Final consonants are often
linked to the vowels that follow them.

A: How much are these pants?   A: And how much is this sweater?
B: They're forty-eight dollars.   B: It's thirty-seven dollars.

B *Pair work* Ask and answer four questions about
prices in this unit. Pay attention to the linked sounds.

interchange 3

Swap meet
See what kinds of deals
you can make as a buyer
and a seller. Turn to
pages IC-4
and IC-5.

7 WORD POWER Materials

A *Pair work* Identify these things. Use the words from the list.
What other materials are these things sometimes made of? Make a list.

a **cotton** shirt   **leather** gloves   a **plastic** bracelet   a **silk** scarf
a **gold** ring   **polyester** pants   **rubber** boots   **silver** earrings

1. *a gold ring*   2. *a Plastic bracelet*   3. *a silk scarf*   4. *Polyester Pants*

5. *leather gloves*   6. *a cotton shirt*   7. *silver earrings*   8. *rubber boots*

B *Class activity* Which of the materials can you find in your classroom?

"Juan has a leather bag."

8 CONVERSATION Shopping

A Listen and practice.

Anne: Look! These jackets are nice.
   Which one do you like better?
 Sue: I like the wool one better.
Anne: Really? Why?
 Sue: It looks warmer.
Anne: Well, I prefer the leather one.
   It's more attractive than the wool one.
 Sue: Hmm. There's no price tag.
Anne: Excuse me. How much is this jacket?
Clerk: It's $499. Would you like to try it on?
Anne: Oh, no. That's OK! But thank you anyway.
Clerk: You're welcome.

 B Listen to the rest of the conversation.

1. What does Anne buy?
2. What does Sue think of it?

9 GRAMMAR FOCUS

Preferences; comparisons with adjectives

Which one do you **prefer**?
  I **prefer** the leather one.
 	
Which one do you **like better/more**?
  I **like** the leather one **better/more**.
	That one is **nicer than** the wool one.
	This one is **cheaper than** . . . .
	The leather jacket is **prettier than** . . . .
	It looks **bigger than** . . . .
	It's **more attractive than** . . . .
		nice → nicer
		cheap → cheaper
		pretty → prettier
		big → bigger
		good → better

For more information on comparatives, see the appendix at the back of the book.

A Complete these conversations. Then practice with a partner.

polyester tie   silk tie   medium shirt   large shirt   leather boots   rubber boots

1. A: Which tie is _prettier_ ,
      the orange one or the
      blue one? (pretty)
   B: Well, the blue one is
      silk. And silk is
      nicer than
      polyester. (nice)

2. A: Is this green shirt
      larger than
      that yellow one? (large)
   B: No, the yellow one is
      the largest. It's a _bigger than_
      large. The green one is
      a medium. (big)

3. A: Which are _cheaper_ ,
      the brown boots or the
      black ones? (cheap)
   B: The brown ones are
      leather. And leather is
      more expansive than
      rubber. (expensive)

B Pair work Compare the items above with a partner.
Give your own opinions.

A: Which tie do you like better?
B: I like the orange one better. The design is nicer.

useful expressions

The color is prettier.
The design is nicer.
The style is more attractive.
The material is better.

10 WRITING

How much do these items cost in your country? Fill in the chart.
Then compare the prices in your country with the prices in the U.S.

	Cost in my country	Cost in the U.S.
gasoline	....	$ 1.10/gallon
a compact disc	....	$ 12.99
a haircut	....	$ 23.00
a pair of jeans	....	$ 34.00

Many things are more expensive in
my country than in the United States.
For example, a liter of gas is
about $.66. In the U.S. it's cheaper.
It's about $1.10 per gallon. . . .

11 READING

Shop Till You Drop

Look at the pictures of different kinds of shopping in the United States.
What kind of shopping can you do in your country?

Catalog Shopping

People in the United States often shop from catalogs. There are special catalogs for almost every need – including clothing, furniture, health and beauty products, and things for the kitchen. People also order about 40% of their music from music club catalogs. Customers say that music stores are too noisy.

Television Shopping

Television shopping began in 1986. About 5% to 8% of the American public now shops by television. Some popular shopping channels are the Home Shopping Network and QVC. Customers say that television shopping is easier than shopping in a store. How do they buy things? They make a phone call and charge the item to their credit card. And TV shopping channels are on late at night, so people can "go shopping" anytime.

Computer Shopping

Is computer shopping the way of the future? About 37% of American households now have personal computers. And shopping by computer (or "shopping on-line") is interesting to more people every day. Already, shoppers can use their computers to order many different products, such as computer products, flowers, food, T-shirts, and posters. And new on-line shopping services appear every day. Soon people may be able to shop for anything, anytime, anywhere in the world.

A Read the article. Check (✓) True or False. For the false statements, give the correct information.

	True	False
1. About 60% of music in the United States is sold through music stores.	☐	☐
2. The Home Shopping Network is the name of a computer shopping service.	☐	☐
3. About 37% of American households do their shopping through the computer.	☐	☐

B *Pair work* Talk about these questions.

1. Do you like shopping? How often do you usually shop?
2. What kinds of shopping do you like? Check (✓) the appropriate boxes.

☐ shopping at discount stores
☐ television shopping
☐ shopping at department stores

☐ shopping at small stores
☐ catalog shopping
☐ shopping at secondhand or thrift stores

☐ computer shopping
☐ shopping at a mall

4 Do you like jazz?

1 SNAPSHOT

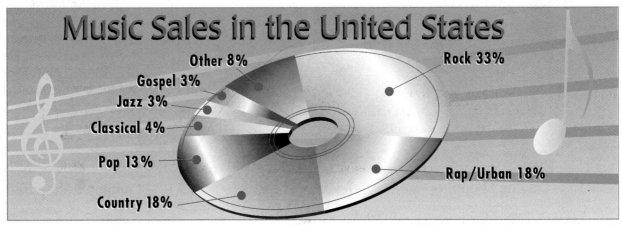

Music Sales in the United States

Other 8%
Gospel 3%
Jazz 3%
Classical 4%
Pop 13%
Country 18%
Rock 33%
Rap/Urban 18%

Source: The Recording Industry Association of America

Talk about these questions.

Which of these kinds of music do people in your country listen to?
What other kinds of music do people in your country like?

Listen and number the musical styles from 1 to 8 as you hear them.

.... *classical*   .... *gospel*   .... *New Age*   .... *rap*
.... *country*   .... *jazz*   .... *pop*   .... *rock*

2 WORD POWER Entertainment

A Complete the chart with words from the list.

classical
game shows
horror films
jazz
news
pop

salsa
science fiction
soap operas
talk shows
thrillers
westerns

B Add three more words to each category. Then compare with a partner.

C Number the items in each list from 1 (you like it the most) to 7 (you like it the least).

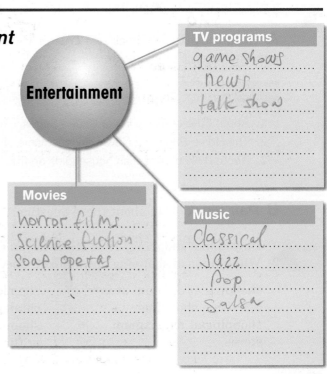

Entertainment

TV programs
game shows
news
talk show

Movies
horror films
science fiction
soap operas

Music
classical
Jazz
Pop
salsa

3 CONVERSATION Likes and dislikes

A Listen and practice.

Liz: Do you like jazz, Tom?
Tom: No, I don't like it very much. Do you?
Liz: Well, yes, I do. I'm a real fan of Wynton Marsalis.
Tom: Oh, does he play the piano?
Liz: No, he doesn't! He plays the trumpet. So, what kind of music do you like?
Tom: I like rock a lot.
Liz: Who's your favorite group?
Tom: The Cranberries. I love their music. How about you? Do you like them?
Liz: No, I don't. I can't stand them!

Wynton Marsalis
The Cranberries

CLASS
AUDIO
ONLY

B Listen to the rest of the conversation.

1. Who is Liz's favorite singer?
2. Does Tom like that singer? Why or why not?

4 GRAMMAR FOCUS

Yes/No and Wh-questions with do

		Object pronouns
Do you **like** jazz? Yes, I **do**. I like it a lot. No, I **don't** like it very much.	**What kind of** music **do** you **like**? I like rock a lot.	me you (singular) him
Does he **play** the piano? Yes, he **does**. No, he **doesn't**.	**What does** he **play**? He plays the trumpet.	her it us
Do they **like** The Cranberries? Yes, they **do**. They love them. No, they **don't** like them very much.	**Who do** they **like**? They like R.E.M.	you (plural) them

Complete these conversations. Then practice with a partner.

1. A: ...Do... you like horror films?
   B: No, I ..don't.. like ..it.. very much. I like comedies.
   A: How about Lisa and Brian? ...do... they like horror films?
   B: Well, I think Brian ..Likes.. Why don't you ask ..them..?

2. A: ...Do... you like the singer Bonnie Raitt?
   B: Yes, I ...do... . I really like ..me.. a lot.   Kaind
   A: What ..kind.. of music ..does.. she sing?
   B: She's a rock singer.
   A: ..does.. she sing country music, too?   it
   B: I don't know. I have her new CD. Let's listen to ....

5 PRONUNCIATION Question intonation

A 📼 Listen and practice. Yes/No questions usually have rising intonation. Wh-questions usually have falling intonation.

Do you like movies?   What kind of movies do you like?

Do you like pop music?   What kind of music do you like?

B Practice these questions.

Do you like TV?   What programs do you like?
Do you like music videos?   What videos do you like?

6 ENTERTAINMENT SURVEY

A *Group work* Write five questions about entertainment and entertainers. Then ask and answer your questions in groups.

Do you like . . . ?
    (pop music, TV, movies, plays)
What kinds of . . . do you like?
    (music, movies, TV programs)
What do you think of . . . ?
    (*Star Trek*, horror films,
    gospel music)

Gloria Estefan

Brad Pitt

Patrick Stewart

B *Group work* Complete this information about your group.

Our Group Favorites	
What's your favorite kind of . . . ?	**Who's your favorite . . . ?**
music:	singer: ....
movie:	actor: ....
TV program:	actress: ....

C *Class activity* Read your group's list to the class. Then find out the class favorites.

useful expressions

Our favorite . . . is . . . .
We all like . . . .
We don't agree on . . . .
We can't stand . . . .

7 *LISTENING* TV game show

A Listen to four people playing *Who's My Date?* Three men want to invite Linda on a date. What kinds of things do they like? What kinds of things does Linda like?

	Music	Movies	TV programs
Bill	*classical*		
John			
Tony			
Linda			

B *Class activity* Who do you think is the best date for Linda?

8 *CONVERSATION* Invitations

 Listen and practice.

Dave: I have tickets to *The Phantom of the Opera* on Friday night. Would you like to go?
Susan: Thanks. I'd love to. What time is the show?
Dave: It's at 8:00.
Susan: That sounds great. So, do you want to have dinner at 6:00?
Dave: Uh, I'd like to, but I have to work late.
Susan: Oh, that's OK. Let's just meet at the theater before the show, around 7:30.
Dave: That sounds fine.

a scene from *The Phantom of the Opera*

9 GRAMMAR FOCUS

Would; verb + to + verb

Would you like to go out on Saturday night? Yes, I would. *encantarta* Yes, I'd love to. Thanks. Yes, I'd really like to go. *gustarte* *me encantarse*	Would you like to see a movie? I'd like to, but I have to work late. I'd like to, but I need to save money. I'd like to, but I want to visit my parents.	Contraction I would = I'd

A Respond to these invitations. Then practice with a partner.

1. A: I have tickets to the baseball game on Saturday. Would you like to go? *safurdey*
   B: _I'd like to, but I want to visit my parents_

2. A: Would you like to come over for dinner tonight?
   B: _I'd like to, but I have to sleep early_

3. A: Would you like to go to the gym with me on Friday night?
   B: _I'd like to, but I have to work late_

4. A: There's a great movie on TV tonight. Would you like to watch it with me?
   B: _Yes, I'd really like to_

B *Pair work* Think of three different things you would like to do. Then invite a partner to do them with you. Ask and answer follow-up questions like these:

When is it?   What time does it start?
Where is it?   What time should I/we . . . ?

10 LISTENING

CLASS
AUDIO
ONLY

Listen to three people inviting friends to events and activities.
Complete the chart. Do the friends accept the invitations?

	Event/Activity	Day	Time	Accept? Yes	No
1. Jake and Paula	movie	friday	friday 9:00 clook	☐	☒
2. Lucy and Chris	Jazz Pianat	thursday	8:30	☑	☐
3. Rich and Ed	Play basebell	saturday	2:00 P.m	☑	☐

11 WRITING

See Interchange 4 for the writing assignment.

interchange 4

**What an invitation!
What an excuse!**

Make up unusual
invitations and funny
excuses. Turn to
page IC-6.

12 *READING*

The Sound of Music

What are some traditional kinds of music in your country?

Do you like popular music from Latin America, the United States, or Asia? Many musicians from around the world blend their country's music with popular sounds.

Caetano Veloso

After thirty years, Caetano Veloso is still one of Brazil's most important musicians. He mixes rock with the music of the Bahia region. Bahia is a state of Brazil that is strongly influenced by African culture. Caetano Veloso is an excellent songwriter and poet. He says of his music, "I make my records like a painter paints his canvas."

Bonnie Raitt

Bonnie Raitt is an American singer, songwriter, and guitarist. Her music blends rock with country and the blues. The blues is a kind of folk music that is often sad. It is usually about love and the problems of life. Bonnie Raitt's strong, rough voice is perfect for singing country and the blues.

Cui Jian

Cui Jian [pronounced "tsay jyan"] is a very important musician in the growth of rock music in China. Western styles, like jazz and rap, clearly influence his music. However, his music is very Chinese in its instruments and sounds. Cui Jian says his music expresses the feelings of Chinese young people.

A Read about the three musicians. Complete the chart.

	Nationality	Types of music he/she blends
1. Caetano Veloso		
2. Bonnie Raitt		
3. Cui Jian		

B *Pair work* Talk about these questions.

1. What do these three musicians have in common?
2. How does Caetano Veloso make his records?
3. Why is Bonnie Raitt's voice good for country and blues music?
4. What does Cui Jian want his music to express?

Review of Units 1-4

1 GETTING TO KNOW YOU

Pair work You are talking to someone at school. Have a conversation.

A: Hi. How are you?
B: . . .
A: By the way, my name is . . . .
B: How do you pronounce your name again?
A: . . . Where are you from?
B: . . .
A: Are you a student here?
B: . . . And how about you? What do you do?
A: . . .
B: Oh, really? And where are you from?
A: . . .
B: Well, nice talking to you. . . .

2 WHAT'S THE QUESTION?

Look at these answers. Write the questions.
Then compare with a partner.

Are you and Teresa in the same class

1. No, Teresa and I aren't in the same class. She's in the morning class.

is your teacher American?

4. No, my teacher isn't American. She's Canadian.

what time do you live home?

6. I leave home at 6:30 in the evening on weekdays.

when Do you leave on weekdays

Where does your sister go to school?

2. My sister? She goes to the University of Toronto.

Would you like to watch see?

7. A video? Sure, I'd love to watch one with you.

Do you like to Rock Music?

5. Rock music is OK, but I like jazz better.

what time do you get up on Sundays?

3. I get up before 11:00 A.M. on Sundays.

wich one is nicer the red or the purple one?

8. The red sweater is nicer than the purple one.

26

3 ROLE PLAY *In a department store*

Pair work Put items "for sale" on your desk or a table –
notebooks, watches, or bags. Use items of different colors.

Student A: You are a clerk. Answer the customer's questions.

Student B: You are a customer. Ask about the price of each item.
Say if you want to buy it.

A: Can I help you?
B: Yes. I like that . . . . How much . . . ?
A: Which one(s)?
B: . . .

Change roles and try the role play again.

4 LISTENING

  Listen to people asking questions at a party. Check (✓) the best response.

1. ☐ I work in an office.
   ☐ Yes, very early. Before 7:00 A.M.

2. ☐ Not very much.
   ☐ Oh, I just stay in and work around the house.

3. ☐ Yes, I have a laptop.
   ☐ A good laptop computer costs over $2,000.

4. ☐ Yes, I'm from Italy.
   ☐ Actually, I work here.

5. ☐ Almost any kind except classical.
   ☐ No, I don't play the piano.

6. ☐ Thanks, I'd love to. What time?
   ☐ It's on at the Varsity Theater.

5 TV AND RADIO

A ***Pair work*** Take turns asking and
answering these questions.

TV

When do you usually watch TV?
What kinds of programs do you prefer?
What's your favorite channel?
What's your favorite program?
What time is it on?
Do you watch . . . (name of program)?

B ***Pair work*** Change partners. Take turns
asking and answering these questions.

Radio

When do you listen to the radio?
What kinds of programs do you listen to?
Do you listen to programs in English?

What's your favorite radio station?
Who are your favorite singers and groups?
What's your favorite radio program?

5 Tell me about your family.

WORD POWER *The family*

A Look at Sam's family tree. How are these people related to him?
Add these words to the family tree.

cousin
father
grandmother
niece
sister-in-law
uncle
wife

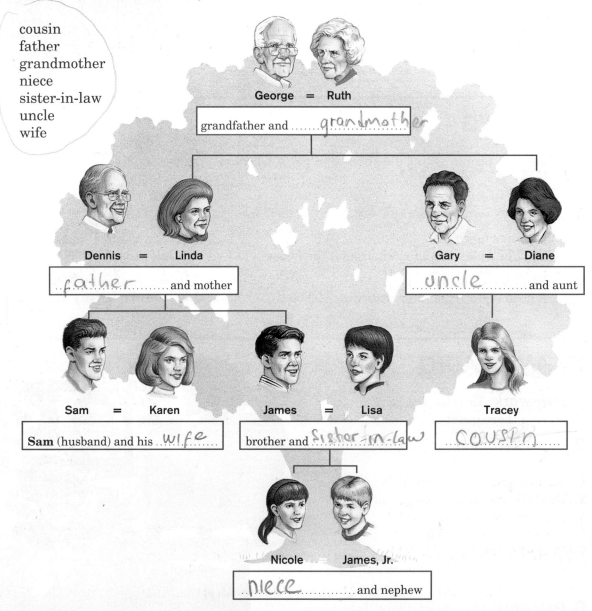

George = Ruth
grandfather and .... *grandmother*

Dennis = Linda
..*father*....and mother

Gary = Diane
uncle....and aunt

Sam = Karen
Sam (husband) and his ..*wife*..

James = Lisa
brother and *sister-in-law*

Tracey
cousin

Nicole = James, Jr.
..*niece*...........and nephew

B *Pair work* Draw your family tree. Then take turns talking about
your families. Ask follow-up questions to get more information.

For a single person:

There are 6 in my family.
I have 2 sisters and a brother.

For a married person:

There are 4 in my family.
We have a daughter and a son.

Follow-up questions:

Where do/does your . . . live?
What do/does your . . . do?

2 **LISTENING** *Hollywood families*

 Listen to two conversations about famous people. How are the people related?

1. Warren Beatty

Shirley MacLaine
sister

Annette Bening
daughter
darer

2. Charlie Sheen

Martin Sheen
father

Emilio Estevez
brother
brader

3 **CONVERSATION** *Asking about families*

eskin aboutfemily

A Listen and practice.

Rita: Tell me about your brother and sister, Sue.
Sue: Well, my sister is a lawyer. *lawyer*
Rita: Really? Does she live here in Seattle? *Seatle* *Su*
Sue: Yes, she does. But she's working in
Washington, D.C., right now.
Her job is top secret. *(sicrit*
Rita: Wow! And what does your brother do?
Sue: He's a painter. He's working in Argentina *Argentine*
this month. He has an exhibition there.
Rita: What an interesting family!
intiristng femily

B Listen to the rest of the conversation.

1. Where do Rita's parents live?
2. What do they do?

4 **PRONUNCIATION** *Blending with* does

Listen and practice. Notice the blending of **does** with other words.

1. A: My brother is married. *married*
   [dəziy] *Dau eng*
   B: **Does he** have any children?
   A: Yes, he does. *ow)*
   [wədəziy]
   B: **What does he** do?
   A: He's a painter.

2. A: My sister lives in Seattle. *Soadle*
   [dəʃiy]
   B: **Does she** live with you?
   A: No, she doesn't.
   [wədəʃiy]
   B: **What does she** do? — *guarassdu*
   A: She's a lawyer.

29

5 GRAMMAR FOCUS

Present continuous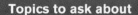

Are you **living** at home now?	Yes, I **am**./No, I'm **not**.	**Some verbs generally not used in the present continuous**
Is she still **working** in Seattle?	Yes, she **is**./No, she **isn't**.	have
Are they **going** to college this year?	Yes, they **are**./No, they **aren't**.	know
		like
Where **are** you **working** this month?	I'm **working** in Japan.	love
What **is** she **doing** these days?	She**'s teaching** at a university.	want
Who **are** they **visiting** this week?	They**'re visiting** their parents.	

A Complete these conversations using the present tense or the present continuous. Then practice with a partner.

1. A: Is anyone in your family looking for a job?
   B: Yes, my sister is. She is working (work) part time in a restaurant now, but she is looking (look) for a job in a theater company. She is love (love) acting.

2. A: What is your brother doing these days?
   B: He is going (go) to college this semester. He is like (like) it a lot. He is studying (study) mathematics.

3. A: Where do your parents live?
   B: They living (live) in Chicago most of the time, but they are staying (stay) in Florida this winter. They have (have) a house there.

B *Pair work* Take turns asking the questions in part A or similar questions of your own. Give your own information when answering.

C *Group work* Take turns. Ask each student about his or her family. Then ask follow-up questions to get more information.

Topics to ask about
traveling
living abroad
taking a class
moving to a new home
going to college or high school
studying a foreign language
looking for a job

A: Is anyone in your family traveling right now?
B: Yes, my father is.
C: Where is he?
B: He's in Bangkok.
D: What's he doing there?
B: . . .

interchange 5

Family facts
Find out some interesting facts about your classmates' families.
Turn to page IC-7.

6 SNAPSHOT

Facts About Families in the United States

Children

57% of children under six have two parents who work or a single parent who works.

63% of women with children work.

50% of working women return to work within a year of having a baby.

Marriage

50% of marriages end in divorce.

80% of divorced people remarry; more than 50% divorce again.

Elderly

60 ~ 70

20% to 30% of the population now cares for an elderly relative, or will within five years.

Source: The Family and Medical Leave Act

Talk about these questions.

Which of these facts surprises you?
Do women with children usually work in your country?
Do people often get divorced?
Do elderly people generally live with relatives?

7 CONVERSATION *Describing family life*

A 🔊 Listen and practice.

Ryan: Look at this headline, Soo Mi.
Soo Mi: Wow! So many people in the United States get divorced!
Ryan: Is it the same in Korea?
Soo Mi: I don't think so. In Korea, some marriages break up, but most couples stay together.
Ryan: Do people get married young?
Soo Mi: Not really. Very few people get married before the age of 20.
Ryan: Hmm. Do women usually work after they get married?
Soo Mi: No, a lot of women stay home and take care of their families. But some work.

CLASS AUDIO ONLY ▶ **B** 🔊 Listen to the rest of the conversation.

What does Ryan say about families in the United States? Write down two things.

I think
Some page

31

8 GRAMMAR FOCUS

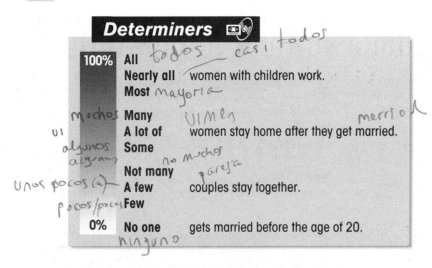

Determiners

100%	All _todos_ _casi todos_	
	Nearly all	women with children work.
	Most _mayoria_	
muchos	Many _vimes_	_merrtod_
_vi_	A lot of	women stay home after they get married.
algunos _algunn_	Some	
	Not many _no muchos_	
unos pocos (a)	A few _pareja_	couples stay together.
pocos/pocas	Few	
0%	No one _ninguno_	gets married before the age of 20.

A Rewrite these sentences using determiners. Then compare with a partner.

1. In Australia, 87% of married couples have children.
   In Australia most of married couples have childres

2. Six percent of 20- to 24-year-olds in the United States are divorced.
   few of 20- to 24 year-olds in the United Stds are divorced

3. Thirty-five percent of the people in Germany live alone.
   Some of the people in Germany live alone

4. In China, 50% of women get married by the age of 22.
   a lot of women get married by the age of 22
   (chaina)

B *Pair work* Rewrite the sentences in part A so
that they are about your country. Then discuss
your information with a partner.

> *In my country, only some married*
> *couples have children.*

useful expressions

Is that right? _estaben_
Do you think so? I think . . . .
I don't agree. _no estoy de acuerdo_
I don't think so. _no pienso eso_
It's different in my country.
es diferente en mi pais

---

9 WRITING

A Write about families in your country. Use some of your ideas from Exercise 8.

> *In my country, most people get married by the*
> *age of 30. Not many women work after they*
> *get married. Grandparents, parents, and children*
> *often live in the same house. . . .*

B *Group work* Take turns reading your compositions.
Then answer any questions from the group.

10 *READING*

The Changing Family

What kinds of problems do parents have in your country?

Now that Judy is working, Steve has to help her more with the housework. He doesn't enjoy it, however.

Judy loves her work, but she feels tired and too busy. She also worries about the children. Judy has to work on Saturdays, so Steve and Judy don't have a lot of free time together.

American families are changing. One important change is that most married women now work outside the home. What happens when both parents work? Read about the Morales family.

Judy and Steve Morales have three children: Josh, 12; Ben, 9; and Emily, 6. Steve is a computer programmer. This year, Judy is working again as a hospital administrator. The family needs the money, and Judy likes her job. Everything is going well, but there are also some problems.

Emily is having a great time in her after-school program. When Judy comes to pick her up, she doesn't want to leave.

Unfortunately, Ben's school doesn't have an after-school program. Right now, he's spending most afternoons by himself in front of the TV.

Josh is enjoying his new freedom after school. He's playing his music louder and spending more time on the phone. He's also doing a few household chores.

A Read the article. What are Steve's and Judy's problems? Complete the chart.

Problems	
1. Steve	....
2. Judy	....
3. Steve and Judy	....

B *Pair work* Talk about these questions.

Homework

1. Which of the problems above do you think is the most serious? Offer some solutions for that problem.
2. Which of the children are benefiting from Judy's working? Which one is not?

6 How often do you exercise?

1 SNAPSHOT

	MALES	FEMALES
Top six sports and fitness activities for teenagers in the United States	1. Football 2. Basketball 3. Weight training 4. Jogging 5. Bicycling 6. Swimming	1. Swimming 2. Basketball 3. Bicycling 4. Aerobics 5. Jogging 6. Regular fitness program

Source: *America's Youth in the 1990s;* George H. Gallup International Institute

Talk about these questions.

Do males and females in your country enjoy any of these sports or activities?
Do you enjoy any of these or other sports or activities? Which ones?

2 WORD POWER *Sports and exercise*

A *Pair work* Which of these activities are popular with the following age groups? Check (✔) the activities. Then compare with a partner.

	Children	Teens	Young adults	Middle-aged people	Older people
aerobics	☐	☐	✓	✓	☐
baseball	☐	✓	☐	☐	☐
bicycling	☐	☐	✓	✓	☐
Rollerblading	☐	☐	☐	☐	☐
soccer	☐	✓	☐	☐	☐
swimming	☐	☐	✓	✓	✓
tennis	☐	☐	✓	☐	✓
weight training	☐	☐	☐	✓	☐
yoga	☐	☐	✓	✓	✓

A: I think aerobics are popular with teens.
B: And with young adults.

B *Pair work* Which of the activities above are used with *do, go,* or *play?*

do aerobics .... *go bicycling* .... *play baseball* ....

do swimming .... *go s* ....

34

3 CONVERSATION *Describing routines*

A 📻 Listen and practice.

Marie: You're really fit, Paul. Do you exercise very much?
Paul: Well, I almost always get up very early, and I lift weights for an hour.
Marie: You're kidding!
Paul: No. And then I often go Rollerblading.
Marie: Wow! How often do you exercise like that?
Paul: About five times a week. What about you?
Marie: Oh, I hardly ever exercise. I usually just watch TV in my free time. I guess I'm a real couch potato!

CLASS AUDIO ONLY ▶ **B** 📻 Listen to the rest of the conversation.

What else does Paul do in his free time?

4 GRAMMAR FOCUS

Adverbs of frequency 📻		
How often do you **usually** exercise? I lift weights **every day.** I go jogging about **once a week.** I play basketball **twice a month.** I exercise about **three times a year.** I don't exercise **very often/very much.**	Do you **ever** watch television in the evening? Yes, I **almost always** watch TV after dinner. I **sometimes** watch TV before bed. **Sometimes** I watch TV before bed.* I **seldom** watch TV in the evening. No, I **never** watch TV. *Sometimes *can begin a sentence.*	**100%** always almost always usually often sometimes seldom hardly ever almost never **0%** never

A Put the adverbs in the correct place. Then practice with a partner.

1. A: What do you do on Saturday mornings? (usually)
   B: Nothing much. I sleep until noon. (almost always)

2. A: Do you go bicycling? (ever)
   B: Yeah, I go bicycling on Saturdays. (often)

3. A: How often do you play sports? (usually)
   B: Well, I play tennis. (twice a week)

4. A: What do you do after class? (usually)
   B: I go out with my classmates. (about three times a week)

5. A: How often do you exercise? (usually)
   B: I exercise. (seldom)

B *Pair work* Take turns asking the questions in part A. Give your own information when answering.

5 PRONUNCIATION Sentence stress

A 🔊 Listen to the syllables stressed in each sentence. Notice that the adverbs of frequency are stressed. Then practice the sentences.

I hardly éver do yóga in the mórning.
I óften go Róllerblading on Sáturdays.
I almost álways play ténnis on wéekends.

B *Pair work* Write four sentences about yourself using adverbs of frequency. Then take turns saying the sentences using the correct stress.

6 FITNESS POLL

A *Group work* Take a poll in your group. One person takes notes. Take turns asking each person these questions.

1. Do you have a regular fitness program? How often do you exercise?

2. Do you ever go to a gym? How often do you go? What do you do there?

3. Do you play any sports? How often do you play?

4. How often do you take long walks? Where do you go?

5. What else do you do to keep fit?

B *Group work* Study the results of the poll. Who in your group has a good fitness program?

7 LISTENING

CLASS
AUDIO
ONLY

🔊 Listen to what Ted, Wanda, and Kim like to do in the evening. Complete the chart.

	Favorite activity	How often?
Ted		
Wanda		
Kim		

8 WRITING Favorite activities

A Write about your favorite activities.

I love to exercise. I usually work out every day. I get up early in the morning and go running for about an hour. Then I often go to the gym and do aerobics. Sometimes I go for a walk in the afternoon. About once a week, I play basketball.

B *Group work* Take turns reading your compositions. Then answer any questions from the group.

9 CONVERSATION Describing exercise

 Listen and practice.

Rod: You're in great shape, Keith.
     Do you work out at a gym?
Keith: Yeah, I do. I guess I'm a real fitness freak.
Rod: So, how often do you work out?
Keith: Well, I do aerobics every day after work.
     And then I play racquetball.
Rod: Say, I like racquetball, too.
Keith: Oh, do you want to play sometime?
Rod: Uh, . . . how well do you play?
Keith: Pretty well, I guess.
Rod: Well, all right. But I'm not very good.
Keith: No problem, Rod. I won't play too hard.

10 LISTENING

CLASS
AUDIO
ONLY

 Listen to John, Anne, and Phil discuss sports and exercise. Which one is a couch potato? a fitness freak? a sports fanatic?

a couch potato   a fitness freak   a sports fanatic

1. .... 2. .... 3. ....

interchange 6

Fitness quiz
Find out how fit you are. Turn to page IC-8.

11 GRAMMAR FOCUS

Questions with how; short answers

How often do you work out?	Twice a week. Not very often.
How much time do you spend at the gym? **How long** do you spend working out?	Around two hours a day. I don't work out.
How well do you play racquetball?	Pretty well. About average, I guess. Not very well.
How good are you at sports?	I'm pretty good at sports. I guess I'm OK. Not too good.

A Complete these questions. Practice with a partner. Then write four more questions.

1. A: .... at volleyball?
   B: I guess I'm pretty good.

2. A: .... swim?
   B: Not very well, but I'd like to learn to swim better.

3. A: .... watch sports?
   B: Pretty often. About three or four times a week.

4. A: .... spend exercising?
   B: I spend about an hour every day.

B *Group work* Take turns asking the questions in part A and your own questions. Give your own information when answering.

Who in your group is a couch potato? a fitness freak? a sports fanatic?

12 READING

Smart Moves

Look at the statements in part A below. Which do you think are true?

It won't surprise fitness freaks to learn that aerobic exercise does more than raise the heart rate: It lifts the spirit and builds confidence. But many brain researchers believe that something else happens, too. Just as exercise makes the bones, muscles, heart, and lungs stronger, researchers think that it also strengthens important parts of the brain.

Research suggests that aerobic exercise helps you learn new things and remember old information better. Aerobic exercise sends more blood to the brain and it also feeds the brain with substances that develop new nerve connections. If the exercise has complicated movements like dance steps or basketball moves, the brain produces even more nerve connections – the more connections, the better the brain can process all kinds of information.

Scientists still don't fully understand the relationship between exercise and brain power. For the moment, people just have to trust that exercise is helping them to learn or remember. Scientific research clearly shows, however, that three or more workouts a week are good for you. A study in the *Journal of the American Medical Association,* for example, shows that walking four to five miles (6.5 to 8 km) an hour for 45 minutes five times a week helps you live longer. So don't be a couch potato. Get out there and do something!

A *Pair work* According to the article, which of these statements are probably true?
Check (✓) the statements. What information helped you determine this?
Underline the information in the article.

Exercise . . .

1. makes you feel happier. ☐
2. makes you feel more self-confident. ☐
3. strengthens the body. ☐
4. can increase your height. ☐
5. can help you learn things better. ☐
6. helps you remember things better. ☐
7. gives you better eyesight. ☐
8. helps you live longer. ☐

B *Pair work* Talk about these questions. Explain your answers.

1. Do you think that exercise helps people to learn and remember better?
2. Can you think of other benefits from exercise?
3. What benefits are most important to you?

7 We had a great time!

1 SNAPSHOT

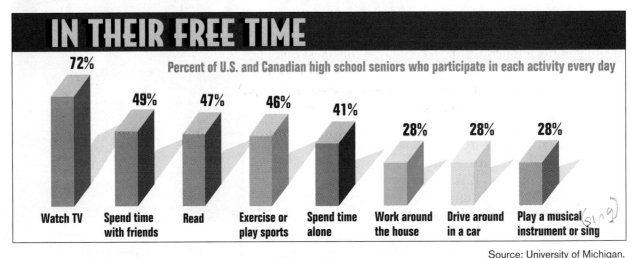

IN THEIR FREE TIME

Percent of U.S. and Canadian high school seniors who participate in each activity every day

- 72% — Watch TV
- 49% — Spend time with friends
- 47% — Read
- 46% — Exercise or play sports
- 41% — Spend time alone
- 28% — Work around the house
- 28% — Drive around in a car
- 28% — Play a musical instrument or sing *(sing)*

Source: University of Michigan, Institute for Social Research

Complete these tasks and talk about them.

Which of these activities do you do every day?
List three other activities you like to do almost every day.
Put the activities you do in order: from the most interesting to the least interesting.

In my free Timo

2 CONVERSATION The weekend

A Listen and practice.

Chris: So, what did you do this weekend, Kate?
Kate: Oh, Diane and I went for a drive in the
country on Saturday.
Chris: That sounds nice. Where did you go?
Kate: We drove to the lake and had a picnic.
We had a great time! How about you?
Did you do anything special?
Chris: Not really. I just worked on my car
all day.
Kate: That old thing! Why don't you just
buy a new one?
Chris: But then what would I do every weekend?

Due herte g. c/

CLASS AUDIO ONLY ▶ **B** Listen to Kate talk about her
activities on Sunday.

1. What did she do?
2. Where did she go?

3 GRAMMAR FOCUS

Past tense 🔊

		Regular verbs
Did you **stay** home on Sunday?	Yes, I **did**. I **watched** a football game on TV.	invite → invited
	No, I **didn't**. I **invited** friends out to dinner.	work → worked
What **did** you **do** on Saturday?	I **worked** on my car.	stay → stayed
	I **stayed** home and **studied**.	study → studied
		Irregular verbs
Did you **do** anything special?	Yes, I **did**. I **drove** to the lake.	drive → drove
	No, I **didn't**. I **had** to baby-sit.	go → went
		have → had
Where **did** you **go** on Sunday?	I **saw** a good movie.	see → saw
	I **went** to a concert.	spend → spent

For a list of irregular past forms and pronunciation rules for
regular past forms, see the appendix at the back of the book.

A Complete these conversations. Then practice with a partner.

1. A: .... you .... (go) out on Friday night?
   B: No, I .... I .... (invite) friends over,
      and I .... (cook) dinner for them.

2. A: How .... you .... (spend) your last birthday?
   B: I .... (have) a party. Everyone .... (enjoy) it,
      but the neighbors .... (complain) about the noise.

3. A: What .... you .... (do) last night?
   B: I .... (go) to the new Tom Cruise film.
      I .... (love) it!

4. A: .... you .... (do) anything special over the weekend?
   B: Yes, I .... I .... (go) shopping. Unfortunately,
      I .... (spend) all my money. Now I'm broke!

B *Pair work* Take turns asking the questions in part A.
Give your own information when answering.

4 PRONUNCIATION *Reduced forms of* did you

A 🔊 Listen and practice. Notice how **did you** is reduced in
the following questions.

[dɪdʒə]   [wədɪdʒə]
Did you have a good time?   **What did you** do last night?

B *Pair work* Practice the questions in the grammar box in Exercise 3.
Pay attention to the pronunciation of **did you**.

5 WORD POWER Collocation

A Find two other words or phrases from the list that are usually paired with each verb.

~~an art exhibition~~   ~~a vacation~~   a party   a trip *viaje*   shopping
a lot of fun   the dishes   dancing   a play   the laundry

did	housework	the dishes	the laundry
went	swimming	dancing	shopping (chaping)
had	a good time	a vacation	a viaje
saw	a movie	an art exhibition	a play
took	a day off	a vacation	a trip

B Write five sentences using words from the list.

I saw a movie last weekend.

6 ANY QUESTIONS?

Group work Take turns. One student makes a statement about the weekend. Other students ask questions. Each student answers at least four questions.

A: I went dancing on Saturday night.
B: **Where** did you go?
A: To the Rock-it Club.
C: **Who** did you go with?
A: I went with my brother.
D: **What time** did you go?
A: We went at around 10:00.
E: **How** did you like it?
A: . . .

7 LISTENING

A 🔊 Listen to John and Laura describe what they did last night. Check (✓) the correct information about each person.

B 🔊 Listen to the conversation again. What did each person do? Take notes. Then take turns telling their stories to a partner.

	John	Laura
had a boring time	✓	☐
had a good time	☐	✓
met someone interesting	✓	☐
got home late	✓	✓

8 **CONVERSATION** *On vacation*

🔊 Listen and practice.

Mike: Hi, Celia! How was your trip to the United States?
Celia: It was terrific. I really enjoyed it.
Mike: Great. How long were you away?
Celia: I was there for about three weeks.
Mike: That's a long time! Was the weather OK?
Celia: Yes, most of the time. But it snowed a lot in Chicago.
Mike: So, what was the best thing about your trip?
Celia: Oh, that's difficult to say. But I guess I liked Nashville the best.

Chicago

Nashville

9 **GRAMMAR FOCUS**

Past tense of be 🔊

Were you away last week?	Yes, I **was**.	**Contractions**
Was your brother away . . . ?	No, he **wasn't**.	was not = was**n't**
Were you and your sister away . . . ?	Yes, we **were**.	were not = were**n't**
Were your parents away . . . ?	No, they **weren't**.	
How long **were** you away?	I **was** away for three weeks.	
How **was** your vacation?	It **was** terrific!	

Complete these conversations. Then practice with a partner.

1. A: How long .... your parents in Europe?
   B: They .... there for a month.
   A: .... they in London the whole time?
   B: No, they .... They also went to Paris and Madrid.

2. A: .... you away last weekend?
   B: Yes, I .... I .... in San Francisco.
   A: How .... it?
   B: It .... great!
   A: How .... the weather?
   B: Oh, it .... foggy and cool as usual.

3. A: I .... in Istanbul last summer.
   B: Really? How long .... you there?
   A: For six weeks.
   B: .... you there on business or on vacation?
   A: I .... there on business.

Istanbul
London
San Francisco

10 VACATIONS

A *Group work* Take turns talking about vacations.
Ask these questions and others of your own.

Where did you spend your last vacation?
How long were you away?
Were you with your family?
What did you do there?

How was the weather? the food?
Did you buy anything?
Do you want to go there again?

B *Class activity* Who in your group had the most
interesting vacation? Tell the class who and why.

interchange 7

Vacation photos

Use the vacation photos
to tell a story. Student A
turns to page IC-9.
Student B turns
to page IC-10.

11 LISTENING

CLASS
AUDIO
ONLY

 Listen to Jason and Barbara talk about their vacations.
Complete the chart.

	Vacation place	Enjoyed it?		Reason(s)
		Yes	No	
Jason	....	☐	☐	....
Barbara	....	☐	☐	....

12 WRITING

A Read this postcard.

Dear Richard,
Greetings from Acapulco! I'm having a
great time! Yesterday I went on a tour
of the city, and today I went shopping.
I bought some beautiful jewelry. Oh,
and last night, I heard some Mariachi
singers on the street. They were terrific.
That's all for now.

Love,
Kathy

B *Pair work* Write a postcard to a partner about your last vacation
or an interesting place you visited recently. Then exchange postcards.

13 **READING** *Vacation postcards*

Paula,
I can't believe my trip is over.
I arrived in Egypt just two
weeks ago! I was with a
group from the university. We
went to the desert to dig in
some old ruins. I didn't find
anything, but I learned a lot.
I'm tired, but I loved every
minute of my trip.
Take care, Margaret

Hi, Luis!

My Hawaiian vacation just ended,
and I am very relaxed! I spent my
whole vacation at a spa in Koloa,
Kauai. Every day for a week I exercised,
did yoga, meditated, and ate vegetarian
food. I also went swimming and
snorkeling. I feel fantastic!

Love, Sue

Dear Michael,

Alaska is terrific! I was just on a trip
in the Arctic National Wildlife Refuge.
There were six people on the trip. We
hiked for ten days. Then we took rafts
to the Arctic Ocean. I saw a lot of
wildlife. Now I'm going to Anchorage.
See you in 3 weeks!

Kevin

A Read the postcards. Then check (✓) the statements that are true.

☐ 1. Margaret had a very relaxing vacation.
☐ 2. Margaret enjoyed her vacation.
☐ 3. Sue was in Hawaii for two weeks.
☐ 4. Sue got a lot of exercise.
☐ 5. Kevin spent his vacation alone.
☐ 6. Kevin's vacation is over.

B *Group work* Talk about these questions. Explain your answers.

1. Which person learned a lot on vacation?
2. Who had a vacation that was full of adventure?
3. Who had a very relaxing vacation?
4. Which vacation sounds the most interesting to you?

8 How do you like the neighborhood?

1 WORD POWER Places

A Match the words and the definitions. Then practice asking the questions with a partner.

pleis wer

What's a . . . ? (*barber chop*)   *It's a place where you . . .*

1. barber shop .... a. wash and dry clothes.
2. laundromat .... b. buy food.
3. library .... c. buy cards and paper.
4. stationery store *c* ...... d. get a haircut.
5. travel agency *agency* e. see a movie or play.
6. grocery store .... f. make reservations for a trip.
7. theater .... g. borrow books. *Prestamo buks*

B *Pair work* Write definitions for these places.

teach money

bank   coffee shop   drugstore   gym   post office
bookstore   dance club   gas station   hotel   restaurant
                              file

> It's a place where you keep your money. (bank)

C *Group work* Read your definitions in groups. Can others guess what each place is?

2 CONVERSATION The neighborhood

Listen and practice.

Jack: Excuse me. I'm your new neighbor, Jack. I just moved in.
Woman: Oh. Yes?
Jack: I'm looking for a grocery store. Are there any around here?
Woman: Yes, there are some on Pine Street.
Jack: OK. And is there a laundromat near here?
Woman: Well, I think there's one across from the shopping center.
Jack: Thank you. *Aproposito*
Woman: By the way, there's a barber shop in the shopping center, too.
Jack: A barber shop?

46

3 *GRAMMAR FOCUS*

There is, there are; one, any, some 🔊

Is there a laundromat near here?
 Yes, **there is.** There's **one** across from the shopping center.
 No, **there isn't**, but there's **one** next to the library.

Are there any grocery stores around here?
 Yes, **there are.** There are **some** on Pine Street.
 No, **there aren't**, but there are **some** on Third Avenue.

Prepositions

on
next to
across from/opposite
in front of
in back of/behind
near/close to
between
on the corner of

A Write questions about these places in the neighborhood map below.

| a bank | a department store | a gym | a laundromat | a post office |
| gas stations | grocery stores | hotels | a pay phone | restaurants |

Is there a pay phone around here?

Are there any restaurants on Maple Avenue?

B *Pair work* Ask and answer the questions you wrote in part A.

A: Is there a pay phone around here?
B: Yes, there is. There's one across from the post office.

4 PRONUNCIATION *Reduced forms of* there is/there are

 Listen and practice. Notice how **there is** and **there are** are reduced in conversation.

There's a gym across from the shopping center.
There's a bookstore near the laundromat.

There are some restaurants on Elm Street.
There are some grocery stores across from the post office.

5 IN YOUR NEIGHBORHOOD

Group work Take turns asking and answering questions about places like these in your neighborhood.

a bookstore	dance clubs	a coffee shop	a music store	stationery stores
a gym	drugstores	movie theaters	a pay phone	a travel agency

A: Is there a good bookstore in your neighborhood?
B: ...
A: And are there any drugstores?
B: ...

useful expressions
Sorry, I don't know.
I'm not sure, but I think . . . .
Of course. There's one . . . .

6 LISTENING

CLASS
AUDIO
ONLY

 Some hotel guests are asking about places to visit in the neighborhood. Complete the chart.

Place	Location	Interesting? Yes	No
Hard Rock Cafe	....	☑	☐
Science Museum	....	☐	☑
Aquarium	.......next to..........	☑	☐

7 SNAPSHOT

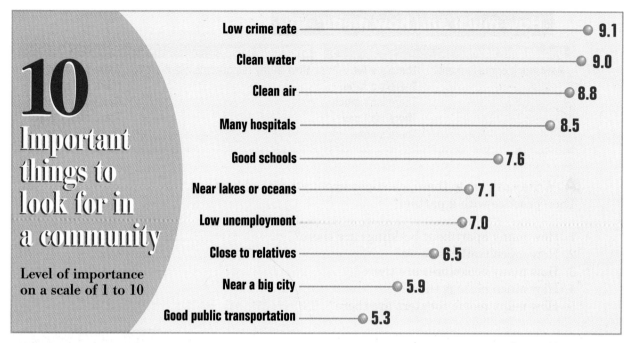

10 Important things to look for in a community

Level of importance on a scale of 1 to 10

Low crime rate	9.1
Clean water	9.0
Clean air	8.8
Many hospitals	8.5
Good schools	7.6
Near lakes or oceans	7.1
Low unemployment	7.0
Close to relatives	6.5
Near a big city	5.9
Good public transportation	5.3

Source: *Money* Magazine

Complete these tasks and talk about them.

*What is important to you in a community? Rank the features above
  from the most important (1) to the least important (10).*
List three other things you think are important in a community.

8 CONVERSATION *Describing neighborhoods*

A Listen and practice.

Dan: Where do you live, Kim?
Kim: I live in an apartment downtown.
Dan: Oh, that's convenient, but . . . how
   much crime is there?
Kim: Not much. But there is a *lot* of traffic.
   I can't stand the noise sometimes!
   Where do you live?
Dan: I have a house in the suburbs.
Kim: Oh, I bet it's really quiet.
   But is there much to do there?
Dan: No, not much. In fact, nothing ever
   really happens. That's the trouble.
Kim: Hey. Let's trade places one weekend!
Dan: OK. Great idea!

B Listen to the rest of the conversation.

What do Dan and Kim say about restaurants
in their neighborhoods?

9 GRAMMAR FOCUS

How much *and* how many

Uncountable nouns		Countable nouns	
How much crime is there?	There's **a lot**.	**How many** restaurants are there?	There are **a lot**.
	There's **a little**.		There are **a few**.
	There isn't **much**.		There aren't **many**.
	There isn't **any**.		There aren't **any**.
	There's **none**.		There are **none**.

A Write answers to these questions about your neighborhood.
Then practice with a partner.

1. How many apartment buildings are there? ....
2. How much traffic is there? ....
3. How many bookstores are there? ....
4. How much noise is there? ....
5. How many movie theaters are there? ....

B *Pair work* Write questions like those in part A about
these topics. Then ask and answer the questions.

crime   parks   pollution   restaurants   schools   stores

interchange 8

Neighborhood survey

Compare two
neighborhoods in
your city. Turn to
page IC-11.

10 WRITING

A *Group work* Talk about where you live.
Discuss these questions in groups.

Do you live in a house or an apartment?
Where is it?
How many rooms are there?
How much noise is there?
Are there any good restaurants nearby?
How many clubs/theaters/gyms are there
  in your neighborhood?
Is there any public transportation near
  your home?
How do you like it there?

B Write a paragraph about where you live.
Use the information you discussed in part A.

I live in a big apartment building in the city. There are two bedrooms,

a living room, a dining room, and a kitchen. There's a lot of noise in

my neighborhood because there's a dance club across from my building. . . .

11 READING

City Scenes

What are cities like in your country?

In many countries around the world, more and more people live in cities. Cities share many characteristics, but are also different from country to country.

Mexico Mexico's cities are modern but have traditional Indian and Spanish influences. The most important buildings are around a central square, which also serves as a place to meet with friends. There are outdoor marketplaces, where people can find almost anything they need. On Sundays, parks are a popular place for family outings. Many people move to Mexico City from rural areas. It has a lot of excitement, but also lots of traffic and air pollution.

Japan Japan's cities also have a mix of traditional and modern characteristics. There are tall office and apartment buildings as well as traditional wooden houses. Many people prefer to live near the center of cities, but because houses there are expensive, they often commute from suburbs. Traffic, pollution, and crowds are problems.

However, there is little crime, and even very crowded cities have many parks and gardens.

Australia Although 80% of Australians live near cities, the cities are not as large as those in some other countries. Most people live in houses in suburbs – not in apartments. The suburbs usually have their own churches, schools, and shopping centers. They also have recreational facilities. In large cities, like Sydney, the suburbs are often far from the center of town. Because many people commute to work, traffic is slow and there are many traffic jams.

A Read the article and complete the chart. Write one positive feature and one negative feature of cities in the countries described.

	Positive	Negative
1. Mexico	....	....
2. Japan	....	....
3. Australia	....	....

B *Pair work* Find five characteristics of the cities above that are also true of cities in your country.

Review of Units 5-8

1 DO YOU DANCE?

A *Class activity* Does anyone in your class do these things?
How often and how well do they do them? Go around the class
and find one person for each activity.

	Name	How often?	How well?
dance	....	....	....
play basketball	....	....	....
do karate	....	....	....
play computer games	....	....	....
swim	....	....	....
play the piano	....	....	....

A: Do you dance?
B: Yes, I do.
A: How often do you go dancing?
B: Every weekend.
A: And how well do you dance?
B: Actually, not very well. But I enjoy it!

B *Group work* Tell your group what you found out.

2 LISTENING

A A thief robbed a house on
Saturday. Detective Dobbs is
questioning Frankie. The
pictures show what Frankie did
on Saturday. Listen to their
conversation. Are Frankie's
answers true (**T**) or false (**F**)?

B *Pair work* Answer these questions.

1. What did Frankie do after he
   cleaned the house?
2. Where did he go? What did he do?
   When did he come home?

1:00 P.M.   **T F**   3:00 P.M.   **T F**   5:00 P.M.   **T F**

6:00 P.M.   **T F**   8:00 P.M.   **T F**   10:30 P.M.   **T F**

3 *WHAT CAN YOU REMEMBER?*

A *Pair work* Talk about what you did yesterday. Take turns asking these questions. Give as much information as possible.

What time did you get up yesterday?
What did you wear?
Were you late for class?
Did you meet anyone interesting?
How many phone calls did you make?
Did you drive or take the bus anywhere?
Did you buy anything?
How much money did you spend yesterday?
Did you watch TV? What programs did you watch?
Did you do any exercise?
Were you in bed before midnight?
What time did you go to sleep?

B *Group work* Close your books. Take turns. How many questions can you ask?

4 *ROLE PLAY* *What's it like?*

Student A: Imagine you are a visitor in your city.
You want to find out more about it.
Ask the questions in the box.

Student B: You are a resident of your city.
A visitor wants to find out more about it.
Answer the visitor's questions.

Change roles and try the role play again.

Questions to ask

What's it like to live here?
How much unemployment is there?
How much crime is there?
How many good schools are there?
Is traffic a problem?
What's public transportation like?
Are there many places to shop? Where?

5 *WHAT'S GOING ON?*

A 🔊 Listen to the sounds of four people doing different things. What do you think each person is doing?

What's going on?	
1.	3. ....
2.	4. ....

B *Pair work* Compare your answers with a partner.

A: In number 1, someone is shaving.
B: I don't think so. I think someone is . . . .

9 What does he look like?

1 WORD POWER Appearance

A Look at these expressions. Can you add three more words or expressions to describe people? Write them in the box below.

Height

short | fairly short (short jait) | medium height (jait) | pretty tall (tot) | tall

Age

young (yong) | middle aged (midl) | elderly (e'lderly)

Looks

handsome | good-looking | pretty

Other words or expressions

....

....

....

Hair

straight black hair (stret) | curly red hair (karly) (jell) | short blond hair (blond)

long brown hair (braun) | bald (bold) | a mustache and beard (mastach) (bierd)

B *Pair work* Choose at least four expressions to describe yourself and your partner. Then compare. Do you agree?

A: You have curly blond hair and a beard. You're young and good-looking.

B: I agree! / I don't agree. My hair isn't very curly.

Me	My partner
short black hair	bold
– middle aged	– elderly
– medium height	– medium height

54

2 CONVERSATION *Describing someone*

Listen and practice.

Clerk: Good afternoon. Can I help you?
Jean: Yes, I'm looking for someone.
His name is Martin Bock.
I'm afraid I missed him.
Clerk: Well, what does he look like?
Jean: Let's see. He's about 35, I guess.
He's pretty tall, with red hair.
Clerk: Oh, are you Jean Taylor?
Jean: Yes, that's right!
Clerk: He asked for you a few minutes ago.
I think he's in the restaurant.
Jean: Thanks. I'll go and look for him.

3 GRAMMAR FOCUS

Questions for describing people

General appearance		Hair	
What does he **look like**?	He's pretty tall, with red hair.	**What color** is her hair?	Light brown.
Does he wear glasses?	Yes, he does.		She has dark brown hair.
Does he have a mustache?	No, he doesn't.	**How long** is her hair?	It's medium length.
Age		Height	
How old is he?	He's about 25.	**How tall** is she?	She's fairly short.
	He's in his twenties.		She's 152 cm (five feet).

her hair

A Write questions to match these statements. Then compare with a partner.

1. ....? My brother is 26.
2. ....? I'm 173 cm (five feet eight).
3. ....? Julia has brown hair.
4. ....? No, she wears contact lenses.
5. ....? He's tall and very handsome.
6. ....? I have brown eyes.

B *Pair work* Write five questions about your teacher's or a classmate's appearance. Then take turns asking and answering your questions.

What color is Aki's hair?

4 WHO IS IT?

A Listen to the speakers describe these people.
Number the people from 1 to 5.

B *Pair work* Choose a person in your class.
Don't tell your partner who it is. Take turns.
Ask questions to guess the person your partner chose.

A: Is it a man or a woman?
B: A man.
A: How tall is he?
B: He's fairly short.
A: What color is his hair?
B: . . .

interchange 9

Find the differences
Compare two pictures of a
party. Student A turns to
page IC-12. Student
B turns to page
IC-14.

5 WRITING

A Write a description of a person in your class.
Don't put the person's name on it.

> He's in his twenties. He's quite good-looking. He's tall, and
> he has short blond hair. He's wearing a red shirt, a black
> jacket, and khaki pants. He's sitting next to the window.

B *Group work* Read your description to the group.
Can they guess who you are describing?

6 SNAPSHOT

THIRTY YEARS OF FASHION

1950s — cap, T-shirt, black leather jacket, gloves, jeans, heavy boots

1960s — hat (*hat*), teased hair, sunglasses, mini dress, wide belt, miniskirt (*skirt*), knee socks (*Knee*), tights (*tights*)

1970s — polyester shirt, three-piece suit: jacket, vest, flared pants

Talk about these questions.

Which of these items are in style now? out of style?
What are three more things that are in style today?
What are two things you wear now that you didn't wear five years ago?

7 CONVERSATION *Identifying people*

A 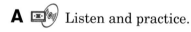 Listen and practice.

Sarah: Hi, Raoul! Good to see you!
Where's Margaret?
Raoul: Oh, she couldn't make it.
She went to a concert
with Alex.
Sarah: Oh! Well, why don't you go
and talk to Judy? She doesn't
know anyone here.
Raoul: Judy? Which one is she?
Is she the woman wearing
glasses over there?
Sarah: No, she's the tall one in jeans.
She's standing near the window.
Raoul: Oh, I'd like to meet her.

B Listen to the rest of the conversation.

(Label)

Can you label Kevin, Michiko, Rosa, and John in the picture?

8 GRAMMAR FOCUS

Modifiers with participles and prepositions 📼

		Participles
Who's Raoul?	He's **the man**	**wearing** glasses.
Which one is Raoul?	He's **the one**	**talking** to Sarah.
		Prepositions
Who's Sarah?	She's **the woman**	**with** the short black hair.
Which one is Judy?	She's **the tall one**	**in** jeans.
Who are the Smiths?	They're **the people**	**next to** the window.
Which ones are the Smiths?	They're **the ones**	**on** the couch.

A Rewrite these statements using modifiers with participles or prepositions. Then compare with a partner.

1. Jim is the tall guy. He's wearing glasses.
   Jim is the tall guy wearing glasses.

2. Bob and Louise are the good-looking couple. They're talking to Jim.
   Bob and Louise are the good-looking couple talking to Jim

3. Lynne is the young woman. She's in a T-shirt and jeans.
   Lynne is the young woman in a Tshirt and jeans

4. Maria is the attractive woman. She's sitting to the left of Carlos.
   Maria is the attractive woman sitting to the left of Carla

5. Tom is the serious-looking person. He's listening to Maria.
   Tom is the serious-looking person listening to Maria

B *Pair work* Complete these questions and add two questions of your own. Use the names of people in your class. Then take turns asking and answering the questions.

1. Who is _the young woman sitting to the (left) of Armando?_ ?   4. Who's the woman wearing _hair_ ... ?
2. Which one is _the woman whit the brye bown?_ ?   5. .... ?
3. Who's the man sitting next to _Milan_ ? ?   6. .... ?

---

9 PRONUNCIATION Contrastive stress

A 📼 Listen and practice. Notice how the stress changes to emphasize a contrast.

A: Is Raoul the one wearing the red **shírt**?   A: Is Judy the short one in **jéans**?
B: No, he's the one wearing the **bláck** shirt.   B: No, she's the **táll** one in jeans.

B 📼 Mark the stress changes in these conversations. Listen and check. Then practice the conversations.

1. A: Is Rose the one sitting next to Kate?   2. A: Is Brian the man on the couch?

   B: No, she's the one standing next to Kate.   B: No, Brian's the man behind the couch.

10 *READING*

Hip-Hop Fashions

What kinds of clothing styles do you like to wear?
Do you like to "dress up" or "dress down"?

Teenagers who listen to the same music often have a common "look." One hot style in music and fashion is hip-hop. Hip-hop is a type of urban music with a heavy beat. The lyrics are very important in this music. Hip-hop fashions are large or loose-fitting street clothes. The style includes baggy jeans, sweatshirts, hiking boots, and baseball caps (usually worn backward). However, teens add other clothing items like flannel shirts, jackets with sports logos, and athletic shoes. In the hip-hop style, boys and girls dress the same.

African American kids in Detroit and Chicago first made hip-hop fashions popular – they wore baggy street clothes to dance clubs. Then North American and European bands also began wearing this style. These bands influenced one another's music and clothing. This mixture made hip-hop into an international fashion sensation.

Hip-hop is now a teen fashion from Britain to Japan. Melanie Borrow, 17, of Manchester, England, says, "My pride and joy in life are my Levi's jeans." In Japan, hip-hop is replacing the usual outfit for teenage girls: blouses and skirts with cartoon characters on them. And in the United States, teens spend a lot of money on hip-hop fashions. David Bowen, 17, of Evanston, Illinois, has five pairs of hiking boots at $100 each. Bowen says, "They're popular because a lot of hip-hop performers wear them. They even rap about them."

A Read the article. Then look at these pictures and label them. According to the article, which of the clothing items are hip-hop fashions? Check (✓) the correct items.

baggy jeans ☐ .... ☐ .... ☐ hiking boots ☐ baseball ☐

.... ☐ sweatshirt ☐ .... ☐ .... ☐ .... ☐

B *Pair work* Talk about these questions.

1. Do you ever listen to urban or hip-hop music?
2. Do you ever wear hip-hop fashions? Describe what you wear.
3. What do you wear when you dress up or dress down?

10 Have you ever ridden a camel?

1 SNAPSHOT

Unusual Ways to Spend Time

Singapore:
Eat at a bird-singing cafe

New York City:
Go to a TV talk show

New Zealand:
Try bungee jumping

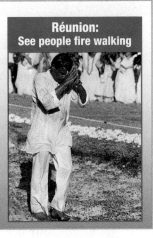
Réunion:
See people fire walking

Talk about these questions.

Which of these activities would you like to try? Why?
What are three unusual things you can do in your city or country?

2 CONVERSATION Going out

A Listen and practice.

>   *enjoing*
> **Ted:** Are you enjoying your trip to New Orleans?
> **Brenda:** Oh, yes. I really like it here.
> **Ted:** Would you like to do something tonight?
> **Brenda:** Sure. I'd love to.
> **Ted:** Let's see. Have you been to a jazz club yet?
> **Brenda:** Yes. I've already been to several clubs here.
> **Ted:** OK. What about an evening riverboat tour?
> **Brenda:** Uh, actually, I've gone twice this week.
> **Ted:** So, what *do* you want to do?
> **Brenda:** Well, I haven't been to the theater in a long time.
> **Ted:** Oh, OK. I hear there's a terrific show at the Saenger Theater.
> **Brenda:** Great! Let's make a reservation.

CLASS AUDIO ONLY ▶ **B** Listen to Ted call the Saenger Theater.

1. What's playing tonight?
2. Where is the theater?

60

3 GRAMMAR FOCUS

Present perfect; already, yet

The present perfect is formed with the verb **have** + the past participle form of a verb.		Contractions
Have you **been** to a jazz club?	Yes, I**'ve already been** to several.	I have = I**'ve**
Have they **seen** the play?	No, they **haven't seen** it **yet**.	have not = haven**'t**
Has she **gone** on a riverboat tour?	Yes, she**'s gone** twice this week.	she has = she**'s**
Has he **called** his parents lately?	No, he **hasn't called** them.	has not = hasn**'t**

Regular past participles	Irregular past participles			
call → call**ed**	be → **been**	have → **had**
hike → hik**ed**	do → **done**	make → **made**
jog → jog**ged**	eat → **eaten**	see → **seen**
try → tr**ied**	go → **gone**	

For a list of irregular past participles, see the appendix at the back of the book.

A How many times have you done these things in the past week?
Write your answers. Then compare with a partner.

1. clean the house
2. make your bed
3. cook dinner
4. do laundry
5. wash the dishes
6. go grocery shopping

> **useful expressions**
> once *de una vez, una, uno*
> *tuais* twice *dos veces*
> three times
> every day

> *I've cleaned the house once this week.*
> **OR**
> *I haven't cleaned the house this week.*

B Complete these conversations using the present perfect.
Then practice with a partner.

1. A: Have you done much exercise this week?
   B: Yes, I have already been to aerobics
      class four times. (be)

2. A: Have you played any sports this month?
   B: No, I haven't the time. (have)

3. A: How many movies have you been to this month?
   B: Actually, I haven't see any yet. (see)

4. A: Have you been to any interesting parties lately?
   B: No, I haven't gone to any parties for a while. (go)

5. A: Have you called any friends today?
   B: Yes, I have already made three calls. (make)

6. A: How many times have you gone out to eat this week?
   B: I have eaten at fast-food restaurants a couple of
      times. (eat)

C *Pair work* Take turns asking the questions in part B.
Give your own information when answering.

4 CONVERSATION *Describing events*

A  Listen and practice.

Dave: So, how was your weekend?
Sue: Oh, really good. I went to see David Copperfield.
Dave: The magician?
Sue: That's right. Have you ever seen him?
Dave: Yes, I have. I saw his show in Las Vegas last year. He's terrific.
Sue: Yeah. He does some incredible things.
Dave: Have you ever been to Las Vegas?
Sue: No, I've never been there.
Dave: You should go sometime. It's an interesting city, and the hotels are wonderful.

B Have you ever seen a magician? When? Where? What did you think of the magician?

David Copperfield

5 GRAMMAR FOCUS

Present perfect and past tense

Use the present perfect for an indefinite time in the past. Use the past tense for a specific event in the past.

Have you ever **seen** a magic show?	Yes, I **have**.	I **saw** a magic show last year.
	No, I **haven't**.	But my sister **saw** David Copperfield.
Have you ever **been** to Las Vegas?	Yes, I **have**.	I **went** there in September.
	No, I **haven't**.	I**'ve** never **been** there.

A Complete these conversations. Use the present perfect and the past tense of the verbs given and short answers. Then practice with a partner.

1. A: Have you ever gone skiing? (go)
   B: Yes, I have. I went skiing once in Colorado.

2. A: Have you ever lost something valuable? (lose)
   B: No, I haven't. But my brother lost his camera on a trip once.

3. A: Have you ever gotten a traffic ticket? (get)
   B: Yes, I have. Once I got a ticket and had to pay $50.

4. A: Have you ever seen a body-building competition? (see)
   B: Yes, I have. I saw the National Championships this year.

5. A: Have you ever been late for an important appointment? (be)
   B: No, I haven't. But my sister went 30 minutes late for her wedding!

B *Pair work* Take turns asking the questions in part A. Give your own information when answering.

6 *PRONUNCIATION* Have

A 🔊 Listen and practice. In questions, **have** is usually reduced to /həv/. In short answers, **have** is not reduced.

A: **Have** you ever been in a traffic accident?
B: Yes, I have.

A: **Have** you ever eaten Greek food?
B: No, I haven't.

B *Pair work* Write four questions like those in part A. Take turns asking and answering the questions. Pay attention to the pronunciation of **have**.

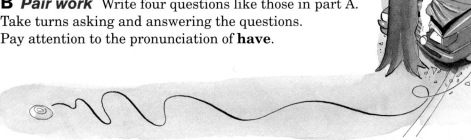

7 *LISTENING*

🔊 Listen to Clarice and Karl talk about interesting things they've done recently. Complete the chart.

	Where he/she went	Why he/she liked it
Clarice		
Karl		

8 *WORD POWER* Collocation

A Find two words or phrases in the list that are usually paired with each verb.

a camel	a hill	kiwi fruit	~~a mountain~~	rice wine	a truck
<u>goat's milk</u>	your keys	<u>a motorcycle</u>	<u>raw fish</u>	a sports car	your wallet

climb ~~repair~~ a mountain   climbed
drink goat's milk
drive a motorcycle
eat raw fish
lose a sports car
ride a truck

B Write the past participle forms of the verbs above. Then compare with a partner.

9 *HAVE YOU EVER...?*

A *Group work* Ask your classmates questions about each of the things in Exercise 8. Take notes on the answers.

A: Have you ever ridden a camel?
B: Yes, I have.
A: Really? Where were you?
B: . . .

B *Class activity* Tell the class one interesting thing you learned about a classmate.

10 *WRITING* *I've never . . . .*

A Write a paragraph describing something that you've never done but would like to do. Explain why you want to do it.

> I've never gone white-water rafting. I'd like to because it sounds exciting. My brother was on vacation in Canada two years ago and decided to try it. . . .

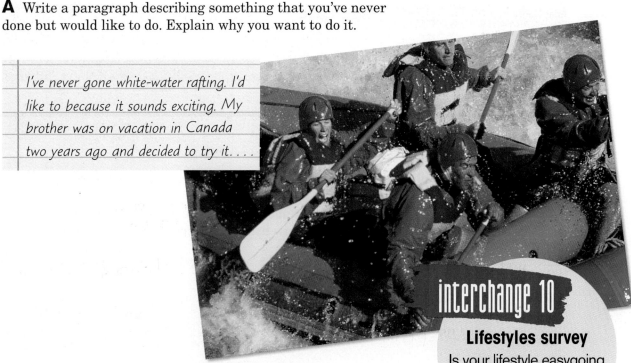

interchange 10

Lifestyles survey
Is your lifestyle easygoing and relaxed or busy and fast-paced? Turn to page IC-13.

B *Pair work* Exchange your compositions. Take turns asking and answering questions with a partner.

11 *READING*

Taking the Risk

Have you ever participated in a risky sport? What was it?

Sports World magazine spoke with Jenny Adams, Tom Barker, and Ray Lee about risky sports.

SW: Hang gliding is a dangerous sport. Jenny, what do you enjoy about the sport, and have you ever had an accident?

Jenny: No, I've never been seriously injured. Maybe I've just been lucky. Once, my glider turned upside down, and I lost control. I almost crashed, but I parachuted away just in time. And I've always felt hang gliding is quite safe – though landing is sometimes difficult. But it's fantastic to be able to fly like a bird!

SW: Tom, you've been mountain climbing for years now. What are some of the dangers that you've experienced?

Tom: High altitudes are hard on the human body. I've experienced lack of oxygen, tiredness, and dehydration. I've lived through storms, avalanches, and strong winds. But that's what I like about mountain climbing – overcoming danger.

SW: What exactly are the bends, Ray? And have you ever experienced them while scuba diving?

Ray: You get the bends when you've been deep under water. If you come up out of the water too quickly, bubbles form in your blood. The bends can be serious, and they can even cause death. But the bends are rare. Scuba diving isn't really dangerous. And it lets you explore another world.

A Read the article. What do Jenny, Tom, and Ray enjoy about the sports they describe? What is dangerous about each sport? Complete the chart.

	Sport	What they enjoy	The danger(s)
1. Jenny	....	....	....
2. Tom	....	....	....
3. Ray	....	....	....

B *Pair work* Talk about these questions.

1. Have you ever tried any of the sports described? What was it like?
2. Which of the sports would you like to try? Why?

11 It's a very exciting city!

1 WORD POWER Adjectives

A *Pair work* Match each word in column A with its opposite in column B. Then add two more pairs of adjectives to the list.

A
1. beautiful (h)
2. big .... (F)
(Chip) 3. cheap barato (D)
4. clean ...... (C)
5. hot (h)
6. interesting (a)
(seif) 7. safe seguro (b)
8. relaxing (e)
9. ....
10. ....

B
a. boring aburrido
b. dangerous
c. dirty sucio
d. expensive caro
e. stressful estresante
f. small pequeña
g. ugly feo
h. cold
i. ....
j. ....

B Choose four adjectives from part A that describe your city. Then compare with a partner.

2 CONVERSATION Describing cities

A Listen and practice.

Linda: Where in Canada are you from, Ken?
  Ken: I'm from Toronto.
Linda: Oh, I've never been there. What's it like?
  Ken: It's a fairly big city, but it's not *too* big.
        The nightlife is good, too.
Linda: Is it expensive there?
  Ken: No, it's not too bad.
Linda: And what's the weather like in Toronto?
  Ken: Well, it's pretty cold in the winter, and
        very hot and humid in the summer.
        It's nice in the spring and fall, though.

CLASS AUDIO ONLY ► **B** Listen to the rest of the conversation.

What does Ken say about entertainment in Toronto?

Toronto

66

3 GRAMMAR FOCUS

Adverbs and adjectives; conjunctions 🔊

It's a **very** exciting city. It's **too** expensive, **however.** *dungue (bo)*
It's **not very** exciting. It's **really** beautiful, **though.**
It's a **fairly** big city, **but** it's **not too** big.
It's **pretty** safe, **and** it's **very** friendly.
segura

A Match the questions with the answers. Then practice
the conversations.

1. What's Hong Kong like?
   Is it an interesting place? ...*c*....

2. Do you like your hometown? ....

3. What's Sydney like?
   I've never been there. ...*a*....

4. Have you ever been to
   São Paulo? ....

✓ a. Oh, really? It's beautiful, and it's very clean.
   It has a great harbor and beautiful beaches.

b. Yes, many times. It's a very modern city.
   It's too hot in the summer, though.

✓ c. Yes, it is. It's very exciting.
   It's really crowded, however.

d. No, I have it. It's not too small, but it's
   pretty boring. That's why I moved away.

B *Pair work* What do you think of these cities? Take turns describing them.

"San Francisco is a really exciting city, and it's very clean."

4 LISTENING

🔊 Listen to Joyce and Nick talk about their hometowns. What do they say?
Check (✓) the correct boxes.

	Big?		Interesting?		Expensive?		Beautiful?	
	Yes	No	Yes	No	Yes	No	Yes	No
1. Joyce	☐	☐	☐	☐	☐	☐	☐	☐
2. Nick	☐	☐	☐	☐	☐	☐	☐	☐

5 HOME SWEET HOME

Group work Take turns. Ask one student about his or her hometown.
Then ask follow-up questions to get more information.

What's your city like?

Is it an interesting place?   Is it very expensive?
Is it very big?   What's the nightlife like?
Is it safe?   What's the weather like?
Is it clean?   Do you like it there?

6 WRITING

Pair work Think of an interesting city in
your country. Write a short composition
about it. Then exchange compositions.
Can your partner suggest any information
to add?

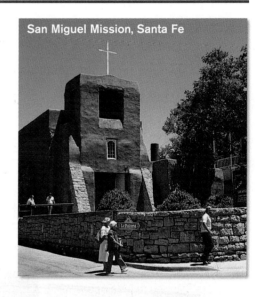
San Miguel Mission, Santa Fe

My favorite city in the United States is Santa Fe.
It's in New Mexico. It's an old city with lots
of interesting Native American and Spanish
buildings. It's fairly small, and it's really beautiful. . . .

7 SNAPSHOT

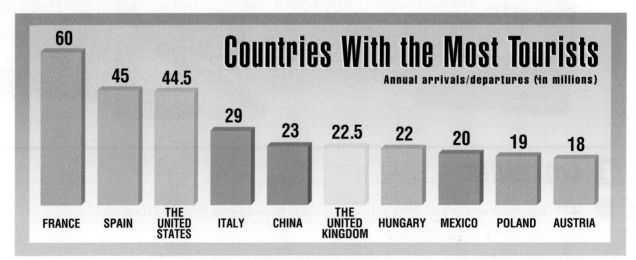

Countries With the Most Tourists
Annual arrivals/departures (in millions)

FRANCE	SPAIN	THE UNITED STATES	ITALY	CHINA	THE UNITED KINGDOM	HUNGARY	MEXICO	POLAND	AUSTRIA
60	45	44.5	29	23	22.5	22	20	19	18

Source: World Tourism Organization

Talk about these questions.

Why do you think France has the most tourists?
Which countries on this list would you most like to visit? Rank the countries from 1 to 10.
Which country did you rank number 1? Why?

8 CONVERSATION *Giving suggestions*

A Listen and practice.

David: Can you tell me a little about Mexico City?
Maria: Sure I can. What would you like to know?
David: Well, what's a good time to visit?
Maria: I think you can go anytime. The weather is always nice.
David: Oh, good! And what should I see there?
Maria: Well, you should visit the National Museum and go to the Palace of Fine Arts.
David: What else?
Maria: Oh, you shouldn't miss the Pyramid of the Sun. It's very interesting.
David: It all sounds really exciting!

the Palace of Fine Arts

CLASS AUDIO ONLY ▶ **B** Listen to the rest of the conversation.

1. Where is David from?
2. What should you do there?

the Pyramid of the Sun

9 GRAMMAR FOCUS

Modal verbs can and should

Can you tell me about Mexico? What **can** you do there?	Yes, I **can**./No, I **can't**. You **can** see the Palace of Fine Arts.
Should I go to the Palace of Fine Arts? What **should** I see there?	Yes, you **should**./No, you **shouldn't**. You **should** visit the National Museum. You **shouldn't** miss the Pyramid of the Sun.

A Complete these sentences about things to do in France. Use the verbs from the list.

1. You .... Paris.
2. You .... the Eiffel Tower.
3. You .... French food.
4. You .... shopping at the flea markets.
5. You .... a boat ride on the Seine River.
6. You .... a morning at the Louvre Museum.

should spend
can see
can go
should visit
should try
shouldn't miss

B *Pair work* Write answers to these questions about your country. Then compare with a partner.

1. What time of year should you go there?
2. What are three things you can do there?
3. Can you buy anything special?
4. What shouldn't a visitor miss?
5. What shouldn't people do?

1. You should go in the spring.

69

10 *PRONUNCIATION* Can't *and* shouldn't

A Listen and practice these sentences. Notice how the *t* in **can't** and **shouldn't** is pronounced.

You can't walk home on the streets late at night.
You shouldn't miss the night markets.
You can't go shopping on Sundays.
You shouldn't swim at the beaches.

B *Class activity* Are any of these statements true about your city?

interchange 11

City guide
Make a guide to fun and interesting places in your city. Turn to page IC-15.

11 *LISTENING*

CLASS AUDIO ONLY

A Listen to three speakers talk about Japan, Argentina, and Italy. Complete the chart.

	Capital city	What visitors should see or do
1. Japan	....	....
2. Argentina	....	....
3. Italy	....	....

CLASS AUDIO ONLY

B Listen again. One thing about each country is incorrect. What is it?

12 *ON VACATION*

Group work Has anyone in your group visited an interesting country or place in your country? Find out more about it. Start like this and ask questions like the ones below.

A: I visited Malaysia last summer.
B: Did you enjoy it?
A: Yes, I did.
C: . . .

What's the best time of year to visit?
What's the weather like then?
What should tourists see and do there?
What special foods can you eat?
What's the shopping like?
What things should people buy?
What else can visitors do there?

Kuala Lumpur, Malaysia

a market in Kuala Lumpur

13 *READING*

FAMOUS CITIES

What cities are famous in your country? Why are they famous?

1.

2.

3.

This beautiful city in northeastern Italy is built on about 120 small islands. The city has no roads. Instead, people use boats to travel along the canals. Flat-bottomed boats called gondolas were once the main means of transportation, but today motorboats are more popular. You should see St. Mark's Square – the center of activity in this city. It has wonderful Renaissance buildings.

Which city:
- ☐ Paris
- ☐ Venice
- ☐ Rome

This American city is the main business and cultural center of the Midwest. It is famous for its music, opera, and theater. It also has excellent museums. When shopping in this city, you can visit a long row of fashionable stores on North Michigan Avenue. This area is called the Magnificent Mile. One of the world's tallest buildings, the John Hancock Center, is also on this avenue.

Which city:
- ☐ New York
- ☐ San Francisco
- ☐ Chicago

Travelers use many words to describe this South American city: beautiful, glamorous, sunny, friendly, and exciting. It is the city of the Carnival, when everyone dances the samba in the streets. Tourists also love to visit its fabulous beaches and mountains. You shouldn't miss the National Park of Tijuca – one of the largest city parks in the world.

Which city:
- ☐ Mexico City
- ☐ Rio de Janeiro
- ☐ Havana

A Read descriptions of the three cities. Check (✓) the correct city to match each description.

B Complete the chart with information about each city.
Then compare with a partner.

	Where is this city?	What is special about this city?	What should visitors do there?
1.			
2.			
3.			

C *Class activity* Which city would you like to visit? Why?

12 It really works!

1 **SNAPSHOT**

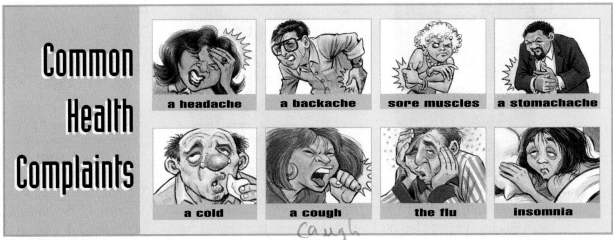

Common Health Complaints

a headache   a backache   sore muscles   a stomachache

a cold   a cough   the flu   insomnia

Source: National Center for Health Statistics

Talk about these questions.

Have you had any of these health problems recently? Which ones?
How many times have you been sick in the past year?
What do you do when you have a headache? a cold? insomnia?

2 **CONVERSATION** *Health problems*

A Listen and practice.

Joan: Hi, Craig! How are you?
Craig: Not so good. I have a terrible cold.
Joan: Really? That's too bad! You should
     be at home in bed. It's really important
     to get a lot of rest.
Craig: Yeah, you're right.
Joan: And have you taken anything for it?
Craig: No, I haven't.
Joan: Well, it's helpful to chop up some garlic
     and cook it in chicken stock. Then drink
     a cup every half hour. It really works!
Craig: Ugh!

CLASS
AUDIO
ONLY

B Listen to advice from two more of
Craig's co-workers.

What do they suggest?

72

3 GRAMMAR FOCUS

Infinitive complements

What should you do for a cold?   **It's important** to get a lot of rest.
It's a good idea to take some vitamin C.
It's useful to get some cold medicine. *Es util tomar algo de medicine*
It's helpful to chop up some garlic and cook it. *Es util pical*

A Look at these health problems. Choose several pieces of good advice for each problem.

a sore throat

a fever

a toothache

a burn

Problems

1. a sore throat *gargante* C
2. a cough .... *tos* ...... j
3. a backache .... b
4. a fever .... f
5. a toothache i
6. a bad headache .... g
7. a burn .... f
8. the flu .... a

Advice

a. take some vitamin C
b. put some ointment on it
c. drink lots of liquids
d. go to bed and rest
e. put a heating pad on it
f. put it under cold water
g. take some aspirin
h. get some medicine from the drugstore
i. see the dentist
j. see the doctor

B *Group work* Talk about the problems in part A and give advice. What other advice do you have for each problem?

A: What should you do for a sore throat?
B: It's a good idea to get some medicine from the drugstore.
C: Yes. And it's important to drink lots of liquids.
D: Well, I think it's useful to . . . .

C Write advice for these problems. (You will use this advice in Exercise 4.)

a cold
insomnia
sore eyes
sore muscles
stress

For a cold, it's a good idea to . . . .

stress

sore eyes

4 **PRONUNCIATION** *Reduced form of* to

A  Listen and practice. In conversation, **to** is usually reduced to /tə/.

A: What should you do for a fever?
B: It's important **to** take some aspirin.
   And it's a good idea **to** see the doctor.

B *Pair work* Now look back at part C of Exercise 3. Ask for and give advice about the health problems you wrote about. Pay attention to the pronunciation of **to**.

interchange 12

Talk radio
Imagine you are a talk show host. Give advice to some callers. Turn to page IC-16.

5 **WHAT DID YOU DO?**

A *Pair work* Take turns talking about these problems.

a stomachache   an insect bitc   a sore throat   the hiccups

A: Have you ever had a stomachache?
B: Sure I have. Just last night, actually.
A: What did you do?
B: I took some antacid.

B *Group work* Compare with other pairs. Tell what you did for each problem.

6 **WORD POWER** *Containers and medicines*

A Use the words in the list to complete these expressions. Then compare with a partner.

bottle   box   can   package   tube

1. a ....*tube*.... of ointment
2. a ..*bottle*.. of aspirin
3. a ....*box*.... of bandages
4. a ....*can*.... of foot spray
5. a *package* of tissues

B What is one more thing you can buy in each of the containers above?

C What common items do you have in your medicine cabinet?

7 *CONVERSATION* *Giving suggestions*

A 🔊 Listen and practice.

Pharmacist: Hi. Can I help you?
Mrs. Webb: Yes, please. Could I have something for a cough? I think I'm getting a cold. *box*
Pharmacist: Well, I suggest a box of these cough drops. And you should get a bottle of vitamin C, too.
Mrs. Webb: Thank you. And what do you have for dry skin? *lotion*
Pharmacist: Try some of this new lotion. It's very good.
Mrs. Webb: OK. Thanks a lot. *lot*

CLASS AUDIO ONLY ▶ **B** 🔊 Listen to the pharmacist talk to the next customer. *cliente*

What does the customer want?

8 *GRAMMAR FOCUS*

Modal verbs* can, could, may *for requests; suggestions 💿

Can/May I help you?	What do you have/suggest for dry skin?
Can I have a box of cough drops? *drop*	Try some of this lotion. *Pulsen vaselina/one*
Could I have something for a sore throat?	I suggest some ointment.
May I have a bottle of aspirin? *bott*	You should get some skin cream. *crem*

Complete these conversations with the verbs *can, could, may, have, suggest, try,* or *should.* Then compare and practice with a partner.

1. A: ....**Can**.... *May* I help you?
   B: Yes. ...**could**.... I have something for tired eyes?
   A: Sure. I ...**have**.... a bottle of eye drops.

2. A: What do you ...**suggest**... for sore muscles?
   B: You ...**should**.... try a tube of this ointment. It's excellent. *Probar*
   A: OK. I'll take it.

3. A: ....**May**.... I have a box of cold tablets, please?
   B: Here you are.
   A: And what do you ...**suggest**... for insomnia?
   B: ...**try**.... some of these sleeping pills.
   A: OK. Thanks.

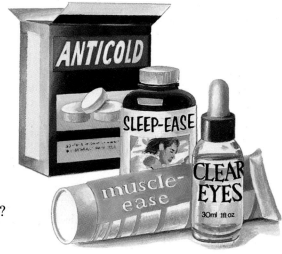

ANTICOLD
SLEEP-EASE
muscle-ease
CLEAR EYES
30ml 1fl oz

9 LISTENING

  Listen to people talking about things in a drugstore. Check (✓) the items they buy.

1.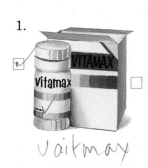

vaitmax

2.

3.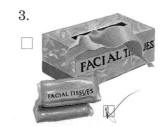

4.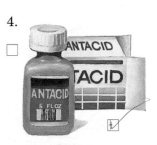

10 ROLE PLAY _Can I help you?_

Student A: You are a customer in a drugstore. You need:

      something for a sunburn
      something for sore muscles
      something for a sore throat ✓

Ask for some suggestions.

Student B: You are a pharmacist in a drugstore. A customer needs some things. Make some suggestions.

   a can of sunburn spray   a tube of muscle ointment   a bottle of throat spray

Change roles and try the role play again. Make up your own information.

11 WRITING

A Write about an interesting home or folk remedy.

> _I have a good home remedy for a sore throat. I learned about it from my grandmother. Cut slices of meat, put pepper on them, and then tie them around your throat with a cloth. It's also a good idea to go to bed and rest. This always works (my grandmother says!)._

B _Pair work_ Take turns reading your compositions. Which home remedy is the most interesting?

12 *READING*

Grandma knows best!

When you have a minor health problem, do you usually go to the doctor, get something from the drugstore, or use a home remedy?

When people have a cold, a fever, or the flu, they usually go to the doctor for help, or they get some medicine from the drugstore. But many people also use home remedies for common illnesses. Here are some simple home remedies.

Bee stings and insect bites

Wash the sting or bite. Put some meat tenderizer on a handkerchief and then put the handkerchief on the bite for half an hour. To avoid insect bites, it's helpful to eat garlic or take garlic pills.

Burns

Put the burn under cold water or put a cold handkerchief on it. It's important not to put ice on the burn.

Colds

Lots of people eat hot chicken soup when they have a cold. They find it clears the head and the nose. Some people rub oil on their chest for a cold. Other people drink a mixture of red pepper, hot water, sugar, lemon juice, and milk or vinegar.

Cough

Drink warm liquids or take some honey.

Headaches

Apply an ice pack or cold cloth to your head, or splash your face with cold water. It's also a good idea to put your hands into hot water and leave them there for several minutes. Also, you shouldn't read or watch TV.

Insomnia

Drink a large glass of warm milk. It's also a good idea to soak in a warm bath.

A *Pair work* Read the article. Then cover the article and complete the chart. What problems are these things good for?

Advice	Problem
1. hot chicken soup / rubbing oil on your chest	Colds
2. a warm bath / warm milk	Insomnia
3. garlic / meat tenderizer	Bee stings
4. an ice pack / putting your hands in hot water	burns
5. cold water / cold handkerchief	headaches
6. honey / warm liquids	cough

B *Group work* Do you use any of these remedies? What other home remedies do you use?

Review of Units 9-12

1 WHAT WAS IT LIKE?

Group work Ask these questions around the group.

Have you ever . . . ?

been on a camping trip
gotten a famous person's
    autograph
given first aid to someone
been on a blind date
lost your credit cards

gone windsurfing
been in an accident
had food poisoning
kept a diary
fainted

When someone answers "Yes," he or she
explains what happened, and the other
students ask for more information.

A: **Have you ever** gone windsurfing?
B: Yeah, I have. I tried it last year in Hawaii.
   It was really fun!
C: **What was it like?** Was it difficult?
B: Yes, it was at first. Has anyone else ever
   gone windsurfing?
D: . . .

2 ROLE PLAY *Missing person*

Student A: You are visiting an amusement
park with your English class.
One of your classmates is lost.
You are talking to a security
officer. Answer the officer's
questions and describe one of
your classmates. (Don't
give the student's name.)

Student B: You are a security officer at
an amusement park. Someone
is talking to you about a lost
classmate. Ask questions to
complete the form. Then look
around the class. Can you find
the lost student?

Change roles and try the role play again.

MISSING PERSONS REPORT

Name	
Age	
Height	
Hair	
Eyes	
Clothing	

3 WHICH ONE IS BILL?

Pair work Look at this picture of a party. Write sentences identifying each person.

Kate   Louisa   Bill   Maggie   Robert

> *Bill is the man in the black shirt./Bill is the one sitting next to Louisa.*

4 LISTENING

CLASS
AUDIO
ONLY

Listen to Jenny talking about Honolulu. What does she say about these things? Complete the chart.

What she says about	
1. size	
2. weather	
3. prices	
4. a famous place	

5 DIFFICULT SITUATIONS

difficult situations

A ***Group work*** What do you do in these situations? Discuss each situation using expressions from the box. Write down your ideas.

What do you do when . . . ?

1. you have an argument with a friend
2. it's 2:00 A.M. and you can't sleep
3. you feel very stressed
4. you can't remember someone's name
5. you need to study, but you can't concentrate

> *1. It's a good idea to apologize right away.*

useful expressions

It's useful to . . . .
It's helpful to . . . .
It's a good idea to . . . .
You can . . . .
You should . . . .

B ***Class activity*** Read your group's ideas to the class.

13 May I take your order, please?

1 SNAPSHOT

Favorite Kinds of Ethnic Foods in the United States

Percentage of people preferring each kind of food

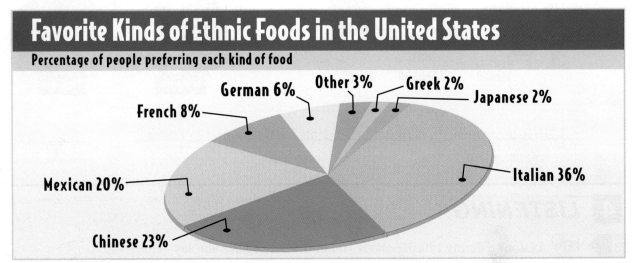

French 8%
German 6%
Other 3%
Greek 2%
Japanese 2%
Mexican 20%
Italian 36%
Chinese 23%

Source: National Restaurant Association

Talk about these questions.

Are there restaurants in your city that serve these kinds of foods?
Which of the foods have you tried? Which would you like to try?
What other kinds of foods do you like?

2 CONVERSATION *Going out for dinner*

A 🔊 Listen and practice.

Sandy: Say, do you want to go out to dinner tonight?
Bob: Sure. Where would you like to go?
Sandy: Well, what do you think of Indian food?
Bob: I love it, but I'm not really in the mood for it today.
Sandy: Yeah. I'm not either, I guess. It's a bit spicy.
Bob: Hmm. How do you like Japanese food?
Sandy: Oh, I like it a lot.
Bob: I do, too. And I know a nice Japanese restaurant near here – it's called Iroha.
Sandy: Oh, I've always wanted to go there.
Bob: Terrific! Let's go!

CLASS AUDIO ONLY ▶ **B** 🔊 Listen to the rest of the conversation.

1. What time do they decide to have dinner? Why?
2. Where do they decide to meet?

3 GRAMMAR FOCUS

So, too, neither, either

I like Japanese food a lot.	I don't like greasy food.
So do I./I do, **too**.	**Neither** do I./I don't **either**.
Really? I don't like it very much.	Oh, I like it a lot.
I'm crazy about dessert.	I'm not in the mood for Indian food.
So am I./I am, **too**.	**Neither** am I./I'm not **either**.
Oh, I'm not at all.	Really? I am.
I can eat really spicy food.	I can't stand fast food.
So can I./I can, **too**.	**Neither** can I./I can't **either**.
Oh, I can't.	Oh, I love it!

healthy   greasy   salty   rich   spicy   delicious   bland

A Write responses to show agreement with these statements.
Then compare with a partner.

1. I'm not crazy about French food. ....
2. I can eat any kind of food. ....
3. I think Mexican food is delicious. ....
4. I can't stand greasy food. ....
5. I don't like salty food. ....
6. I'm in the mood for something spicy. ....
7. I'm crazy about Korean food. ....
8. I don't enjoy rich food very much. ....
9. I always eat healthy food. ....
10. I can't eat bland food. ....

B *Pair work* Take turns responding to the statements in part A again.
Give your own opinion when responding.

C Write statements about these things. (You will use the statements
in Exercise 4.)

1. two kinds of food you like
2. two kinds of food you can't stand
3. two kinds of food you are in the mood for

4 PRONUNCIATION Stress in responses

A 🔊 Listen and practice. The last word of each response is usually stressed.

So do **Í**.	I do, **tóo**.	Neither am **Í**.	I'm not **éither**.
Neither do **Í**.	I don't **éither**.	So can **Í**.	I can, **tóo**.
So am **Í**.	I am, **tóo**.	Neither can **Í**.	I can't **éither**.

B *Pair work* Take turns reading the statements you wrote in part C of Exercise 3. Pay attention to the stress in your responses.

A: I don't really like greasy food.
B: I don't **éither**. (Neither do **Í**.) It's not very healthy.

5 WORD POWER Restaurant orders

A *Pair work* Complete the chart with words from the list. Then add two more words to each category. What's your favorite food in each category?

apple pie   cold pasta salad   chicken broth   chocolate cake   coffee
cole slaw   onion soup   grilled salmon   hamburger & fries   ice cream
iced tea   milk   mixed greens   roast turkey   clam chowder

Soups	Salads	Main dishes	Desserts	Beverages
onion soup	cold pasta salad	chicken broth	apple pie	iced tea
col	cole slaw	grilled salmon	ice cream	milk
	mixed greens	hamburger & fries		chocolate cake
		roast turkey		coffee
				clam chowder

B What foods do you think these people like best? Use items from the chart above or your own ideas.

Jenny

Brenda

Grant

Mr. and Mrs. Dobson

1. ....   2. ....   3. ....   4. ....

CLASS AUDIO ONLY ▶ **C** 🔊 Listen to each of the people above talking about their favorite foods and take notes. How similar were your guesses?

6 CONVERSATION *Ordering a meal*

 Listen and practice.

Waiter: May I take your order?
Customer: Yes. I'd like a hamburger and a large order of french fries, please.
Waiter: All right. And would you like a salad?
Customer: Yes, I'll have a mixed green salad.
Waiter: OK. What kind of dressing would you like? We have vinaigrette, Italian, and French.
Customer: Italian, please.
Waiter: And would you like anything to drink?
Customer: Yes, I'd like a large soda, please.

7 GRAMMAR FOCUS

Modal verbs would *and* will *for requests*

What **would** you **like** to eat?	**I'd like** a hamburger. **I'll have** a small salad.	*Contractions* I will = **I'll** I would = **I'd**
What kind of dressing **would** you like?	**I'd like** Italian, please. **I'll have** French.	
What **would** you **like** to drink?	**I'd like** a large soda. **I'll have** coffee.	
Would you **like** anything else?	Yes, please. **I'd like** some water. No, thank you. That **will be** all.	

Complete this conversation. Then practice with a partner.

Waitress: What _would_ you like to order?
Customer: I _'ll_ have the fried chicken.
Waitress: _Would_ you like rice or potatoes?
Customer: Potatoes, please.
Waitress: What kind of potatoes would you _like_?
Mashed, baked, or french fries?
Customer: I _'d_ like french fries.
Waitress: OK. And what will you _have_ to drink?
Customer: I guess I _'ll_ have a cup of coffee.
Waitress: Would you _like_ anything else?
Customer: No, that _will_ be all for now, thanks.

Later

Waitress: Would you _like_ dessert?
Customer: Yes, I _'d_ like ice cream.
Waitress: What flavor _would_ you like?
Customer: Hmm. I _'ll_ have chocolate, please.
Waitress: OK. I'll bring it right away.

bring it

8 ROLE PLAY *In a coffee shop*

Student A: You are a customer in a coffee shop.
This is what you want to order for lunch:

tomato and cucumber salad   garlic bread
spaghetti and meatballs   iced tea with lemon

Student B: You are the waiter or waitress.
Take your customer's order.

Change roles and try the role play again. Make up your own information.

9 LISTENING

A 🔊 Listen to Tom and Tina ordering in a restaurant. What did each of them order? Fill in their orders.

B 🔊 Listen to the rest of the conversation. What happened?

Phil's Diner   No. 399825

Date _____

Thank You!   **Total** _____

10 WRITING *Restaurant reviews*

A Have you eaten out at a restaurant recently? How was it?
Write a review of the restaurant and the meal you had there.

> *The Surf and Turf Restaurant*
>
> I had lunch at the Surf and Turf Restaurant last week. It's a steak and seafood restaurant. I ordered a steak and a Caesar salad. For dessert, I had chocolate cake and coffee. My meal cost about $24 with the tip.
>
> The waiter was helpful. The coffee wasn't very good, but the salad and steak were delicious. I'd go back to the Surf and Turf.

Are you ready to order?
Have lunch at The Corner Cafe. Student A turns to page IC-17. Students B and C turn to page IC-18.

B *Group work* Take turns reading your reviews to the group. Is there a restaurant you would like to try?

11 *READING*

To Tip or Not to Tip?

Do you tip for services in your country? When?

Canadians and Americans usually tip in places like restaurants, airports, hotels, and hair salons because many people who work in these places get low salaries. A tip shows that the customer is pleased with the service.

At airports, porters usually get a dollar tip for each bag. Hotel bellhops usually get a dollar for carrying one or two suitcases. A hotel door attendant or parking valet also gets about a dollar for getting a taxi or for parking a car. Many people also tip hotel room attendants, especially when they stay in a hotel for several days. They usually leave a dollar for each day.

The usual tip for other kinds of services – for example, for taxi drivers, barbers, hairdressers, waiters, and waitresses – is between 10 and 20 percent of the bill. The size of the tip depends on how pleased the customer is. In most restaurants, the check does not include a service charge. If the group is large, however, there may be an added service charge. There is no tipping in cafeterias or fast-food restaurants.

A *Pair work* Read the article. Then talk about these questions.

1. How much should you tip someone in North America who:

   takes your bag at an airport?
   parks your car at a hotel or restaurant?
   serves you in a fast-food restaurant?

2. What tip should you leave for the following:

   a $27 haircut?
   a $50 restaurant check?
   a $14 taxi fare?

B *Group work* Do you think tipping is a good or bad custom? Why?

14 The biggest and the best!

1 WORD POWER Geography

A Circle the word that doesn't belong in each list. Then compare with a partner.

1. canyon
   cliff
   swamp
   valley

2. lake
   plateau
   river
   sea

3. hill
   mountain
   volcano
   ocean

4. desert
   forest
   plains
   waterfall

B Find examples of some of the words above in this picture.
What other geography words can you think of?

C Add two names to these lists. Then compare with a partner.

Mountains	Rivers	Continents	Oceans
Mount Everest	the Amazon River	Africa	the Pacific Ocean

2 CONVERSATION *Describing countries*

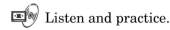 Listen and practice.

Paul: I'm going to Australia next year. Aren't you from "down under," Kelly?

Kelly: That's right.

Paul: I hear there's not much pollution, and the beaches are clean and beautiful.

Kelly: Oh, yes. Australia has some of the most famous beaches in the world – like Bondi Beach.

Paul: What else should I see?

Kelly: Well, the Great Barrier Reef is there. It's the <u>longest coral reef</u> in the world.

Paul: Wow! It sounds beautiful. You're lucky to be an Australian.

Kelly: Thanks, but actually, I'm a New Zealander.

the Great Barrier Reef

3 GRAMMAR FOCUS

Comparisons with adjectives

Adjective	Comparative	Superlative
large	larger	the largest
long	longer	the longest
dry	drier	the driest
big	bigger	the biggest
beautiful	more beautiful	the most beautiful
famous	more famous	the most famous
good	better	the best
bad	worse	the worst

Which country is **larger**, Canada or China?
   Canada is **larger than** China.

Which country is **the largest**: Russia, Canada, or China?
   Russia is **the largest** country of the three.

What is **the most beautiful** mountain in the world?
   I think Fujiyama is **the most beautiful**.

For more information on comparatives and superlatives, see the appendix at the back of the book.

A Complete questions 1 to 4 with comparatives. Complete questions 5 to 8 with superlatives. Then ask and answer the questions. Check your answers in the appendix.

1. Which country is ...smaller..., Monaco or Vatican City?   (small)
2. Which waterfall is ...higher..., Niagara Falls or Angel Falls?   (high)
3. Which city is ...more crowded..., Hong Kong or Cairo?   (crowded)
4. Which lake is ...larger..., the Caspian Sea or Lake Superior?   (large)
5. Which mountain is ...tallest...: Mount McKinley, Mount Everest, or Fujiyama?   (tall)
6. What is ...longest... river in the world, the Nile or the Amazon?   (long)
7. Which country is ...the most popular... with tourists: Spain, France, or Italy?   (popular)
8. What is ...deepest... ocean in the world, the Pacific or the Atlantic?   (deep)

B *Class activity* Write four questions like those in part A about your country or other countries. Then ask your questions around the class.

4 PRONUNCIATION *Questions of choice*

Listen to the intonation of questions where there is a choice.
Then practice the questions.

Which country is bigger, China or Russia?

Which is the largest desert in the world, the Australian or the Sahara?

Which country is the most interesting: Korea, Brazil, or France?

5 IN YOUR OPINION

Group work Answer these questions about your country.
Be ready to explain your answers. Then compare in a group.

What are the three most interesting places in your country?
What's the best time of year to visit?
What are the most famous tourist attractions?
What's the most beautiful place in your country?

interchange 14

How much do you know?

You probably know more than you think you do! Take a quiz. Turn to page IC-19.

6 WRITING

A Write about one of the places or things you discussed in Exercise 5.

> I think the most beautiful place in my country is a town called Ubud on Bali. It's located in the mountains, and there are lots of rice fields. Many artists live and work there. . . .

B *Pair work* Exchange papers and read each other's compositions.

Ubud, Bali, Indonesia

7 LISTENING *TV game show*

CLASS AUDIO ONLY

Three people are playing a TV game show. Listen to each question, and check (✓) the correct answer.

1. ☑ the Statue of Liberty
   ☐ the Eiffel Tower
   ☐ the Empire State Building

2. ☐ Concorde
   ☑ 747
   ☐ DC-10

3. ☐ gold   *libro oro*
   ☑ butter   *4.b monle*
   ☑ feathers *Plms*

4. ☐ the U.S.
   ☐ China
   ☑ Canada

5. ☐ Moscow
   ☑ New York
   ☐ Shanghai

6. ☐ Australia
   ☑ Argentina *ciudad + pequeña*
   ☐ Brazil

8 SNAPSHOT

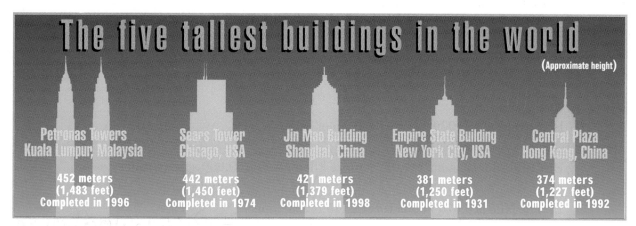

The five tallest buildings in the world

(Approximate height)

Petronas Towers Kuala Lumpur, Malaysia	Sears Tower Chicago, USA	Jin Mao Building Shanghai, China	Empire State Building New York City, USA	Central Plaza Hong Kong, China
452 meters (1,483 feet) Completed in 1996	442 meters (1,450 feet) Completed in 1974	421 meters (1,379 feet) Completed in 1998	381 meters (1,250 feet) Completed in 1931	374 meters (1,227 feet) Completed in 1992

Source: Council on Tall Buildings and Urban Habitats

Talk about these questions.

Would you like to visit any of these places? Which ones? Why?
Can you identify these buildings in your city?
  The tallest building: ....
  The oldest building: ....
  The most beautiful building: ....

9 CONVERSATION *Distance and measurements*

A Listen and practice.

Paul: So, what's New Zealand like?
Kelly: Oh, it's beautiful. It has lots of farms,
and it's very mountainous.
Paul: Mountainous? Really? I didn't know that.
How high are the mountains?
Kelly: Well, the highest one is Mount Cook.
It's about 3,800 meters high.
Paul: Hmm. How far is New Zealand from Australia?
Kelly: Well, I live in Auckland, and Auckland
is about 2,000 kilometers from Sydney.
Paul: Well, maybe I should visit you next year, too.
Kelly: That would be great!

CLASS AUDIO ONLY ▶ **B** Listen to the rest of the conversation.

What are some things New Zealand is famous for?

Auckland, "the City of Sails"

10 GRAMMAR FOCUS

Questions with how

How far is New Zealand from Australia?	It's about 2,000 kilometers.	(1,200 miles)
How big is Singapore?	It's 620 square kilometers.	(239 square miles)
How high is Mount Everest?	It's 8,848 meters **high.**	(29,028 feet)
How deep is the Grand Canyon?	It's about 1,900 meters **deep.**	(6,250 feet)
How long is the Mississippi River?	It's about 6,019 kilometers **long.**	(3,740 miles)
How hot is New Zealand in the summer?	It gets up to about 23° Celsius.	(74° Fahrenheit)
How cold is it in the winter?	It goes down to about 10° Celsius.	(50° Fahrenheit)

farenheit

A Write the questions to these answers. Then practice with a partner.

1. A: *How high is Angel falls* ?
   B: Angel Falls is 979 meters (3,212 feet) high.
2. A: *How big is California?* ?
   B: California is about 411,000 square kilometers (159,000 square miles).
3. A: *How long is the Nile River?* ?
   B: The Nile is 6,670 kilometers (4,145 miles) long.
4. A: *How hot is Washington D.C in the Summer?* ?
   B: Washington, D.C., gets up to about 32° Celsius (90° Fahrenheit) in the summer.

B *Group work* Think of five questions with *how* about places in your country
or other countries you know. Ask and answer your questions in groups.

"How cold is Seoul in the winter?"

11 *READING*

Things You Can Do to Help the Environment

Is pollution in your country: ■ **serious?** ■ **under control?** ■ **increasing?** ■ **decreasing?**

Our environment is in trouble. People and industries are polluting the air, rivers, lakes, and seas. You may think that there's nothing you can do to help. That's not true. In fact, there are many things you can do to help the environment. Here are a few.

Cars

The burning of gasoline is one of the biggest sources of carbon monoxide (CO) in the atmosphere. Some people believe that CO is causing global warming. They think CO thins the ozone layer, which protects us from the sun's rays. So try to walk, bicycle, or use public transportation. And if you drive a car, drive at a steady speed – this is more efficient than speeding up and slowing down.

Products

Don't use disposable products. In a single year, people in the United States use enough disposable diapers to reach to the moon and back seven times. If you use disposable products, use products made from recycled materials. Also, recycle whenever possible. Recycling one aluminum can saves enough energy to run a TV for three hours.

Energy

The biggest use of home energy is for heating and cooling homes. So turn the heat down, especially at night. Replace regular light bulbs with fluorescent or halogen bulbs, which use less energy.

Water

Showers use a lot of water. In one week a typical American family uses as much water as a person drinks in three years! Buying a special "low-flow" shower head or taking shorter showers can cut this use in half. Also, fix any leaky faucets.

A *Pair work* Read the article. Then talk about these questions.

1. Which of the advice above is new to you?
2. Do you follow any of the advice in the article?
3. Which are the three best pieces of advice?
4. What are two other things people can do to protect the environment?

B *Group work* Look at the photos in the article. Which ones show environmental problems? Which show solutions? Describe what is right or wrong in each photo.

15 I'm going to see a musical.

1 SNAPSHOT

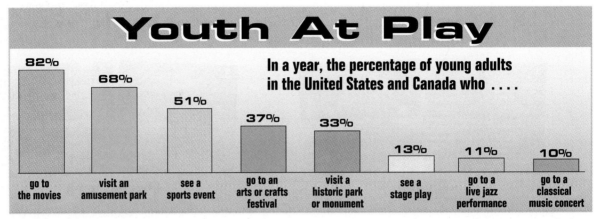

Youth At Play

In a year, the percentage of young adults in the United States and Canada who . . . .

82%	68%	51%	37%	33%	13%	11%	10%
go to the movies	visit an amusement park	see a sports event	go to an arts or crafts festival	visit a historic park or monument	see a stage play	go to a live jazz performance	go to a classical music concert

Source: National Endowment for the Arts

Talk about these questions.

Which of these activities have you done in the past year?
Which of these activities would you like to do?
What other activities do you like to do?

2 CONVERSATION *Talking about plans*

A Listen and practice.

Tony: Say, Anna, what are you doing tonight? Would you like to go out?

Anna: Oh, sorry, I can't. I'm going to work late tonight. I have to finish this report.

Tony: Well, how about tomorrow night? Are you doing anything then?

Anna: No, I'm not. What are you planning to do?

Tony: I'm going to see a musical. Would you like to come?

Anna: Sure, I'd love to! But let *me* pay for the tickets this time. It's my turn.

Tony: All right! Thanks!

CLASS AUDIO ONLY ▶ **B** Listen to the rest of the conversation.

1. What musical are they going to see?
2. What are they doing before the musical?
3. Where are they going to meet?
4. What time are they meeting?

3 GRAMMAR FOCUS

Future with present continuous and be going to

With present continuous
What **are** you **doing** tonight?
  I'm going to a movie.

Are you **doing** anything tomorrow night?
  No, I'm not.

With be going to + verb
What **is** she **going to do** tonight?
  She**'s going to work** late.

Are they **going to see** a musical tomorrow night?
  Yes, they are.

Time expressions
tonight
tomorrow
on Friday
this weekend
next week

A Complete the invitations in column A with the present continuous used as future. Complete the responses in column B with *be going to*.

A

1. What ..are.. you ..doing.. (do) tomorrow? Would you like to go out?

2. ..Are.. you ..doing.. (do) anything on Saturday night? Do you want to see a movie?

3. We ..are having.. (have) friends over for a barbecue on Sunday. Would you and your parents like to come?

B

a. Well, my father ..is going to visit.. (visit) my brother at college. But my mother and I ..are going to be.. (be) home. We'd love to come!

b. Sorry, I can't. I ..am going work.. (work) overtime. How about Saturday?

c. Can we go to a late show? I ..m going to stay.. (stay) at the office till 7:00. After that I ..am going to go.. (go) to the gym.

B Match the invitations in column A with the responses in column B. Then practice with a partner.

4 WORD POWER *Leisure activities*

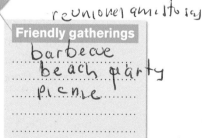

A Complete the word map with activities from the list. Then add two more words to each category.

- art show
- barbecue
- baseball game
- beach party
- car show
- comedy act
- craft fair
- hockey game
- picnic
- play
- rock concert
- tennis tournament

Leisure activities

Exhibitions
art show
craft fair
car show

Friendly gatherings *reuniones amistosas*
barbecue
beach party
picnic

B *Pair work* Are you going to do any of the activities on the chart? When are you doing them? Talk with a partner.

A: I'm going to see a rock concert.
B: Really? When?
A: On Friday.
B: . . .

Spectator sports
baseball game
hockey game
play
tennis tournament

Live performances *espectáculos en vivo*
comedy act
rock concert

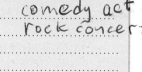

5 ROLE PLAY *An invitation*

Student A: Choose an activity from Exercise 4 and invite a partner to go with you. Be ready to say where and when the activity is.

> A: Say, are you doing anything on . . . ?
> Would you like to . . . ?

Student B: Your partner invites you out. Either accept the invitation and ask for more information, or say you can't go and give an excuse.

Accept	*Refuse*
B: That sounds interesting. Where is it?	B: Oh, I'm sorry, but I can't go. I'm . . . .

Change roles and try the role play again.

6 CONVERSATION *Telephone messages*

 Listen and practice.

Secretary: Good morning, Parker Industries.
Mr. Kale: Hello. May I speak to Ms. Graham, please?
Secretary: I'm sorry. She's not in. Can I take a message?
Mr. Kale: Yes, please. This is Mr. Kale.
Secretary: Is that G-A-L-E?
Mr. Kale: No, it's K-A-L-E.
Secretary: All right.
Mr. Kale: Please tell her our meeting is on Friday at 2:30.
Secretary: Friday at 2:30.
Mr. Kale: And would you ask her to call me this afternoon? My number is 356-4031.
Secretary: 356-4031. Yes, Mr. Kale. I'll give Ms. Graham the message.
Mr. Kale: Thank you. Good-bye.
Secretary: Good-bye.

interchange 15

What are you going to do?

Find out what your classmates are doing over the weekend. Turn to page IC-20.

To: *Ms. Graham*
Date: *August 10*   Time: _____

WHILE YOU WERE OUT

From: *Mr. Kale*
of: _____
Phone: *356-4031*   ext: _____
Message: _____
The meeting is on Friday at 2:30.
Please call him this afternoon.
Taken by: _____

7 GRAMMAR FOCUS

Tell _and_ ask 🔊

Statement	Messages with a statement
The meeting is on Friday.	**Please tell Ann (that)** the meeting is on Friday.
	Would you tell her (that) . . . ?
	Could you tell her (that) . . . ?
Request	Messages with a request
Call me this afternoon.	**Please ask him to** call me this afternoon.
	Would you ask him to . . . ?
	Could you tell him to . . . ?

Look at the message slips. Ask someone to pass on these messages.
Use the words in parentheses. Then compare with a partner.

1.
> Kim -
> The movie is at
> 7:00 tonight.

(could) _Could you tell Kim the movie is at 7:00?_

2.
> Mike -
> Pick me up at home
> around 4:00.

(would) would you Ask Mike to Pickme up at home around 4:00

3.
> Maria -
> The concert on Saturday
> is canceled.

(please) Please ask Maria the concert on saturday is canceled

4.
> Jim -
> Bring the tickets for the
> hockey game tonight.

(could)

5.
> Ann -
> The museum opens at
> 10:00 tomorrow morning.

(would)

6.
> Alex -
> Meet us in front of the
> cafeteria at 12:15.

(please)

8 WRITING

Pair work You want to give messages to people in your class. Write a
request to your partner. Ask him or her to give the messages for you.

> Dear Su Hee,
>
> I'm not going to be in class tomorrow. Would you please ask Ms. King to save any
> handouts for me? Also, could you tell Steve that I can't meet him for dinner after class?
>
> Thanks,
>
> Juan

9 PRONUNCIATION *Reduced forms of* could you *and* would you

A Listen and practice. Notice how **could you** and **would you** are reduced in conversation.

/cʊdʒə/
Could you tell Matt the meeting is at 5:00?

/wʊdʒə/
Would you ask him to pick me up at 4:30?

B Practice these questions with reduced forms.

Could you ask her to return my dictionary?
Would you tell him there's a picnic tomorrow?

10 LISTENING *Take a message*

CLASS AUDIO ONLY ▶ Listen to telephone calls to Mr. Kim and Ms. Carson, and write down the messages.

1.
To: _Mr. Kim_
Date: _____ Time: _____
WHILE YOU WERE OUT
From: _Mis Paris_
of: _City Car center_
Phone: _Pl_ ext: _____
Message: _5543290_
Call Mrs. Carson
Pleae ask Mr. Kim talkme at 3:30pm
as very important
Taken by: _____

2.
To: _Wendy_ ~~Mrs Carson~~
Date: _____ Time: _____
WHILE YOU WERE OUT
From: _Sandy_
of: _first National Bank_
Phone: _482_ ext: _313_
Message: _Pleae Ask her_
to call sandy of the
first National Bank
Taken by: _____

11 ROLE PLAY *Who's calling?*

Student A: Call your friend David to tell him this:

There's a party at Bob's house on Saturday night.
Bob's address is 414 Maple St., Apt. 202.
Pick me up at 8:00 P.M.

Student B: Someone calls for your brother David. He isn't in.
Take a message for him.

Change roles and try another role play.

Student A: Someone calls for your sister Carol. She isn't in.
Take a message for her.

Student B: Call your friend Carol to tell her this:

There's no class next Friday afternoon.
The class is going to a movie at Westwood Theater.
Meet us in front of the theater at 4:30.

useful expressions
May I speak to . . . ?
Can I take a message?
I'll give . . . the message.

12 READING

Ways to Keep Phone Calls Short

Do you like to talk on the phone?
Do you think that you spend too much time on the phone?

The phone rings. It's a friend who wants to tell you about his or her latest health problem. You hate to be rude and cut your friend off, but what can you do? Time management consultant Stephanie Winston, author of *Stephanie Winston's Best Organizing Tips,* offers this advice:

1. Don't ask questions like "What's new?" They give the impression that you have time to chat. After "hello," get right to the heart of the matter.

2. Time *your* calls intelligently. If you make a call right before lunch or dinner, or at the end of the workday, people chat less.

3. Set a time limit. Start with, "Hi, I've only got a few minutes, but I wanted to talk to you about …." Or, "Gee, I'd love to talk more, but I only have a couple of minutes before I have to run errands."

4. Jump on a pause. Even the most talkative caller has to pause now and then. Quickly say, "It has been great talking with you." Then end the conversation.

5. Forget niceties. Some people just don't take a hint. Interrupt your caller and say, "I'd like to talk to you longer, but I'm pressed for time. Good-bye." Then hang up. Don't ask for permission to end the conversation.

6. Find a "partner in crime." If nothing else works, ask someone in your home to help you. For example, one woman signals her husband, who yells, "Jane, I think the roast is burning!"

7. Avoid the phone completely. Use an answering machine to screen calls. If you have an important message for a chatterbox, leave the message when he or she isn't in.

A Read the article. Then look at these sentences. Check (✓) the things you can say to keep phone calls short.

- ☐ 1 I'm glad you feel better. What can I do for you?
- ☐ 2. I have to go now. Good-bye.
- ☐ 3. Hi. How are things?
- ☐ 4. I need to get off the phone now. There's someone at the door.
- ☐ 5. So, what else is new?
- ☐ 6. No, I'm not busy right now.
- ☐ 7. I'm sorry to call you at dinnertime, but I have just one question.
- ☐ 8. I only have three minutes before I have to leave.

B *Pair work* Talk about these questions.

1. Which advice have you used sometimes?
2. Which do you think are the three best pieces of advice?
3. What else can you do to keep phone calls short?

16 A change for the better!

1 SNAPSHOT

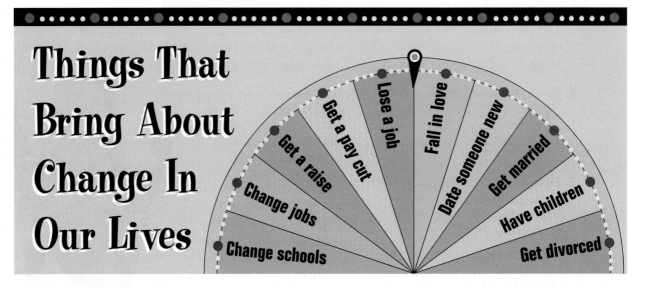

Things That Bring About Change In Our Lives

Change schools
Change jobs
Get a raise
Get a pay cut
Lose a job
Fall in love
Date someone new
Get married
Have children
Get divorced

Talk about these questions.

Have any of these things happened to you in the last few years?
How have they changed you?
What other things bring about change in our lives?

2 CONVERSATION *Catching up*

A Listen and practice.

Brian: Diane Grant? I haven't seen you for ages.
Diane: Brian! How have you been?
Brian: Pretty good. Say, you've really changed!
Diane: Oh, well, I've lost some weight. And my hair is longer than before.
Brian: Well, you look great! How are you?
Diane: I'm doing really well. I got married about three years ago. I have two kids now.
Brian: That's terrific!

B Listen to the rest of the conversation.

How has Brian changed?

CLASS AUDIO ONLY ▶

98

3 GRAMMAR FOCUS

Describing changes

With the present tense	With the comparative	With the past tense	With the present perfect
I **have** two kids now.	My job is **more stressful** (now).	I **got** married.	I**'ve lost** weight.
I **don't smoke** anymore.	My hair is **longer** (**than** before).	I **moved** to a new city.	I**'ve grown** a mustache.

A How have you changed in the last five years? Check (✓) the statements that are true for you. If a statement isn't true, give the correct information.

- ☑ 1. I've changed my hairstyle.
- ☑ 2. I dress differently now.
- ☑ 3. I've lost weight.
- ☑ 4. I moved into my own apartment.
- ☑ 5. I got married.
- ☑ 6. I'm more outgoing than before.
- ☐ 7. I don't go to many parties anymore.
- ☐ 8. My life is easier now.

B *Pair work* Compare your responses in part A. Have you changed in similar ways?

C *Group work* Write five sentences describing other changes in your life. Then compare in groups. Who in the group has changed the most?

4 LISTENING *Memory lane*

CLASS AUDIO ONLY

Linda and Scott are looking through a photo album. Listen to their conversation. How have they changed? Write down three changes.

Changes
- the hair more shorter now
- you can wait now
-

5 WORD POWER Things that change

A Complete the word map with the phrases from the list. Then add two more examples to each category.

- ~ cut my hair short
- ↶ do aerobics
- ↶ eat more vegetables
- ↶ get dressed up
- ↶ get up early
- ↶ grow a beard
- ↶ learn to swim
- ↶ learn to type
- quit smoking
- speak English
- start cooking
- wear contact lenses

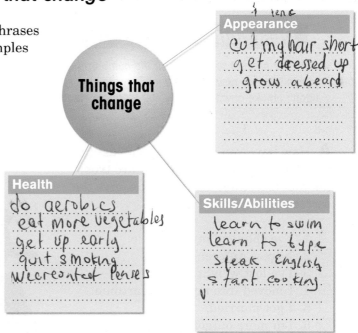

Things that change

Appearance
ↁ ıene
cut my hair short
get dressed up
grow a beard

Health
do aerobics
eat more vegetables
get up early
quit smoking
wecreontect lenses

Skills/Abilities
learn to swim
learn to type
speak English
start cooking

B *Pair work* Have you changed in any of these areas? Tell your partner about a change in each category.

"I get up earlier in the morning. I've started cooking. And I get dressed up for work now."

6 CONVERSATION Planning your future

A Listen and practice.

Alex: So what are you going to do after graduation, Susan?

Susan: Well, I've saved some money, and I think I'd really like to travel.

Alex: Lucky you. That sounds exciting!

Susan: Yeah. Then I plan to get a job and my own apartment.

Alex: Oh, you're not going to live at home?

Susan: No, I don't want to live with my parents – not after I start to work.

Alex: I know what you mean.

Susan: What about you, Alex? Do you have any plans yet?

Alex: I'm going to get a job *and* live at home. I'm broke, and I want to pay off my student loan!

CLASS AUDIO ONLY ▶ **B** Listen to the rest of the conversation.

1. What kind of job does Alex want?
2. Where would Susan like to travel?

7 *GRAMMAR FOCUS*

Verb + infinitive

What **are** you **going to do** after graduation?
I'm (not) **going to get** a job right away.
I (don't) **plan to get** my own apartment.
I (don't) **want to live** with my parents.
I **hope to get** a new car.
I'd **like to travel** this summer.
I'd **love to move** to a new city.

A Complete these statements so that they are true for you. Use information from the grammar box. Then add three more statements of your own.

1. I *'m going to* move to a new city.
2. I *'m plan* get married.
3. I *'m wun to* have a large family.
4. I *hope to* find a job where I can travel.
5. I *hope to* make a lot of money!
6. I *'d like to* become very successful.
7. I *'d like to* retire at an early age.
8. _____
9. _____
10. *I'd like to visit a new place*

B *Pair work* Compare your responses with a partner. How are you the same? How are you different?

8 *PLAN ON IT*

Group work What are your plans for the future? Ask and answer these questions.

What are you going to do after this English course is over?
Do you plan to study here again next year?
What other languages would you like to learn?
What countries would you like to live in? Why?
What countries wouldn't you like to live in? Why?
Do you want to get a (new) job in a few years?
What kind of job do you hope to get?

9 *PRONUNCIATION* *Reduced form of* to

A Listen and practice. Notice that **to** is reduced to /tə/.

I hope **to** get married.   I'd love **to** move to a new city.
I plan **to** have a large family.   I'd like **to** live in a small town.

B *Pair work* Write four statements about yourself using the verbs above. Take turns reading your statements with a partner. Pay attention to the pronunciation of **to**.

10 *WRITING*

A Write about your plans for the future.

> *I would like to join the Peace Corps for a couple of years. I have a degree in biology, so I hope to work in forestry or environmental education. I'd like to work with people in . . . .*

B *Pair work* Compare your composition with a partner's. Ask and answer questions about each other's plans.

working in the Peace Corps

interchange 16

Unfold your future!
Imagine you could do anything, go anywhere, and meet anybody.
Turn to page IC-21.

11 *LISTENING*

CLASS
AUDIO
ONLY

A Listen to three people discussing their plans for the future. What do they plan to do? What don't they want to do? Take notes.

	Plans to	Doesn't want to
1. Charlie	....	....
2. Leon	....	....
3. Marie	....	....

B *Group work* Which person do you think is most like you? Do your classmates agree?

12 READING

The Future Looks Bright

Do you like to set goals for yourself? What important goals have you reached recently?

Balamurati Krishna Ambati

At age three, Balamurati Krishna Ambati was badly burned and spent several months in the hospital. He decided then that he wanted to be a doctor. A few years later, he read in the *Guinness Book of Records* that the youngest doctor in the world was 18 years old. So he decided to become a doctor by the age of 17. Many people thought this was impossible, but at 11, Ambati was in college. He graduated from college at 14 and from medical school at 17. Now that he is a doctor, Ambati plans to go for advanced training in Boston.

Catherine Charlton

Catherine Charlton is studying engineering at Cornell University, but she has already achieved an important goal: She has worked for NASA (the National Aeronautics and Space Administration). Charlton's achievements aren't only in engineering, however. She is also a successful pianist and composer. Charlton hopes to combine her talents for engineering and music someday. For example, she would like to design concert halls or manufacture pianos.

Jasmin Sethi

The Scholastic Aptitude Test is the test American students take to enter college; each year, only a few students get a perfect score. One of those students was Jasmin Sethi. Her achievement was especially remarkable because she is blind. To take the test, someone read the test questions to her, and she gave the answers. She even solved difficult math problems in her head. Sethi has been the editor of her school newspaper and has organized food collections. She wants to go to a top university next year. Sethi would like to be a lawyer.

A Read the article. What are each student's interests? What goals has each student set?

	Interests	Goals
1. Balamurati	....	....
2. Catherine	....	....
3. Jasmin	....	....

B *Pair work* Talk about these questions.

1. Do you think Balamurati is too young to be a doctor?
2. What other careers would allow Catherine to combine her interests?
3. How do you think someone like Jasmin overcomes his or her disabilities?
4. How old were you when you started to think about your career goals?
5. Have you achieved a goal you set? What was it?
6. What other goals do you have?

Review of Units 13-16

1 FAVORITE RESTAURANT

A *Group work* Take turns talking about your favorite place to eat. One student makes a statement about a favorite restaurant. Other students ask questions.

My favorite place to eat is . . . .

Where is it?
What kind of food do they serve?
Does it have a nice atmosphere?
Is it expensive?

How much does dinner cost?
When is it open?
How often do you go there?
What do you usually order?

B *Class activity* Which place is the most interesting to you? Tell the class why.

2 LISTENING

CLASS AUDIO ONLY   Listen and check (✓) the best response.

1. ☐ Yes, this way, please.
   ☐ Yes, please.

2. ☐ No, I don't.
   ☐ Yes, I'll have tea, please.

3. ☐ I'd like a steak, please.
   ☐ Yes, I would.

4. ☐ I'll have a cup of coffee.
   ☐ Italian, please.

5. ☐ Carrots, please.
   ☐ Yes, I will.

6. ☐ Yes, I'd like some water.
   ☐ No, I don't think so.

3 INTERESTING ADDRESSES

A *Pair work* Ask and answer questions about these places in your city.

Buildings

the biggest hotel
the most famous building
the oldest building

Streets

the busiest street
the best street for restaurants
the best street for shopping

Entertainment

the best place to go dancing
the best place to listen to music
the most interesting tourist spot

A: What's the biggest hotel?
B: I think it's the Hilton.
A: I do, too. / So do I. /
    Oh, I don't. I think it's the . . . .

B *Class activity* Compare your answers around the class.

4 THE WEEKEND

Pair work Which of the activities listed are you going
to do this weekend? What else are you going to do?
Talk with a partner.

A: I'm seeing a concert this weekend.
B: What concert are you going to see?
A: A guitar concert at school.
B: Really? When is it?
A: It's on Saturday night. I'm going with my brother.

Some activities
see a concert
meet someone special
go out to eat
work
play a sport or exercise
make a long-distance call

5 ROLE PLAY *Inviting a friend*

A ***Pair work*** Take turns inviting your
partner to do something.

A: Hello?
B: Hi, ... This is . . . .
A: Oh, hi!
B: Say, are you doing anything (on) . . . ?
A: Oh, yes. I'm sorry. I'm . . . .
B: Well, how about (on) . . . ?
A: No. What would you like to do?
B: Let's . . . .
A: I'd love to! What time . . . ?
B: . . .
A: And where . . . ?
B: . . .
A: OK. See you on . . . . Bye!
B: Bye-bye.

B ***Pair work*** Change roles and try the
conversation with a different partner.

6 INTERVIEW

A ***Pair work*** Find out more about a classmate. Ask your partner
these questions or questions of your own.

Where have you lived?
What schools have you gone to?
What did you study? / What do you study now?
Are you married? / Do you hope to get married?
Do you have any children? / Do you want to have children?
What would you like to do in five years? ten years? when you retire?

B ***Class activity*** Tell the class about your partner.

Interchange Activities

GETTING TO KNOW YOU

A *Class activity* Go around the class and find this information. Write a classmate's name only once.

Find someone who . . .	Name
1. . . . has the same first name as a famous person. **"What's your first name?"**	....
2. . . . has an unusual nickname. **"What do people call you?"**	....
3. . . . has an interesting middle name. **"What's your middle name?"**	....
4. . . . has the same last name as a famous person. **"What's your last name?"**	....
5. . . . is named after his or her father or mother. **"Are you named after your father or mother?"**	....
6. . . . always remembers people's names. **"Are you good with names?"**	....
7. . . . is from a beautiful city or town. **"Where are you from?"**	....
8. . . . speaks two foreign languages. **"What languages do you speak?"**	....

B *Pair work* Compare your information with a partner.

interchange 2 | *COMMON GROUND*

A Complete this chart with information about yourself.

	Time
I usually get up at	. . . .
I have breakfast at	. . . .
I leave for work or school at	. . . .
I have dinner at	. . . .
I go to bed during the week at	. . . .
I go to bed on weekends at	. . . .

B *Class activity* Take a survey. Ask five classmates for this information.

Names:	. . . .	. . . .	. . . .	. . . .	. . . .
What time do you . . . ?	**Times**				
get up	. . . .	. . . .	. . . .	. . . .	. . . .
have breakfast	. . . .	. . . .	. . . .	. . . .	. . . .
leave for work or school	. . . .	. . . .	. . . .	. . . .	. . . .
have dinner	. . . .	. . . .	. . . .	. . . .	. . . .
go to bed during the week	. . . .	. . . .	. . . .	. . . .	. . . .
go to bed on weekends	. . . .	. . . .	. . . .	. . . .	. . . .

C *Class activity* Compare the times you do things with the times your classmates do things. Whose schedule is the most like yours? Tell the class.

"Keiko and I have a similar schedule. We both get up at six and have breakfast at seven A.M. . . ."

useful expressions
We both . . . at . . . .
We . . . at different times.
My schedule isn't like anyone else's.

interchange 3 *SWAP MEET*

Student A

A You want to sell these things. Write an appropriate price for each item.

binoculars

price: ....

tennis racket

price: ....

radio

price: ....

camera

price: ....

VCR

price: ....

Student B

A You want to sell these things. Write an appropriate price for each item.

bicycle

price: ....

blender

price: ....

answering machine

price: ....

CD player

price: ....

TV

price: ....

Students A and B

B *Pair work* Discuss the price of each thing and choose at least three things that you want to buy. Get the best price you can. Be prepared to haggle.*

A: How much is the . . . ?
B: It's only $ . . . .
A: Wow! That's expensive!
B: Well, how about $ . . . ?
A: No. That's still too much. What about the . . . ?
B: You can have it for $ . . . .
A: OK. That's reasonable.
B: And how much is the . . . ?
A: . . .

* *haggle:* Buyers and sellers suggest other amounts until both agree on a lower price.

interchange 4 *WHAT AN INVITATION! WHAT AN EXCUSE!*

A Make up three invitations to interesting or unusual activities.
Write them on cards.

Godzilla Meets Mightyman is at the Plaza Theater tonight at 8:00. Would you like to see it?	*There's a dog and cat show at City Stadium on Saturday. It's at 3:00. Do you want to go?*	*I want to see the Turtle Races tomorrow. They're at 1:00 at the Civic Hall. Would you like to go?*

B Write three response cards. One is an acceptance card.

That sounds great! What time do you want to meet?

The other two cards are refusals. Think of silly or unusual excuses.

I'd like to, but I want to take my bird to a singing contest.	*I'm sorry. I'd like to, but I have to wash my hair.*

C *Class activity* Put all the invitation cards
in one pile and all the response cards in another
pile facedown. Shuffle each pile. Each student
takes three invitation cards and three
response cards.

Go around the class. Invite people to do
the things on your invitation cards.
Use the response cards to accept
or decline any invitation.

interchange 5 *FAMILY FACTS*

A *Class activity* Go around the class and find this information.
Write a classmate's name only once. Ask follow-up questions of your own.

Find someone . . .	Name
1. . . . who is an only child. **"Do you have any brothers or sisters?"**	....
2. . . . who has more than two brothers. **"How many brothers do you have?"**	....
3. . . . who has more than two sisters. **"How many sisters do you have?"**	....
4. . . . whose brother or sister is studying abroad. **"Are any of your brothers or sisters studying abroad? Where?"**	....
5. . . . who lives with his or her grandparents. **"Do you live with your grandparents?"**	....
6. . . . who has a great-grandparent still living. **"Is your great-grandmother or great-grandfather still living?"**	....
7. . . . who has a family member with an unusual job. **"Does anyone in your family have an unusual job?"**	....
8. . . . whose mother or father is working abroad. **"Is either of your parents working abroad? Where?"**	....

B *Group work* Compare your information in groups.

interchange 6 *FITNESS QUIZ*

A *Pair work* Interview a partner using this simple quiz. Then add up your partner's score, and find his or her rank below.

Fitness Quiz

Your Nutrition	Points
1. How many meals do you eat during a day?	
• Five or six small meals	6
• Three meals	3
• One or two meals	0
2. Do you eat at regular times during the day (not too early or too late)?	
• Almost always	6
• Usually	3
• Seldom	0
3. How many servings of fruits and vegetables do you usually have a day?	
• Five or more	6
• Two to four	4
• One or none	1
4. How much fatty food do you eat?	
• Very little	6
• About average	3
• A lot	0
5. Do you take vitamins every day?	
• Always	6
• Often	4
• Sometimes	2
6. Do you take more vitamins when you are sick?	
• Yes	4
• No	2

Rank your partner.

55 to 70 points: Super job! Keep up the good work!

35 to 54 points: Good job! Your health and fitness are above average.

15 to 34 points: Your health and fitness are below average. Try to learn more about health and fitness.

14 points and below: You seem to be out of shape. Now is the time to start making changes. See your doctor or other professionals if you need help.

Your Fitness	Points
7. How often do you exercise?	
• Three or more days a week	6
• One or two days a week	3
• Never	0
8. Which best describes your fitness program?	
• Both weight training and aerobic exercise	6
• Weight training or aerobic exercise only	3
• None	0
9. How important is your fitness program to you?	
• Very important	6
• Somewhat important	3
• Not very important	0

Your Health	Points
10. Which best describes your weight?	
• Within 6 pounds (3 kg) of my ideal weight	6
• Within 10 pounds (4.5 kg) of my ideal weight	3
• More than 12 pounds (5.5 kg) over or under	0
11. How often do you have a complete physical?	
• Once a year	6
• Every two or three years	3
• Almost never go to the doctor	0
12. How often do you smoke?	
• Never	6
• Hardly ever	1
• Often	0

Total Points

B *Group work* Compare your scores in groups. Who is the fittest? What can you do to improve your fitness?

"I need to . . . ."

interchange 7 VACATION PHOTOS

Student A

A *Pair work* You went on a vacation to Mexico and took these photos. First, think about these questions. Then use the photos to tell your partner about your vacation. Give as much information as you can, and answer your partner's questions.

"I had a really interesting vacation. I went to Mexico . . . ."

Where did you go?
How long were you there?
Who did you go with?
What did you do there?
Did you enjoy it?
Where did you take this picture?
Who is this/that?
Is this a . . . ?

shopping

a bullfighter

the Pyramid of the Moon

Mexico City – a beautiful night

some Mariachis

B *Pair work* Listen to your partner talk about his or her vacation. Ask questions like the ones in part A about the vacation.

interchange 7 *VACATION PHOTOS*

Student B

A *Pair work* Listen to your partner talk about a recent vacation.
Ask questions about the vacation and the photos.

Where did you go?
How long were you there?
Who did you go with?
What did you do there?
Did you enjoy it?
Where did you take this picture?
Who is this/that?
Is this a . . . ?

B *Pair work* Look at these photos of your vacation in Thailand.
First, think about the questions in part A. Then use the photos to
tell your partner about your vacation. Give as much information
as you can, and answer your partner's questions.

"I had a really interesting vacation recently, too. I went to Thailand . . . ."

interchange 8 *NEIGHBORHOOD SURVEY*

A *Group work* Imagine you are looking for a new home. You need to decide where you want to live. Compare two different neighborhoods in your city or town. Talk with your group and complete the survey.

What kinds of people live in each neighborhood – families,
   young people, working people, retired people?
Compare the neighborhoods' recreation facilities, stores,
   schools, and public transportation.
How much noise is there? pollution?
What's one advantage of living in each neighborhood?
   What's one disadvantage?

	Neighborhood 1:	Neighborhood 2:
	....	....
people		
recreation facilities		
stores		
schools		
public transportation		
noise		
pollution		
an advantage of living in the neighborhood		
a disadvantage of living in the neighborhood		

A: What neighborhoods do you want to compare?
B: Let's look at Parkside and downtown.
C: OK. So what kinds of people live in Parkside?
D: There are lots of retired people. There aren't very
   many young people with families.
A: That's true. What about downtown?
C: . . .

B *Class activity* Study the results of the survey. Which neighborhood would you prefer to live in? Tell the class where and why.

interchange 9 FIND THE DIFFERENCES

Student A

A *Pair work* How many differences can you find between your picture here and your partner's picture? Ask questions like these to find the differences. (Look only at the people with names.)

How many people are there in your picture?
How many are standing? Who?
How many are sitting? Who?
What color is Dave's T-shirt? Kate's sweater?
Who is holding a drink?
What does . . . look like?
Does . . . wear glasses?
Does . . . have a beard?
What color is . . .'s hair?
How long is . . .'s hair?

Picture 1

B *Class activity* How many differences are there in the pictures? What are they?

"In picture 1, Dave's T-shirt is . . . . In picture 2, it's . . . ."

interchange 10 *LIFESTYLES SURVEY*

A *Pair work* What kind of lifestyle does your partner have: easygoing and relaxed or busy and fast-paced? Interview your partner using this survey.

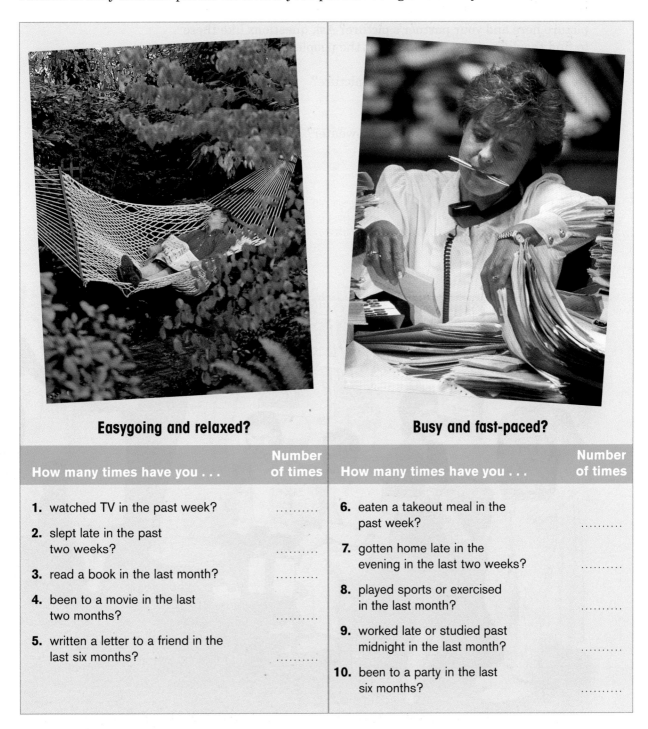

Easygoing and relaxed?

How many times have you . . .	Number of times
1. watched TV in the past week?	....
2. slept late in the past two weeks?	....
3. read a book in the last month?	....
4. been to a movie in the last two months?	....
5. written a letter to a friend in the last six months?	....

Busy and fast-paced?

How many times have you . . .	Number of times
6. eaten a takeout meal in the past week?	....
7. gotten home late in the evening in the last two weeks?	....
8. played sports or exercised in the last month?	....
9. worked late or studied past midnight in the last month?	....
10. been to a party in the last six months?	....

B *Group work* Tell the group what you think your partner's lifestyle is like and why.

"Juan's lifestyle is busy and fast-paced. He hardly ever has time to watch TV, read a book, or go to the movies. He works late a lot, and he often eats takeout meals. . . . "

interchange 9 FIND THE DIFFERENCES

Student B

A Pair work How many differences can you find between your picture here and your partner's picture? Ask questions like these to find the differences. (Look only at the people with names.)

How many people are there in your picture?
How many are standing? Who?
How many are sitting? Who?
What color is Dave's T-shirt? Kate's sweater?
Who is holding a drink?
What does . . . look like?
Does . . . wear glasses?
Does . . . have a beard?
What color is . . .'s hair?
How long is . . .'s hair?

Picture 2

B Class activity How many differences are there in the pictures?
What are they?

"In picture 1, Dave's T-shirt is . . . . In picture 2, it's . . . ."

interchange 11 *CITY GUIDE*

A Where can you get information about your city? buy souvenirs?
see historical sights? Complete the "City Guide" with information
about your city.

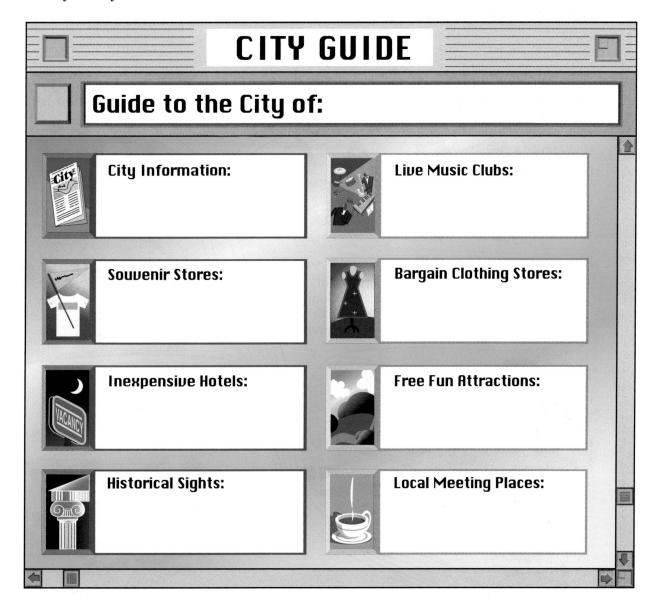

CITY GUIDE

Guide to the City of:

City Information:

Live Music Clubs:

Souvenir Stores:

Bargain Clothing Stores:

Inexpensive Hotels:

Free Fun Attractions:

Historical Sights:

Local Meeting Places:

B *Group work* Compare your "City Guides" in groups. Ask these
questions and your own questions. Add any additional or interesting
information to your guide.

Where can you get information about your city?
Where can you buy souvenirs?
Are there any inexpensive hotels?
What historical sights should you see?
What's a good place to hear local music?
What's a cheap place to shop for clothes?
What fun things can you do for free?
Where do people often meet?

interchange 12 *TALK RADIO*

A *Group work* Look at the four questions that people called a radio program about. What advice would you give each caller? Discuss suggestions to give each caller, and then choose the best one.

Caller 1: I'm visiting the United States. I'm staying with a couple of families while I'm here. What small gifts can I get for the families I stay with?

Caller 2: My dog barks loudly all night long. The neighbors are complaining about him. What can I do?

Caller 3: My doctor says that I'm not in good shape, and I need to lose about four and a half kilos (10 pounds). I don't like exercising though. Do you have any advice?

Caller 4: My school wants to buy some new gym equipment, so we want to have a fundraiser. What are some good ways to raise money?

useful expressions

I think it would be useful to . . . .
One thing you could do is . . . .
It's a good idea to . . . .
It's important to . . . .
You should . . . .

B *Class activity* Share your group's advice for each problem with the class.

interchange 13 ARE YOU READY TO ORDER?

Student A

You are the waiter or waitress at The Corner Cafe.
Take your customers' orders.

Taking the order
- Greet your customers.
- Ask what they would like. Write down each person's order on a separate piece of paper. (Use the menu to write down the orders and amounts.)
- Check the orders like this: "You ordered . . . ." and "You wanted . . . ."
- Ask if your customers want anything else (such as something to drink, a salad, or dessert).
- Go and get their orders.

Delivering the order
- Bring the orders to your customers. (You make a mistake. You give one customer the wrong thing.)
- Go and get the right order and bring it back.

Bringing the check
- Give each customer his or her check with a total at the bottom. (You make a mistake. You did not correctly add up one of the checks.)
- Walk away and wait for the customers to put the checks and money on the table.
- Pick up the checks and money. Bring back each customer's change.

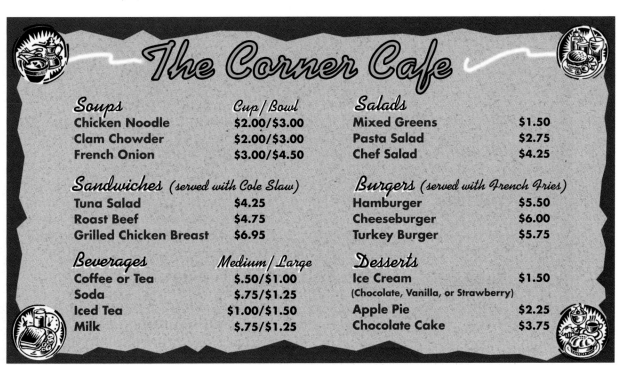

The Corner Cafe

Soups	Cup / Bowl
Chicken Noodle	$2.00/$3.00
Clam Chowder	$2.00/$3.00
French Onion	$3.00/$4.50

Salads	
Mixed Greens	$1.50
Pasta Salad	$2.75
Chef Salad	$4.25

Sandwiches (served with Cole Slaw)	
Tuna Salad	$4.25
Roast Beef	$4.75
Grilled Chicken Breast	$6.95

Burgers (served with French Fries)	
Hamburger	$5.50
Cheeseburger	$6.00
Turkey Burger	$5.75

Beverages	Medium / Large
Coffee or Tea	$.50/$1.00
Soda	$.75/$1.25
Iced Tea	$1.00/$1.50
Milk	$.75/$1.25

Desserts	
Ice Cream	$1.50
(Chocolate, Vanilla, or Strawberry)	
Apple Pie	$2.25
Chocolate Cake	$3.75

interchange 13 *ARE YOU READY TO ORDER?*

Students B and C

You are hungry customers in The Corner Cafe. You are having lunch.
The waiter or waitress comes to take your order.

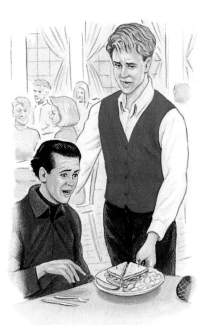

Ordering
- Look at the menu below. Order something to eat and drink.
- Ask the waiter or waitress to bring you something extra (such as a glass of water or another fork).

Being served
- The waiter or waitress brings your order. Is it correct? If not, tell him or her like this: "Sorry, I didn't order . . . . I ordered . . . ."

Paying the check
- The waiter or waitress brings a check for each of you. Are they correct? If not, tell him or her like this: "Excuse me. This isn't right. It should be . . . ."
- Put the checks and money on the table for the waiter or waitress to pick up.

Tipping
- The waiter or waitress brings your change.
- Decide how much to leave for a tip.

The Corner Cafe

Soups	Cup / Bowl	*Salads*	
Chicken Noodle	$2.00/$3.00	**Mixed Greens**	$1.50
Clam Chowder	$2.00/$3.00	**Pasta Salad**	$2.75
French Onion	$3.00/$4.50	**Chef Salad**	$4.25

Sandwiches (served with Cole Slaw)		*Burgers* (served with French Fries)	
Tuna Salad	$4.25	**Hamburger**	$5.50
Roast Beef	$4.75	**Cheeseburger**	$6.00
Grilled Chicken Breast	$6.95	**Turkey Burger**	$5.75

Beverages	Medium / Large	*Desserts*	
Coffee or Tea	$.50/$1.00	**Ice Cream**	$1.50
Soda	$.75/$1.25	(Chocolate, Vanilla, or Strawberry)	
Iced Tea	$1.00/$1.50	**Apple Pie**	$2.25
Milk	$.75/$1.25	**Chocolate Cake**	$3.75

interchange 14 | *HOW MUCH DO YOU KNOW?*

Pair work Take turns asking and answering these questions.
Check (✓) the correct answer. If you and your partner don't
agree, check (✓) the answer you think is correct.

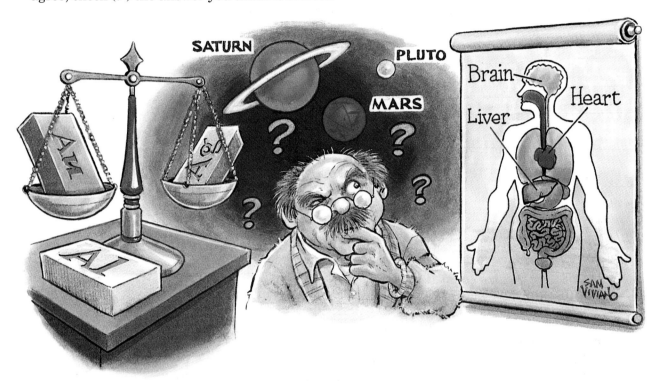

World Knowledge Quiz

1.	Which metal is the heaviest?	☐ gold	☐ silver	☐ aluminum
2.	Which planet is the coldest?	☐ Neptune	☐ Saturn	☐ Pluto
3.	Which one is the biggest?	☐ Jupiter	☐ the Earth	☐ Mars
4.	Which animal lives the longest?	☐ a whale	☐ an elephant	☐ a tortoise
5.	Which one is the tallest?	☐ an elephant	☐ a giraffe	☐ a camel
6.	Which of these is the heaviest?	☐ the brain	☐ the heart	☐ the liver
7.	Which drink has the most calories?	☐ 1 liter of wine	☐ 1 liter of beer	☐ 1 liter of soda*
8.	Which country is the driest?	☐ Egypt	☐ Peru	☐ Chile
9.	Which one is closest to the equator?	☐ Malaysia	☐ Colombia	☐ India
10.	Which shape has the most sides?	☐ a pentagon	☐ an octagon	☐ a hexagon
11.	Which measurement is the longest?	☐ a yard	☐ a kilometer	☐ a mile
12.	Which era is the oldest?	☐ the Renaissance	☐ the Dark Ages	☐ the Middle Ages

*1 liter = 35 ounces

Correct answers

How many did you get correct? (See the appendix at the back of the book for the answers.)

12	Perfect! Brilliant! You should be a teacher.	**5–8**	Just OK. How often do you go to the library?
9–11	Very good! Do you watch lots of TV game shows?	**0–4**	You should never be on a quiz show.

interchange 15 WHAT ARE YOU GOING TO DO?

A *Class activity* What are your classmates' plans for the weekend?
Go around the class and find people who are going to do these things.
Ask for further information.

Find someone who is going to . . . next weekend.	Name
go on a date	....
stay out all night	....
go to an amusement park	....
go to a party	....
visit friends out of town	....
compete in a sports event	....
see a play	....
go to a garage sale	....

A: Are you going to an amusement park this weekend?
OR
A: Are you going to go to an amusement park this weekend?
B: Yes, I am, actually.
A: Oh, you are? Who are you going with?
B: . . .

B *Pair work* Compare your information with a partner.

interchange 16 *UNFOLD YOUR FUTURE!*

A Complete this chart with information about yourself.

My Possible Future	
What are two things you plan to do next year?	....
	....
What are two things you aren't going to do next year?	....
	....
What is something you would like to change?	....
	....
What is something you hope to buy in the next year?	....
	....
What is a place you want to visit someday?	....
What is a place you would like to move to?	....
Who would you like to take a vacation with?	....
What famous person would you like to meet?	....

B *Group work* Compare your information in groups.
Be prepared to explain the future you have planned.

A: What are two things you plan to do next year?
B: Well, I'm going to travel to Italy and meet
  someone new.
C: Oh, really? Who are you going to meet?
B: I don't know, yet! What about you? What are
  two things you plan to do next year?
C: . . .

Unit Summaries

Unit Summaries contain lists of key vocabulary and functional expressions, as well as grammar extensions for each unit. For Grammar Focus models, please refer to the appropriate unit page.

1 PLEASE CALL ME CHUCK.

KEY VOCABULARY

Nouns
back
bow *reverencia*
cheek *mejilla*
class
Dad
engineering
female *(Fimei)*
friend
greeting *saludos*
handshake
hug
kiss
male
Mom *Mam*
(first/last/full) name
nickname *sobrenombre*
parents
pat
student
(baseball/volleyball) team
women *gumen*

Titles
Miss
Mr.
Mrs. *mises*
Ms. *mises*

Adjectives
married *merried*
same *igual*
single

Articles
a
the *la*

Verbs
am
are
is

Adverbs
here
(over) there *(alla)*
too *van outv*

Prepositions
from (Paris/France)
in (English 102/Canada)
on (the volleyball team/
    the back)

Conjunctions
and
but

Interjections
oh
well

EXPRESSIONS

Greeting someone *somuan*
Hello.
Hi.

**Exchanging personal
information**
What's your name?
  I'm . . . ./My name is . . . .
Where are you from?
  I'm from . . . .
How's everything?/
How are you?
  Not bad.
  Pretty good, thanks. *very muy bien*

Introducing someone
This is . . . ./These are . . . .
  Nice to/Pleased to/
  Good to meet you.

Asking about someone
Who's that?
  That's . . . .
Who are they?
  Their names are . . . and . . . .

Checking information
How do you pronounce . . . ?
  It's Mandel, with the accent
  on "del."
How do you spell . . . ?
What do people call you?
  Please call me . . . .
  You can call me . . . .
  Everyone calls me . . . .
Excuse me, what's . . . again?
  It's . . . .
Are you studying . . . ?/
Are you on vacation?
  Yes, I am./No, I'm not.

Agreeing
That's right.
OK.

GRAMMAR EXTENSION Sentences with be

My name **is** Amy.
          be + noun

I **am** from Korea.
    be + prepositional phrase

I **am** Korean.
    be + adjective

HOW DO YOU SPEND YOUR DAY?

KEY VOCABULARY

Nouns	*Workplaces*	food	**Verbs**	**Adverbs**
Jobs/Professions	airline	high school	answer	a lot
announcer Comunicador	(construction/	house	arrive (at)	early
architect	electronics)	instruction	build	exactly
carpenter	company	lunch	care for	home
chef	department store	music	cook	late
company director	hospital	(news)paper	do	only
disc jockey	office	passenger	get (home)	pretty (late)
doctor	radio station	patient	get up	then
engineer	(fast-food)	people	go (to bed/to	
flight attendant	restaurant	phone	school/to work)	**Prepositions**
(tour) guide	school	snack	have (a job/lunch)	about/around
nurse		tour	leave	(10:00/noon)
police officer	*Classes*	TV	like	after (midnight)
professor	business	weather report	love	at (night/7:00/
receptionist	computer science	work	play (music)	noon/midnight)
sales manager	mathematics		read	before (noon)
salesman		**Adjectives**	sell	for (an hour)
salesperson	*Time*	average	serve	in (the morning/
secretary	day	full-time	sleep	the afternoon/
security guard	holiday	great	sound (interesting)	the evening)
supervisor	hour	interesting	spend (your day)	like (Peru)
teacher	week	little	start	on (weekends/
travel agent	year	long	stay up	weekdays/
word processor		part-time	study	weeknights/
	Other		take	Sundays)
	clothes	**Article**	teach	until (midnight)
	country	an	wake up	
	(computer)		watch	**Interjection**
	equipment		work	so

EXPRESSIONS

Describing work/school
What do you do?
  I'm a/an . . . .
Where do you work?
  I work at/in/for . . . .
Where do you go to school?
  I go to . . . .

Asking for more information
What about . . . ?
Which . . . ?

Asking for and giving opinions
How do you like . . . ?
  I like . . . a lot./I love . . . .
  It's a great . . . .

Expressing interest
Really?
Oh, really?
That sounds interesting.

Talking about daily schedules
How do you spend your day?
  Well, I . . . . Then I . . . .
What time do you go to work/school?
  I leave at . . . .
And when do you get home?
  I get home around . . . .

Apologizing
Gee, I'm sorry.

GRAMMAR EXTENSION

1. Prepositions in sentences about work/school

I work	**for** Toyota.	*for* + name of company
	for Ms. Jones.	*for* + name of person
	for a lawyer.	*for* + person's job

I work	**in** a bank.	*in/at* + workplace
	at a restaurant.	

I work	**in** the sales department.	*in* + department/section
	in the front office.	

I go **to** Columbia University.   *to* + name of school

2. Articles

Indefinite articles
I'm **a** student.   *a* before consonants
He's **an** engineer.   *an* before vowel sounds

Definite article
I work for **the** *Daily News.*   *the* + specific place
  in **the** sales department.

KEY VOCABULARY

Nouns	*Materials**	*Other*	**Adjectives**	**Verbs**
Clothes and jewelry	cotton	adult	attractive	buy
backpack	gold	color	bad	get
bag	leather	compact disc	big	have on
boots	plastic	cost	cheap	let (me) + verb
bracelet	polyester	(room) decor	dark	look (= seem)
cap	rubber	design	different	look at
earrings	silk	dollar	each	pay (for)
gloves	silver	entertainment	expensive	prefer
jacket	wool	(for) example	good	spend (money)
(pair of) jeans		expenses	large	try on
necklace	*Names of	(gallon of) gas	light	
pants	materials can	haircut	medium	**Adverbs**
ring	be used as nouns	health	nice	almost
Rollerblades	or adjectives.	money	OK	better
scarf		(birthday) present	perfect	more
shirt		price	pretty	right there
(athletic) shoes		salary	reasonable	
sunglasses		savings	small	**Preposition**
sweater		style	warm	for (you)
tie		(price) tag	yearly	
watch		taxes		**Conjunction**
		thing		or
		transportation		

EXPRESSIONS

Talking about prices
How much is this sweater?
    It's . . . .
That isn't bad.
How much are those shoes?
    They're . . . .
That's expensive.

Comparing
The black boots are more
attractive/prettier than the
brown ones.

Identifying things
Which one?
    The wool one.
Which ones?
    The blue ones.

Talking about preferences
Which one do you like better/more?
    I like the . . . one better/more.
Which ones do you prefer?
    I prefer the . . . ones.

Getting someone's attention
Excuse me.
Hey.
Look!

Making and declining an offer
Would you like to . . . ?
    Oh, no. That's OK.

Thanking someone
Thank you (anyway).
    You're welcome.

Asking for more information
Why?
Do you mean . . . ?
Oh, these?

Expressing doubt
Hmm.
I'm not sure.

Expressing surprise
Are you kidding?

GRAMMAR EXTENSION *Comparative of adjectives*

Adjectives with -er
Add *-er:*   cheap → cheap**er**
Add *-r:*   nice → nic**er**
Drop *y* and add *-ier:*   pretty → prett**ier**
Double the final consonant and add *-er:*   big → big**ger**

Adjectives with more
more + adjective: **more** perfect
                              more expensive

For more information on comparatives, see the appendix at the back of the book.

4 DO YOU LIKE JAZZ?

KEY VOCABULARY

Nouns
*Music**
classical
country
gospel
jazz
New Age
pop
rap/urban
rock
salsa

*Names of musical
styles can be used as
nouns or adjectives.

Movies
comedy
horror film
science fiction
thriller
western

TV programs
game show
news
soap opera
talk show

Entertainers
actor
actress
group
singer

Other
CD
date *~dat~*
dinner
fan
(baseball) game *gem*
gym
kind (of) *kaiia*
piano
play *play*
theater *+*
ticket
trumpet
video

Adjectives
best
favorite
new

Verbs
agree *be acuerdo*
ask
come over *visitarme*
go out *salir*
have to *tenr*
know
listen to
meet *encontrar*
need *necesitv*
play (an instrument)
save *(selv) ahorrar*
sing *sing*
think of
visit
want

Adverbs
just
really *rrilly*
tonight *tonayt*

Prepositions
for (dinner)
on (TV)
with (me) *(u) t mi)*

EXPRESSIONS

Talking about likes and dislikes
Do you like . . . ?
    Yes, I do. I like . . . a lot.
    No, I don't. I can't stand . . . .
    No, I don't like . . . very much.
What kind of . . . do you like?
What do you think of . . . ?
What's/Who's your favorite . . . ?

Giving opinions
I like . . . . Do you?
I can't stand . . . . How about you?
I think . . . .
We don't agree on . . . .

Inviting and accepting/ refusing invitations
Would you like to . . . ?
    Yes, I would./I'd love to.
Do you want to . . . ?
    That sounds great.
    I'd like to, but I have to . . . .

Making suggestions
Why don't you . . . ?
Let's . . . .
    That sounds fine.

Asking about events
When is it?
Where is it?
What time does it start?
Where should we . . . ?

Asking for more information
How about . . . ?

GRAMMAR EXTENSION

1. Plural nouns
Add -s: singer → singers
Add -es: actress → actresses
Drop y and add -ies: comedy → comedies

2. Prepositions
Do you want to go out **on** Saturday?   *on* + day
Let's meet **at** the theater.   *at* + place
          at 7:30.   *at* + time

5 TELL ME ABOUT YOUR FAMILY.

KEY VOCABULARY

Nouns
Family/Relatives
aunt
brother
children
cousin
daughter
father
grandfather
grandmother
grandparents
husband
mother
nephew
niece
sister
sister-in-law
son
uncle
wife

Other
acting
age
college
exhibition
fact
family tree
headline
home
(foreign) language
lawyer
painter
percent
semester
theater company
winter

Pronoun
anyone

Adjectives
divorced
elderly
famous
together
young

Verbs
break up
end
get (married/divorced)
live
look for
move
remarry
return
say
stay
take (a class)
take care of
talk
tell
travel
visit

Adverbs
Time expressions
again
ever
most of the time
never
(right) now
often
still
these days
usually
this month/semester/
    winter/year

Other
abroad
alone

Prepositions
at (a university/home)
by (the age of . . .)

EXPRESSIONS

Asking about someone
Tell me about . . . .
What is . . . doing these days?

Exchanging information about the present
Are you still looking for a job?
    Yes, I am./No, I'm not.
What are you studying this year?
    I'm studying a foreign language.
Is anyone in your family . . . right now?
    Yes, my . . . is.

Expressing interest
Is that right?
What an interesting . . . !
Wow!

Disagreeing
Do you think so? I think . . . .
I don't agree.
I don't think so.
It's different in my country.
Not really.

GRAMMAR EXTENSION Present participles

Add -*ing:*

go → go**ing**

work → work**ing**

Drop *e* and add -*ing:*

live → liv**ing**

Double the final consonant and add -*ing:*

get → get**ting**

shop → shop**ping**

6 HOW OFTEN DO YOU EXERCISE?

KEY VOCABULARY

Nouns
Sports and fitness activities
aerobics
basketball
bicycling
football
jogging
racquetball
Rollerblading
soccer
swimming
tennis
weight training
yoga

Other
classmate
couch potato
fitness freak
free time
(fitness) program
sports fanatic
teen(ager)

Pronoun
nothing

Adjectives
good (at sports/for you)
fit
in (great) shape
middle-aged
old
popular
regular

Verbs
exercise
guess
keep
learn
lift (weights)
play (a sport)
stay
take (a walk)
work out

Adverb
hard
just (= only)
sometime
too

Prepositions
in (my free time)
for (a walk)
like (that)

Interjection
say

EXPRESSIONS

Talking about routines
How often do you . . . ?
  Three times a week/day/month.
  I don't . . . very often.
Do you ever . . . ?
How much time do you spend . . . ?
  Around two hours a day.

Talking about abilities
How well do you . . . ?
  Pretty well.
  Not very well.
How good are you at . . . ?
  I'm pretty good, I guess.
  Not too good.

Asking for more information
What else . . . ?

Expressing surprise
You're kidding!

Agreeing
All right.
No problem.

GRAMMAR EXTENSION Placement of adverbs of frequency

Questions
Is   he   usually at the gym after work?
be + subject + adverb

Statements
He   is   usually at the gym after work.
subject + *be* + adverb

He   isn't   usually there on weekends.
subject + negative *be* + adverb

Questions
Does he   usually go to the gym after work?
does + subject + adverb + verb

Statements
He   usually goes to the gym after work.
subject + adverb + verb

He   usually doesn't   go on weekends.
subject + adverb + *doesn't* + verb

Always usually goes between *don't/doesn't* and the main verb.

He   doesn't   always   go to the gym on weekends.
subject + *doesn't* + adverb + verb

7 WE HAD A GREAT TIME!

KEY VOCABULARY

Nouns
car
city
concert
(the) country
dancing
dishes
drive
housework
lake
neighbor
noise
party
picnic
trip
weather

Pronouns
anything
everyone
someone

Adjectives
all
boring
broke
cool
difficult
foggy
special
terrific

Verbs
baby-sit
complain
drive
enjoy
go shopping
have (someone) over
have (a[n] . . . time/
  [a lot of] fun)
invite (someone) out
see
snow
take (a day off)
work on

Adverbs
Time expressions
all day/month/year
all the time
as usual
last night/summer/weekend
the whole time
yesterday

Other
also
around
away
unfortunately

Prepositions
in (the country)
on (a trip/business/vacation)
over (the weekend)

EXPRESSIONS

Talking about past activities
Did you go out on Saturday?
What did you do . . . ?
How did you spend . . . ?
Where did you go . . . ?
What time did you go . . . ?
How long were you . . . ?

Giving opinions about past experiences
How did you like . . . ?/
How was . . . ?
  It was . . . . /I really enjoyed it.
What was the best thing about . . . ?
  It's difficult to say.
Was the . . . OK?

Making and responding to suggestions
Why don't you (just) . . . ?
  But then what would I do . . . ?

GRAMMAR EXTENSION Sentences about the weather

	it + be
How was the weather?	It was cool/cold/freezing.
	warm/hot.
	sunny/clear.
	cloudy/rainy.
	windy/foggy.

it + verb
It rained/snowed.

KEY VOCABULARY

Nouns
Neighborhood/
Community places
apartment (building)
aquarium
bank
barber shop
bookstore
cafe
coffee shop
dance club
drugstore
gas station
grocery store
hotel
laundromat
library
(science) museum
park
pay phone
post office
shopping center

stationery store
street
travel agency

Other
air
bedroom
book
card
crime
dining room
idea
kitchen
living room
ocean
paper (= stationery)
pollution
public transportation
suburbs
traffic
unemployment
water

Adjectives
busy
clean
close
convenient
important
low
near
quiet
safe *seguro*

Verbs
borrow *prestar*
dry *secar*
happen
make (a reservation)
move in
trade (places) *cambiar*
wash

Adverbs
downtown
nearby

Prepositions
in (the shopping center/
  your neighborhood)
on (Pine Street/Third
  Avenue)

Interjections
by the way *a proposito/hablamb de eso*
in fact
of course

EXPRESSIONS

Asking for and giving locations
Is there a/an . . . around here?
  Yes, there is. There's one . . . .
  No, there isn't, but there's one . . . .
  Sorry, I don't know.
Are there any . . . near here?
  Yes, there are. There are some . . . .
  No, there aren't, but there are some . . . .
  I'm not sure, but I think . . . .

Complaining
That's the trouble.

Asking about quantities
How much . . . is there?
  There's a lot/a little/none.
  There isn't much/any.
How many . . . are there?
  There are a lot/a few/none.
  There aren't many/any.

Giving opinions
I bet . . . .

GRAMMAR EXTENSION

1. Countable and uncountable nouns

Countable

Singular	Plural
a bookstore	(**some**) bookstores
an apartment	(**some**) apartments

Uncountable

Singular	Plural
(**some**) traffic	–
(**some**) noise	–

2. *Some* and *any*

Questions
Is there **a** bookstore?
Are there **any** bookstores?

Questions
Is there   traffic?
         any traffic?

Statements
There are **some** bookstores.

Statements
There is **some** traffic.

Negatives
There aren't **any** bookstores.

Negatives
There isn't **any** traffic.

WHAT DOES HE LOOK LIKE?

KEY VOCABULARY

Nouns
beard
centimeter (cm) *lentes contacto*
contact lenses
couch
couple
eye
fashion
foot/feet
glasses
guy
hair
hand *mano*
height *altura*
length
man
mustache
person
T-shirt
window
woman

Adjectives
bald
blond
curly
good-looking
handsome
khaki
serious-looking
short
straight
tall

Verbs
ask for
change
miss
sit
stand
wear

Adverbs
ago
fairly
pretty
quite

Prepositions
in (a T-shirt and jeans/his thirties)
on (the couch)
to (the left [of])
with (red hair)

EXPRESSIONS

Greeting someone
Good afternoon.
Good to see you.

Offering help
Can I help you?
  Yes, I'm looking for . . . .

Asking about someone's appearance
What does she look like?
How old is she?
What color is her hair/are her eyes?
How tall is she?

Identifying people
Which one is Judy?
  She's the one talking to Tom.
Who's Brian?
  He's the man with curly blond hair/in jeans/
  behind the couch.

Expressing Intention
I'll go and . . . .

Expressing regret
I'm afraid . . .

Hesitating
Let's see.

Confirming information
Are you . . . ?
  Yes, that's right.

GRAMMAR EXTENSION Be *and* have *to describe someone*

be + adjective
I'm 18.
He**'s** bald.
She**'s** tall.
They**'re** medium height.

have + noun
I **have** brown hair.
He **has** a mustache and a beard
She **has** blue eyes.
They **have** curly black hair.

10 HAVE YOU EVER RIDDEN A CAMEL?

KEY VOCABULARY

Nouns
accident
appointment
audience
bird
breakfast
bungee jumping
camel
camera
(body-building)
  competition
(a) couple (of)
fire
fish
grocery shopping
hill
kiwi (fruit)
laundry
magic
magician
(goat's) milk
motorcycle
mountain

pastime
pleasure
riverboat
skiing
sports car
truck
wallet
way
wedding
(a) while
white-water rafting
(rice) wine

Pronouns
several
something

Adjectives
every
exciting
incredible
raw
several
unusual
valuable
wonderful

Verbs
call
clean
climb
decide
drink
eat
hike
jog
lose
make (your bed)
ride
try

Adverbs
actually
already
lately
once
recently
today
twice
yet

Prepositions
for (a while)
in (a long time)

Conjunction
because

EXPRESSIONS

Exchanging information about past experiences
Have you ever . . . ?
  Yes, I have./No, I haven't.

Giving a suggestion
You should . . . .

Agreeing
Sure.

Checking and sharing information
The magician?
  That's right.
I hear . . . .

GRAMMAR EXTENSION Time expressions

With present perfect

Time expressions refer to indefinite times in the past.

I've **already** seen that show.
I've seen it **twice**.
I haven't seen it **yet**.
I haven't been to the movies **in a long time**.

With past tense

Time expressions refer to specific times in the past.

I saw it **last night**.
I saw it **yesterday**.
I saw it **last Friday**.
I went to the movies **about a month ago**.

KEY VOCABULARY

Nouns
Seasons
fall
spring
summer
winter

Other
arrival
beach
departure
harbor
hometown
(flea) market
million
nightlife
tourist
visitor

Pronoun
you (= anyone)

Adjectives
beautiful
cold
crowded
dangerous
dirty
friendly
hot
humid
modern
relaxing
stressful
ugly

Verbs
Modals
can
should

Other
hate

Adverb
anytime

Prepositions
at (the beach)
in (the fall)
on (the street)

Conjunctions
however
though

EXPRESSIONS

Describing something
What's . . . like?
  It's . . . , but it's not too . . . .
  It's . . . , and it's . . . .

Asking for a favor
Can you . . . ?
  Yes, I can./Sure I can.
  No, I can't.

**Asking for and giving
suggestions**
What should I . . . ?
  You should . . . .
  You shouldn't . . . .
Should I . . . ?
  Yes, you should./
  No, you shouldn't.

Talking about advisability
What can you do?
  You can . . . .
  You can't . . . .

GRAMMAR EXTENSION *Sentences with* and, but, however, though

These sentences mean the same: They contrast something good *(a beautiful city)* and something bad *(very hot)*.

This is a beautiful city, **but** it's very hot in the summer.
            It's very hot in the summer, **however**.
            It's very hot in the summer, **though**.

In this sentence, the conjunction *and* adds information.

This is a beautiful city, **and** there's always a lot to do.

KEY VOCABULARY

Nouns
Health problems
backache
burn
cold
cough
dry skin
fever
flu
headache
hiccups
insect bite
insomnia
muscle
pain
sore throat
stomachache
stress
sunburn
toothache

Containers and medicines
antacid
aspirin
bandage
bottle
box
can
cold tablets
cough drops
(anti-itch/skin) cream
(eye) drops
heating pad
lotion
ointment
package
sleeping pills
spray
tissue
tube
vitamin (C)

Other
chicken stock
dentist
garlic
liquid
meat
medicine cabinet
pepper
pharmacist
remedy
rest
slice

Adjectives
excellent
folk
half
helpful
lots of
sore
tired
useful

Verbs
Modals
could
may

Other
chop up
cut
get (a cold)
put
rest
take (medicine/
    something for . . .)
tie
suggest
work (= succeed)

Prepositions
in (bed)
under (cold water)

EXPRESSIONS

Talking about health problems
How are you?
    Not so good. I have . . . .
That's too bad.

Offering and accepting assistance
Can/May I help you?
    Yes, please. Could/Can/May I have . . . ?
Here you are.
    Thanks a lot.

Asking for and giving advice
What should you do . . . ?
    It's helpful/a good idea to . . . .

Asking for and giving suggestions
What do you have/suggest for . . . ?
    Try/I suggest/You should get . . . .

Expressing dislike
Ugh!

GRAMMAR EXTENSION Sentences with have got to talk about health problems

What's the matter?   **I've got** a bad cold.   *Contractions*
                        She's got the flu.   I have = **I've**
                                                          She has = **She's**

KEY VOCABULARY

Nouns _beruchey_
Food and beverages
bread
broth _caldo rich_
(chocolate) cake
(clam) chowder _clamatp_
(cup of) coffee
col cole slaw _slow/ensalaca dserpi_
cucumber _pepin_
dessert _postre_
dressing _aderezo_
(ele1vo) flavor _sabor_
(french) fries
(mixed) greens _mixt verde_
hamburger
ice cream
lemon
main dish _plato principal_
meal _mi_
meatballs _mit bolls/albmtip_
milk
pasta

(apple) pie
potato
rice
salad
salmon
seafood
spaghetti
soda
(onion) soup _ceb-vle_
steak _corte carn_
(iced) tea
tomato
turkey _pavo_
vegetable _(Velchteibol)_
vinaigrette

Other
customer
order
tip
waiter
waitress

Pronoun
all

Adjectives
baked
bland
delicious
ethnic
fried
greasy
grilled
healthy
mashed
rich
roast
salty
spicy

Verbs
Modals
will
would

Other
bring
go back
order

Adverbs
a bit
(not) at all
for now
right away

Preposition
with (lemon)

EXPRESSIONS

Expressing feelings
I'm crazy about . . . .
I'm (not) in the mood for . . . .

Agreeing and disagreeing
I like . . . .
   So do I./I do, too.
I don't like . . . .
   Neither do I./I don't either.
I'm crazy about . . . .
   So am I./I am, too.
I'm not in the mood for . . . .
   Neither am I./I'm not either.
I can . . . .
   So can I./I can, too.
I can't . . . .
   Neither can I./I can't either.

Ordering in a restaurant
May I take your order, please?/
What would you like?
   I'd like/I'll have a/an/the . . . .
What kind of . . . would you like?
   I'd like/I'll have . . . , please.
Would you like anything else?
   Yes, please. I'd like . . . .
   No, thank you. That will be all.

GRAMMAR EXTENSION Polite requests

Imperative
Please bring me a glass of water.

Questions with can/could/will/would
Can you please bring me a glass of water?
Could . . . .
Will . . . .
Would . . . .

14 THE BIGGEST AND THE BEST!

KEY VOCABULARY

Nouns

Geography
canyon
cliff
continent
desert
"down under" (= Australia
  and New Zealand)
farm
field
forest
plain
plateau
(coral) reef
river
sea
swamp
valley
volcano
waterfall

Measurements
degree
  (Fahrenheit/Celsius)
kilometer
meter
(square) mile
temperature

Other
artist
attraction
butter
feather
town

Adjectives
deep
far
heavy
high
located
lucky
mountainous

Verbs
get up (to)
go down (to)

Prepositions
in (the mountains/the world)
of (the three)
on (Bali)

EXPRESSIONS

Talking about distance and measurements
How far is . . . from . . . ?
  It's about . . . kilometers/miles.
How big is . . . ?
  It's . . . square kilometers.
How high is . . . ?
  It's . . . meters/feet high.
How deep is (the) . . . ?
  It's . . . meters deep.
How long is (the) . . . ?
  It's . . . kilometers long.
How hot is . . . in the summer?
  It gets up to . . . degrees.
How cold is . . . in the winter?
  It goes down to . . . degrees.

Making comparisons
Which country is larger, . . . or . . . ?
  . . . is larger than . . . .
Which country is the largest: . . . , . . . , or . . . ?
  . . . is the largest of the three.
What is the most beautiful . . . in the world?
  I think . . . is the most beautiful.

GRAMMAR EXTENSION Superlative of adjectives

Adjectives with -est
Add *-est:*   high → high**est**
Add *-st:*   large → larg**est**
Drop *y* and add *-iest:* dry   → dr**iest**
Double the final consonant and add *-est:* big → big**gest**

Adjectives with most
most + adjective: **most** famous
                    most mountainous

See the appendix at the back of the book for a list of adjectives.

KEY VOCABULARY

Nouns
(comedy) act
(leisure) activity
address
amusement park
barbecue
cafeteria
(telephone) call *coll*
dictionary *dicchionary*
(craft) fair
(arts/crafts) festival
gathering *agroparse*
handout *distribedir*

hockey
meeting
message
monument
musical
plan
spectator
(tennis) tournament
turn *turne*

Adjectives
canceled *canceled*
historic
live

Verbs
finish
give
open
pick (someone) up *recoger*
plan
return *regresar*
speak

Adverbs
in
overtime
tomorrow

Prepositions
at (college)
till (7:00) *hasta*

Conjunction
that

EXPRESSIONS

Talking about plans
What are you doing tonight?
    I'm going . . . .
Are you doing anything tomorrow/
tonight?
    No, I'm not.
What is he going to do tonight?
    He's going to . . . .
Is he going to . . . tomorrow night?
    Yes, he is.

Apologizing and giving reasons
I'm sorry, but I can't go.
I'm working late.

**Accepting and refusing
invitations**
Would you like to . . . ?/
Do you want to . . . ?
    I'd love to.
    Oh, sorry, I can't.

Making a business call
Good morning, ...
    Hello. May I speak to . . . , please?
. . .'s not in. Can I take a message?
    Yes, please. This is . . . . Would
you ask . . . to call me? My number
is . . . .
I'll give . . . the message.
    Thank you. Good-bye.

Leaving and taking messages
Can/May I take a message?
    Please tell . . . (that) . . . .
    Please ask . . . to . . . .
    Would/Could you tell . . . (that) . . . ?
    Would/Could you ask . . . to . . . ?

GRAMMAR EXTENSION Future sentences

With be going to

The verb *be* is always used in the *be going to* form – never in the present continuous.

Where **are** you **going to be** tomorrow?
    I'm going to be at home.

With present continuous

Arrive, come, go, leave, and *stay* are usually used in the present continuous.

We**'re arriving** tomorrow.
        coming
        going
        leaving
        staying

KEY VOCABULARY

Nouns	**Adjectives**	**Verbs**	**Adverbs**
biology	dressed up	become	anymore
course	easy	bring about	differently
degree	outgoing	date	for ages
(environmental) education	own	dress	
forestry	successful	fall (in love)	**Prepositions**
graduation		grow	at (an early age)
hairstyle		hope	into (a new apartment)
kid		join	
life/lives		pay off	
(student) loan		quit	
photo album		retire	
weight		smoke	
		start	
		type	

EXPRESSIONS

Exchanging personal information
How have you been?
  Pretty good.
How are you?
  I'm doing really well.

Describing changes
You've really changed!
  I'm married now.
  I don't wear glasses anymore.
  My job is easier (now).
  I'm heavier (than before).
  I got divorced.
  I've grown a mustache.

Talking about plans for the future
I'm (not) going to . . . .
I (don't) plan to . . . .
I (don't) want to . . . .
I hope to . . . .
I'd like/love to . . . .

GRAMMAR EXTENSION Review: Wh-questions

What's your name?
What do you do?
What time do you get up?
What kind of music do you like?
What do you look like?
What color are your eyes?
What are you like?
What are you doing these days?
What did you do last night?
What do you think of Brad Pitt?

When do you get home?
When are you leaving?

Where are you from?
Where do you work?
Where did you go yesterday?
Where were you?
Which jeans do you like better,
  the light ones or the dark ones?
Which one is Tom?

Who is that?
Who's your favorite actress?
Who did you go out with last night?
Who's Sarah?

How do you like your job?
How do you spend your day?
How did you spend your last birthday?
How was your trip?

How much is that blouse?
How much crime is there in your city?
How many restaurants are there in your neighborhood?

How often do you exercise?
How well do you play?
How good are you at sports?
How long do you spend working out?
How long were you away?
How much time do you spend at the gym?
How old are you?
How long is your hair?
How tall are you?

Why don't you buy a new car?

Appendix

COUNTRIES AND NATIONALITIES

This is a partial list of countries, many
of which are presented in this book.

Argentina	Argentine	Germany	German	the Philippines	Filipino
Australia	Australian	Greece	Greek	Poland	Polish
Austria	Austrian	Hungary	Hungarian	Russia	Russian
Brazil	Brazilian	India	Indian	Singapore	Singaporean
Bolivia	Bolivian	Indonesia	Indonesian	Spain	Spanish
Canada	Canadian	Ireland	Irish	Switzerland	Swiss
Chile	Chilean	Italy	Italian	Thailand	Thai
China	Chinese	Japan	Japanese	Turkey	Turkish
Colombia	Colombian	Korea	Korean	Peru	Peruvian
Costa Rica	Costa Rican	Lebanon	Lebanese	the United Kingdom	British
Ecuador	Ecuadorian	Malaysia	Malaysian	the United States	American
Egypt	Egyptian	Mexico	Mexican	Uruguay	Uruguayan
England	English	Morocco	Moroccan		
France	French	New Zealand	New Zealander		

NUMBERS

0	1	2	3	4	5	6	7	8
zero	one	two	three	four	five	six	seven	eight
9	10	11	12	13	14	15	16	17
nine	ten	eleven	twelve	thirteen	fourteen	fifteen	sixteen	seventeen
18	19	20	21	22	30	40	50	60
eighteen	nineteen	twenty	twenty-one	twenty-two	thirty	forty	fifty	sixty

70	80	90	100	1,000
seventy	eighty	ninety	one hundred (a hundred)	one thousand (a thousand)

COMPARATIVE AND SUPERLATIVE ADJECTIVES

1. Adjective with -er and -est

big *grande*	dirty *suci°*	high *jauy* old	tall *toll/alto*
busy *ocupado*	dry *seco*	hot *jati* pretty	ugly *fe°*
cheap *barato*	easy *(isi*	large *larg* quiet	warm *tibio*
clean *limpio*	fast *rapid°*	light *layt* safe	wet *mojado*
close *cerrado*	friendly	long *(long)* scary *(scery)* young *joven*	
cold *(cuid)* *(fresco)*	funny *fany*	mild *mail* short	
cool *(cul)* *frio*	great *great*	new *(niuw)* slow *derpacio*	
deep *dip* *profundo*	heavy *heivy*	nice *naice* small *smol*	

2. Adjectives with *more* and *most*

attractive	exciting	outgoing
beautiful	expensive	popular
boring	famous	relaxing
crowded	important	stressful
dangerous	interesting	difficult
delicious		

3. Irregular adjectives

good → better → best
bad → worse → the worst

Robert

PRONUNCIATION OF REGULAR PAST FORMS

with /d/	*with /t/*	*with /ɪd/*
studied	worked	invited
stayed	watched	visited

IRREGULAR VERBS

Present	Past	Participle		Present	Past	Participle
(be) am/is, are	was, were	been		make	made	made
bring	brought	brought		meet	met	met
buy	bought	bought		put	put	put
come	came	come		quit	quit	quit
cut	cut	cut		read	read	read
do	did	done		ride	rode	ridden
drink	drank	drunk		run	ran	run
drive	drove	driven		see	saw	seen
eat	ate	eaten		sell	sold	sold
fly	flew	flown		set	set	set
fall	fell	fallen		sit	sat	sat
feel	felt	felt		sleep	slept	slept
get	got	gotten		speak	spoke	spoken
give	gave	given		spend	spent	spent
go	went	gone		take	took	taken
grow	grew	grown		teach	taught	taught
have	had	had		tell	told	told
hear	heard	heard		think	thought	thought
keep	kept	kept		wear	wore	worn
lose	lost	lost		write	wrote	written

ANSWER KEY   Unit 14, Exercise 3, page 87

1. Vatican City — (.44 square kilometers/.17 square miles)
2. Angel Falls — (979 meters/3,212 feet)
3. Hong Kong — (247,501 people per square mile)
4. the Caspian Sea — (378,400 square kilometers/146,101 square miles)
5. Mount Everest — (8,848 meters/29,028 feet)
6. the Nile — (6,670 kilometers/4,145 miles)
7. France — (60 million tourists)
8. the Pacific Ocean — (average depth of 4,028 meters/13,215 feet)

ANSWER KEY   Interchange 14, page IC-19

1. gold
2. Pluto (temperature = −230ºC/−382ºF)
3. Jupiter (diameter =142,984 km/88,846 miles)
4. a tortoise (maximum age = 150 years)
5. a giraffe (height = 5.5 meters/18 feet)
6. the liver (weight = 1,560 grams/55 ounces)
7. 1 liter of wine
8. Egypt (rainfall = 100–200 mm/4–8 inches)
9. Colombia (The equator runs through Colombia.)
10. an octagon (An octagon has 8 sides.)
11. a mile (1 mile = 1,760 yards = 1.6 kilometers)
12. the Dark Ages (from around 500–1,000 A.D.)

Acknowledgments

ILLUSTRATIONS

Barbara Griffel 15 *(top)*, 17 *(top)*, 18, 59
Randy Jones 5 *(top)*, 9, 23, 29, 37 *(top)*, 38, 46 *(top)*, 47, 52, 53, 54, 56, 63, 66, 75 *(top)*, 80, 85, 86, 94, 100, 104, IC-4 and IC-5 *(bottom)*, IC-16, IC-20
Mark Kaufman 74, 75 *(bottom)*, 76, 83 *(top)*, 84, IC-4 *(top five items)*, IC-5 *(top five items)*
Kevin Spaulding 3 *(bottom)*, 4, 5 *(bottom)*, 14, 15 *(bottom)*, 28, 37 *(bottom)*, 49, 55, 57, 60, 72 *(bottom)*, 78 *(bottom)*, 79, 92, 98, 105, IC-12, IC-14, IC-17, IC-18
Sam Viviano 2, 3 *(top)*, 11, 17 *(bottom)*, 26, 27, 31, 35, 40, 46 *(bottom)*, 61, 64, 72 *(top)*, 73, 78 *(top)*, 83 *(bottom)*, 89, 97, 99, IC-2, IC-3, IC-6, IC-19

PHOTOGRAPHIC CREDITS

9 *(left to right)* © Jon Riley/Tony Stone Images; © SuperStock; © Bruce Byers/FPG International; © Dennis Hallinan/FPG International; © Michael Krasowitz/FPG International; © Bruce Ayres/Tony Stone Images
10 © Flip Chalfant/The Image Bank
11 © James Levin/FPG International
12 © Jon Riley/Tony Stone Images
13 *(left to right)* © Mary Kate Denny/PhotoEdit; © Peter Correz/Tony Stone Images; © Jeffrey Sylvester/FPG International
16 *(top row, left to right)* Courtesy of IBM Corporation; courtesy of Kmart Corporation; courtesy of Kmart Corporation; courtesy of SWATCH; *(bottom row, left to right)* courtesy of IBM Corporation; Jeans by GUESS, photo © Richard Bachmann; courtesy of Reebok; courtesy of Kmart Corporation
19 *(left to right)* © Michael Keller/The Stock Market; © Ed Bock/The Stock Market; © Cybershop
21 *(top)* © Christian Ducasse/Gamma Liaison; *(bottom)* © Alpha/Globe Photos
22 *(clockwise from top)* © Fitzroy Barrett/Globe Photos; © Alpha/Globe Photos; © Paramount Pictures/Globe Photos
23 A scene from *The Phantom of the Opera*, photograph © Clive Barda
25 *(Bonnie Raitt)* © Alain Benainous/Gamma Liaison; *(Cui Jian)* © Forrest Anderson/Gamma Liaison; *(Caetano Veloso, performing at SummerStage in Central Park)* © Robert L. Smith
27 © Randy Masser/International Stock
29 *(left to right)* © Adam Scull/Globe Photos; © Bob V. Noble/Globe Photos; © Andrea Renault/Globe Photos; © R. Henry McGee/Globe Photos; © Imapress/Globe Photos; © Michael Ferguson/Globe Photos
30 © Chuck Kuhn Photography/The Image Bank
32 © Jim Cummins/FPG International
33 © Rob Gage/FPG International
35 © Donna Day/Tony Stone Images

38 © Paul Loven/The Image Bank
39 © Kevin Horan/Tony Stone Images
41 © Michael Keller/The Stock Market
42 © Peter Ginter/The Image Bank
43 *(ex.8, top)* © Gary Irving/Tony Stone Images; *(ex. 8, bottom)* © Hiroyuki Matsumoto/Tony Stone Images; *(ex. 9, clockwise from top)* © Zeynep Sumen/Tony Stone Images; © Ed Pritchard/Tony Stone Images; © Joe Cornish/Tony Stone Images
44 © Cliff Hollenbeck/Tony Stone Images
45 *(top to bottom)* © Matthew Weinreb/The Image Bank; © Wayne H. Chasan/The Image Bank; © Joseph Van Os/The Image Bank
48 © Schmid-Langsfeld/The Image Bank
50 © Ron Chapple/FPG International
51 © Jose Fuste Raga/The Stock Market
57 *(left to right)* © Springer/Corbis-Bettmann; © Helmut Gritscher/FPG International; © Paramount/The Kobal Collection
60 *(left to right)* © Alain Evrard/Gamma Liaison; © Globe Photos; © Paul McKelvey/Tony Stone Images; © Alexis Orand/Gamma Liaison
62 © Alpha/Globe Photos
64 © Dann Coffey/The Image Bank
65 *(top to bottom)* © Elan Sun Star/Tony Stone Images; © David Madison/Tony Stone Images; © Darryl Torckler/Tony Stone Images
66 © Richard Simpson/Tony Stone Images
67 *(left to right)* © Chip Vinai/Gamma Liaison; © Porter Gifford/Gamma Liaison; © Sylvain Grandadam/Tony Stone Images; © Tony Stone Images
68 © J. Blank/H. Armstrong Roberts
69 *(top)* © Don Klumpp/The Image Bank; *(bottom)* © Poulides/Thatcher/Tony Stone Images
70 *(left)* © Paul Chesley/Tony Stone Images; *(right)* © Glen Allison/Tony Stone Images
71 *(left to right)* © George Hunter/ H. Armstrong Roberts; © Travelpix/FPG International; © Will & Deni McIntyre/Tony Stone Images
74 © Richard Bachmann
81 *(left to right)* © Tony Stone Images; © Laurence Dutton/Tony Stone Images; © Luis Castaneda, Inc./The Image Bank; © James Jackson/Tony Stone Images; © Alberto Incrocci/The Image Bank; © Kenneth Mengay/Gamma Liaison; © Richard Bachmann
82 *(left to right)* © Paul Barton/The Stock Market; © Ron Chapple/FPG International; © Paul Barton/The Stock Market; © Ron Chapple/FPG International
87 © Stephen Frink/Tony Stone Images
88 © R. Kord/H. Armstrong Roberts
90 © Chad Ehlers/Tony Stone Images
91 *(top row, left to right)* © Ed Pritchard/Tony Stone Images ; © Ariel Skelley/The Stock Market; © Stephen Simpson/FPG International; © Mug Shots/The Stock

Market; *(bottom row, left to right)* © Richard Bachmann; courtesy of Philips Lighting Company; © Kevin Laubacher/FPG International; courtesy of Niagara Conservation Corporation
101 *(top to bottom)* © SuperStock; © Tom Wilson/FPG International; © Michael Keller/The Stock Market; © L.O.L. Inc./FPG International
102 © Eddie Adams/The Stock Market
103 *(left to right)* PEOPLE Weekly © 1995 Frank Veronsky; © Ted Rice; © Ed Hill/*The Bergen Record,* Hackensack, NJ
104 © Travelpix/FPG International
IC-7 *(left to right)* © Chuck Mason/International Stock; © Stephen Simpson/FPG International; © Michael Krasowitz/FPG International
IC-9 *(top row, left to right)* © Cliff Hollenbeck/International Stock; © Bruce Byers/FPG International; © Cliff Hollenbeck/International Stock; *(bottom row, left)* © Cliff Hollenbeck/International Stock; *(bottom row, right)* © Cathlyn Melloan/Tony Stone Images
IC-10 *(top row, left to right)* © Telegraph Colour Library/FPG International; © Darryl Torckler/Tony Stone Images; *(bottom row, left to right)* © Telegraph Colour Library/FPG International; © Josef Beck/FPG International; © Hugh Sitton/Tony Stone Images
IC-13 *(left)* © John Terence Turner/FPG International; *(right)* © Bruce Ayres/Tony Stone Images
IC-21 © Vera R. Storman/Tony Stone Images

TEXT CREDITS

The authors and publishers are grateful for permission to reprint the following items.

41 Adapted from "Smart Moves," by Susan Brink, *U.S. News and World Report,* May 16, 1996, page 76.
49 *(Snapshot)* Reprinted from the September 1994 issue of *MONEY* by special permission; copyright 1994, Time Inc.
97 Adapted from *Stephanie Winston's Best Organizing Tips,* by Stephanie Winston, Simon & Schuster, 1995.
103 *(Balamurati Krishna Ambati)* Adapted from "Prodigy, 12, Fights Skeptics, Hoping," by Alessandra Stanley, *New York Times,* May 7, 1990, pages A1, B9. Copyright © 1990 by The New York Times Co. Reprinted by permission. *(Catherine Charlton)* Adapted from "The Top Ten College Winners," *Glamour,* October 1994, Vol. 92, No. 10, page 118. *(Jasmin Sethi)* Adapted from "Blind Student Aces SAT," by Paul J. Toomey, *The Bergen Record* (Hackensack, NJ), November 20, 1995.
IC-7 Adapted from "Lifystyle Quiz," by Linda Henry, *Muscle & Fitness,* September 1994, pages 230–231. Reprinted with permission.

new interchange

Jack C. Richards

*video
activity
book*

1

CAMBRIDGE
UNIVERSITY PRESS

Revised for use with *New Interchange*

Plan of Video Activity Book 1

iii

Introduction

NEW INTERCHANGE

New Interchange is a revision of *Interchange,* one of the world's most successful and popular English courses. *New Interchange* is a multi-level course in English as a second or foreign language for young adults and adults. The course covers the four skills of listening, speaking, reading, and writing, as well as improving pronunciation and building vocabulary. Particular emphasis is placed on listening and speaking. The primary goal of the course is to teach communicative competence, that is, the ability to communicate in English according to the situation, purpose, and roles of the participants. The language used in *New Interchange* is American English; however, the course reflects the fact that English is the major language of international communication and is not limited to any one country, region, or culture. Level One is for students at the beginner or false-beginner level.

Level One builds on the foundations for accurate and fluent communication already established in the *Intro* Level by extending grammatical, lexical, and functional skills. The syllabus covered in Level One also incorporates a rapid review of language from the *Intro* Level, allowing Student's Book 1 to be used with students who have not studied with *Intro*.

THE VIDEO COURSE

New Interchange Video 1 has been revised for use with *New Interchange*. The Video is designed to complement the Student's Book or to be used independently as the basis for a short listening and speaking course.

As a complement to the Student's Book, the Video provides a variety of entertaining and instructive live-action sequences. Each video sequence provides further practice related to the topics, language, and vocabulary introduced in the corresponding unit of the Student's Book.

As the basis for a short, free-standing course, the Video serves as an exciting vehicle for introducing and practicing useful conversational language used in everyday situations.

The Video Activity Book contains a wealth of activities that reinforce and extend the content of the Video, whether it is used to supplement the Student's Book or as the basis for an independent course. The Video Teacher's Guide provides thorough support for both situations.

COURSE LENGTH

The Video contains sixteen dramatized sequences and five documentary sequences. These vary slightly in length, but in general, the sequences are approximately three minutes each, and the documentaries are approximately five minutes each.

The accompanying units in the Video Activity Book are designed for maximum flexibility and provide anywhere from 45 to 90 minutes of classroom activity. Optional activities described in the Video Teacher's Guide may be used to extend the lesson as needed.

MORE ABOUT THE COURSE COMPONENTS

Video

The sixteen video sequences complement Units 1 through 16 of *New Interchange* Student's Book 1. Although each sequence is linked to the topic of the corresponding Student's Book unit, it presents a new situation and introduces characters who do not appear in the text. This element of diversity helps keep students' interest high and also allows the Video to be used effectively as a free-standing course. At the same time, the language used in the video sequences reflects the structures and vocabulary of the Student's Book, which is based on an integrated syllabus that links grammar and communicative functions.

The five documentaries may be used for review or at any point in the course. These sequences correspond to the placement of the review units in the Student's Book, with a fifth "bonus" documentary appearing after Sequence 2. The documentaries are based on authentic, unscripted interviews with people in various situations, and serve to illustrate how language is used by real people in real situations.

Video Activity Book

The Video Activity Book contains sixteen units based on live-action sequences and five documentary units that correspond to the video sequences and documentaries, and is designed to facilitate the effective use of the Video in the classroom. Each unit includes previewing, viewing, and postviewing activities that provide learners with step-by-step support and guidance in understanding and working with the events and language of the sequence. Learners expand their cultural awareness, develop skills and strategies for communicating effectively, and use language creatively.

Video Teacher's Guide

The Video Teacher's Guide contains detailed suggestions for how to use the Video and the Video Activity Book in the classroom, and includes an overview of video teaching techniques, unit-by-unit notes, and a range of optional extension activities. The Video Teacher's Guide also includes answers to the activities in the Video Activity Book and photocopiable transcripts of the video sequences.

■ VIDEO IN THE CLASSROOM

The use of video in the classroom can be an exciting and effective way to teach and learn. As a medium, video both motivates and entertains students. The *New Interchange* Video is a unique resource that does the following:

- Depicts dynamic, natural contexts for language use.

- Presents authentic language as well as cultural information about speakers of English through engaging story lines.

- Enables learners to use visual information to enhance comprehension.

- Focuses on the important cultural dimension of learning a language by actually showing how speakers of the language live and behave.

- Allows learners to observe the gestures, facial expressions, and other aspects of body language that accompany speech.

■ WHAT EACH UNIT OF THE VIDEO ACTIVITY BOOK CONTAINS

Each unit of the Video Activity Book is divided into four sections: *Preview*, *Watch the Video*, *Follow-up*, and *Language Close-up*. In general, these four sections include, but are not limited to, the following types of activities:

Preview

Culture The culture previews introduce the topics of the video sequences and provide important background and cultural information. They can be presented in class as reading and discussion activities, or students can read and complete them as homework.

Vocabulary The vocabulary activities introduce and practice the essential vocabulary of the video sequences through a variety of interesting tasks.

Guess the Story/Guess the Facts The Guess the Story (or in some units Guess the Facts) activities allow students to make predictions about characters and their actions by watching the video sequences without the sound or by looking at photos in the Video Activity Book. These schema-building activities help to improve students' comprehension when they watch the sequences with the sound.

Watch the Video

Get the Picture These initial viewing activities help students gain global understanding of the sequences by focusing on gist. Activity types vary from unit to unit, but typically involve watching for key information needed to complete a chart, answer questions, or put events in order.

Watch for Details In these activities, students focus on more detailed meaning by watching and listening for specific information to complete tasks about the story line and the characters.

What's Your Opinion? In these activities, students respond to the sequences by making inferences about the characters' actions, feelings, and motivations, and by stating their opinions about issues and topics.

Follow-up

Role Play, Interview, and Other Expansion Activities This section includes communicative activities based on the sequences in which students extend and personalize what they have learned.

Language Close-up

What Did They Say? These cloze activities focus on the specific language in the sequences by having students watch and listen in order to fill in missing words in conversations.

Grammar and Functional Activities In these activities, which are titled to reflect the structural and functional focus of a particular unit, students practice, in a meaningful way, the grammatical structures and functions presented in the video sequences.

First day at class

1 CULTURE

In the United States and Canada, most people have three names:

First name   **Middle name**   **Last name**
Anne   Louise   Lucas

In universities, students usually use titles and last names with their teachers:
Hello, Professor Lucas.

Hello, Professor Anne.

In English, do not use a title with a first name.

How many names do people have in your country?
Do you use titles (Ms., Mrs., Mr., Professor) with last names?
*   With first names?*
Do you ever call teachers by their first names?

2 VOCABULARY Nationalities

Pair work When people first meet, they often talk about nationality.
What do you call people from these countries?

Country	Nationality	Country	Nationality	Country	Nationality
Brazil	*Brazilian*	France	....	Mexico	....
Canada	....	Japan	....	Spain	....
England	....	Korea	....	Thailand	....

3 GUESS THE STORY

Watch the first minute of the video with the sound off.
What do you think happens to the young man?
Check (✓) your answer.

☐ He meets an old friend.
☐ He meets the teacher of his class.
☐ He goes to the wrong classroom.

Watch the video

4 GET THE PICTURE

Complete the chart. Then compare with a partner.

First name:
Sachiko

Last name:
Tanaka

Occupation:
Student

First name:
Marie

Last name:
Ouellette

Occupation:
teacher

First name:
RICK

Last name:
?

Occupation:
student

---

5 WATCH FOR DETAILS

Check (✓) the correct answers. Then compare with a partner.

Merrie originals

1) Rick is originally from
   - ✓ Mexico.
   - ☐ the United States.
   - ☐ Canada.

2) Rick now lives in
   - ☐ Mexico.
   - ☒ the United States.
   - ☐ Canada.

3) Marie is originally from
   - ☐ France.
   - ☒ Canada.
   - ☐ the United States.

4) Marie teaches
   - ☐ French. *manechment*
   - ☒ business management. *bisne*
   - ☐ English.

5) Rick and Sachiko are studying
   - ☐ mathematics.
   - ☐ English.
   - ☒ business management.

6 FORMS OF ADDRESS

How do the people in the video address each other? Check (✓) the correct answers. Then compare with a partner. (One item has two answers.)

	First name only	First and last name	Title and last name
1) Marie to Sachiko	☐	☐	✓
2) Marie to Rick	☐	☐	☐
3) Rick to Marie	☐	☐	☐
4) Sachiko to Marie	☐	☐	☐

7 WHAT'S YOUR OPINION?

Check (✓) your opinions. Then compare with a partner.

1) Why do you think Rick introduces himself to Marie?
   - ☒ to make a friend
   - ☐ to meet his teacher
   - ☐ other ....

2) When Rick learns that Marie is his teacher, how do you think he feels?
   - ☐ amused
   - ☐ angry
   - ☒ embarrassed
   - ☐ pleased

3) How do you think Marie feels?
   - ☒ amused
   - ☐ angry
   - ☐ embarrassed
   - ☒ pleased

amused   angry   embarrassed   pleased

aMIUSed   *engry*   *embarred*   *plisd*

 Follow-up

8 ROLE PLAY Meeting people

A *Group work* Imagine you are Rick, Sachiko, or Professor Ouellette. Write three more questions to ask each other.

1) *Where are you from?* ....
2) ....
3) ....
4) ....

B Now introduce yourselves. Have conversations like this:

A: Hello, my name's Rick.
B: Hi, I'm Sachiko.
A: Where are you from, Sachiko?
B: I'm from Japan. . . .

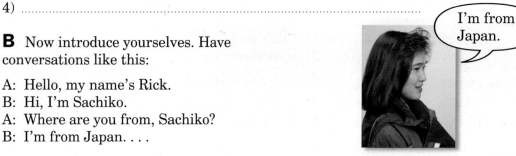

Where are you from?

I'm from Japan.

Language close-up

9 WHAT DID THEY SAY?

Watch the video and complete the conversation. Then practice it.

Rick is introducing himself to Marie Ouellette.

Rick: Hi. ..My.. name's Ricardo, but everybody calls me .....Rick..... .

Marie: Well, nice to .... you, Rick. .... Marie Ouellette.

Rick: It's nice to meet you, Marie. . . . Um, ... are you from, Marie?

Marie: I'm from ....

Rick: Oh, so .... Canadian?

Marie: That's right.

Rick: From what .... ?

Marie: Montreal. How .... you?

Rick: I'm originally .... Mexico City, but my family and I .... up here ....

Marie: Oh, are you a .... here?

Rick: Yes, I ....

10 QUESTIONS WITH BE

A Complete these questions with **is** or **are**.

1) ....Is.... Ms. Tanaka's first name Naomi? *(Mis written above)*
2) ....Are.. Rick and Sachiko students?
3) ..Are.. you Canadian, Marie? *(Canedian ✓ written above)*
4) .....IS.. Rick from Argentina?
5) ....are you a student here, Rick?

B *Pair work* Take turns asking and answering the questions.

A: Is Ms. Tanaka's first name Naomi?
B: No, it isn't. It's . . .

A: H

11 WH-QUESTIONS *Getting to know people*

A Complete these questions with **is**, **are**, or **do**.

1) What ....is..... Sachiko's last name?
2) Where ...are. Rick and Sachiko from?
3) What ......do... you teach, Professor Ouellette?
4) What ...IS.... Rick studying?
5) What ....do... you do, Rick?

B *Pair work* Take turns asking and answering the questions above.

C *Class activity* Now find out about your classmates. Write four more questions. Then go around the class and ask them.

1) *What's your name?*
2) What is Hiram's last name?
3) Where is Maly from?
4) What is Armando studging?
5) What do you do Ana?

2 I need a change!

Preview

1 CULTURE

In the United States and Canada, people usually work from
9 A.M. to 5 P.M. Most people get two weeks of vacation a year.
Sometimes people in offices and businesses work late without
extra pay. People also change jobs quite often. The average
person will change careers – not just jobs – two or three times
in a lifetime.

What hours do people work in your country?
How much vacation do they get?
Do they change jobs often?

THE WORK FORCE IN THE UNITED STATES AND CANADA

1959
70%
30%

1991
51%
49%

2 VOCABULARY Occupations

Pair work Who works in the places below? Put the words in the
chart. (One word can go in both columns.) Can you add three
more words?

Hotel	Office
bellhop	computer programmer
	secretary

bellhop

computer programmer

secretary

office manager

cashier

chef

6

adivina

3 GUESS THE STORY

Watch the first minute of the video with the sound off.
Answer these questions.

1) Where do you think the woman works?

2) What do you think her job is?

3) Do you think she likes her work?

Watch the video

4 GET THE PICTURE

Check (✓) the correct answer. Then compare with a partner.

1) What does Lynn do?
   ☐ She's a hotel worker.
   ☑ She's a manager.
   ☐ She's a salesperson.

2) Why doesn't Lynn like her job?
   ☐ The money isn't good.
   ☐ She doesn't like her boss.
   ☑ She works long hours.

3) What does Lynn want to do?
   ☑ Work in a hotel.
   ☐ Work for an airline.
   ☐ Work in a restaurant.

5 WATCH FOR DETAILS

Check (✓) **True** or **False**. Then correct the false statements.
Compare with a partner.

	True	False	
1) Lynn works at CompuTech.	☐	✓	*Lynn works at AdTech.*
2) The company is a computer software company.	☑	☐	the company is
3) Lynn is a manager in customer service.	☑	☐	Lynn is a manager b
4) Lynn works five days a week.	☐	☑	Lynn work sixs days a week
5) Lynn is studying business.	☑	☐	yes, she is tudying busines
6) Bob's friend works in California.	☐	☑	No, Bob's
7) Bob's friend manages a hotel.	☑	☐	Yes, Bob's friend manages a hotel

6 GIVING REASONS

Pair work Complete the chart. Look at the pictures and put two possible reasons in each column. (Some reasons can go in both columns.)

Reasons why Lynn doesn't like AdTech	Reasons why Lynn wants to work in a hotel
She works on weekends.	She's interested in hotel management.
she works sixs days a week	
she works long hours	

She's interested in hotel management.

She works on weekends.

She wants to do something new.

There's too much telephone and computer work.

She likes to travel.

The company is in a cold climate.

Follow-up

7 ROLE PLAY Jobs

A *Pair work* Imagine you work at AdTech. Talk about your job:

A: Where do you work at AdTech?
B: . . .
A: What do you do in your job?
B: . . .
A: How do you like your job?
B: . . .

B *Group work* Work in groups of four. Choose a job and ask and answer questions about your work. Who has the most interesting job?

Language close-up

8 WHAT DID THEY SAY?

Watch the video and complete the conversation. Then practice it.

Paula sees Lynn in the cafeteria at lunch.

Paula: Hi, Lynn! How are ...*you*... doing?

Lynn: Oh, ... , Paula. Pretty .... , thanks.
How are you?

Paula: Not .... Say, you .... Bob Wallace, don't you?

Lynn: Oh, no, I don't .... so. Hi, ... Lynn Parker.

Bob: Pleased to .... you.

Paula: So, ... everything?

Lynn: .... you really .... to know?

Paula: Of course .... do.

9 WH-QUESTIONS WITH DO; PREPOSITIONS

A Complete the questions in the present tense. Complete the answers
with the prepositions **at**, **in**, or **to**. Then practice the conversations.

1) Bob: Where ......*do you work*...... , Lynn?

   Lynn: I work ...*at*.. AdTech. It's a computer software company.

   Bob: What ...*do you do*... there?

   Lynn: I'm a manager ...*In*... customer service. *servis*

2) Bob: Where *do you go* ... to school, Lynn?

   Lynn: I go ...*to*... Franklin University. I'm studying
   hotel management.

3) Lynn: What ...*do you do*..., Bob? *lawyer*

   Bob: I'm a lawyer.

   Lynn: Oh. Where ....*do you work*...?

   Bob: I work ...*at*... the law firm of Christopher Brown. *for*

Where do
you work?

I work at
AdTech.

B *Pair work* Now have similar conversations using your
own information. (If you don't work, choose a job from page 6.)

10 ASKING ABOUT JOBS

Pair work Bob's friend manages a hotel in Hawaii. Think of three
more questions Lynn can ask him about his job. Then ask and
answer the questions.

1) *How do you like your job?* ....

3) ....

2) ....

4) ....

Documentary 1

Jobs

Preview

1 VOCABULARY Jobs

Pair work Match the jobs and the pictures.

architect   chef   ✓lawyer   photographer   travel agent
cashier   doctor   pianist   teller

1) *lawyer* ....

2) ....

3) ....

4) ....

5) ....

6) ....

7) ....

8) ....

9) ....

2 GUESS THE FACTS

Pair work In this documentary, you are going to meet people with
the jobs above. Which jobs do you think men do? Which do you
think women do?

 **Watch the video**

3 GET THE PICTURE

What do these people do? Write their occupations under the photos.
Then compare with a partner.

1) _reporter_

2) _architect_

3) _lawyer_

4) _pianist_

5) _computer phr_

6) _cashier_

7) _Bank teller_

8) _doctor_

4 WATCH FOR DETAILS

Complete the chart. Then compare with a partner.

Rick Armstrong

1) His job:
Photographer

2) One thing he likes:
meaning many people

3) One thing that's difficult:
It's take 50 o' 60 shots per object

Sylvia Davis

1) Her job:
travel agent

2) One thing she likes:
It's interesting

3) One thing that's difficult:
answer phone and answer fax

 **Follow-up**

5 ROLE PLAY Interview

Class activity Play the role of a reporter and
interview at least three classmates about their
jobs. Have conversations like the one to the right:

A: What do you do?
B: I'm an architect.
A: Do you like your job? . . .

3 At a garage sale

1 CULTURE

In the United States and Canada, people often sell old things, like furniture, jewelry, or clothing, at a "garage" or "yard" sale. They decide on prices, put the things on tables in their garage or yard, and then put a sign in front of their house. People come to look and maybe to buy. Sometimes the old things are antiques and worth a lot of money.

Do people have garage sales in your country?
What old things do you have at home?
What is one thing that you want to sell?

GARAGE SALE
Saturday, 9 A.M. to 5 P.M. Children's clothes, kitchen items, TV.
257 Maple Avenue

YARD SALE
Sunday, 12 P.M. to 6 P.M. Antiques, books, clock, stereo, bicycle. 89 Shadow Oak Drive

2 VOCABULARY Garage sale items

Pair work Put the words in the chart. Can you add six more words? Add things from your home.

Kitchen items	Jewelry	Other
		books

books

a bracelet

a watch   a necklace   a motorcycle   dishes   cups and saucers   a camera

3 GUESS THE STORY

A ***Watch the video with the sound off.*** Which things do you see at the garage sale? Circle them in Exercise 2.

B What do you think the man buys? What does the woman buy? Make a list.

....

....

....

....

....

....

....

new interchange video — *Watch the video*

4 WHAT'S YOUR OPINION?

In the end, do you think Fred and Susan buy any of these things at the garage sale? Check (✓) **Yes** or **No**. Then compare with a partner.

	Yes	No
1) the camera	☐	☐
2) the motorcycle	☐	☐
3) the necklace	☐	☐
4) the bracelet	☐	☐
5) the watch	☐	☐

5 MAKING INFERENCES

Check (✓) the best answers. Then complete item (4) with your opinion. Compare with a partner.

1) Susan thinks the camera is
   ☐ too old.
   ☐ too expensive.

2) Fred thinks the necklace is
   ☐ beautiful.
   ☐ just all right.

3) Fred thinks the watch is
   ☐ beautiful.
   ☐ too expensive.

4) The man tells his wife that ....

....

....

6 GARAGE SALE

A *Pair work* Imagine you are at a garage sale. Number the sentences below (1 to 6) to make conversations. Then practice the conversations.

1) .... And how much are these earrings?
....*1*.... Hello. Can I help you?
.... It's twelve dollars.
.... Yes, how much is this bracelet?
.... They're twenty dollars.
.... Thanks. I'll think about it.

2) .... Can I help you?
.... Oh, that's pretty expensive.
.... OK. I'll take it.
.... Yes, how much is this watch?
.... Well, how about thirty dollars?
.... It's forty dollars.

B *Class activity* Plan a class garage sale. Form two groups. Make a list of things your group will sell, and give each item a price.

Items for sale	Price
....	....
....	....
....	....
....	....
....	....

Now have the garage sale:

Group A: You are the sellers. Try to sell everything on your list to Group B. Then change roles and decide what to buy from Group B.

Group B: You are the buyers. Ask questions and decide what to buy. Then change roles and try to sell everything on your list to Group A.

Language close-up

7 WHAT DID THEY SAY?

Watch the video and complete the conversation. Then practice it.

Fred and Susan are looking at things at the garage sale.

Fred: Hey, Susan, how do you .....*like*...... this?
Susan: Oh, ..., Fred.
Fred: Oh, come on. It's only a .... !
Susan: .... you really .... it, Fred?
Fred: No, I guess .... right.
Vendor: Can I .... you?
Fred: No, thanks .... We're just ....
Susan: Oh, Fred, ... over here. Just look at this lovely,
          old .... !
Fred: Yeah, it's ....
Susan: It's .... just OK, Fred. It's very .... !

8 EXPRESSING OPINIONS

Fred says these sentences. What do they mean in the video?
Check (✓) the correct answer. Then compare with a partner.

1) How do you like this?
   ☐ Can you believe this?
   ☐ What do you think of this?

2) Oh, come on.
   ☐ Please let me [buy it].
   ☐ Are you kidding?

3) Yeah, it's OK.
   ☐ I like it a little.
   ☐ The price is reasonable.

4) Oh, that's not bad.
   ☐ It's nice.
   ☐ The price is reasonable.

5) Susan, are you kidding?
   ☐ I don't believe it!
   ☐ Let's go!

9 HOW MUCH AND HOW OLD

A Complete the conversations with **how much is (are)** or **how old is (are)**.

1) A: *How much is* .... this necklace?
   B: It's only $10.
   A: .... it?
   B: It's twenty years old.

2) A: .... these books?
   B: They're $2 each.
   A: And .... they?
   B: They're about ten years old.

3) A: .... these shoes?
   B: About two years old, I think.
   A: .... they?
   B: They're $20.

B *Pair work* Practice the conversations. Use items of your own.

4 What kind of movies do you like?

Preview

1 CULTURE

Today, there is a video store in almost every neighborhood in the United States and Canada. Nowadays, many people don't go to the movies very often. Instead they prefer to rent a video and watch it at home. Video stores are large, with every type of video for rent. You can also rent videos in some supermarkets.

Do people go to the movies a lot in your country?
Do they rent videos?
What is your favorite movie or video?

Number of stores renting videos (U.S. and Canada)

VIDEO **1993** 82,500

VIDEO **1983** 13,000

Average Price of

A MOVIE TICKET $5.00

A VIDEO RENTAL $2.50

2 VOCABULARY *Kinds of movies*

What kind of movies or videos do you like? Check (✔) your opinions. Then compare answers in groups.

WHAT'S YOUR OPINION?

	I like them.	They're OK.	I don't like them very much.	I can't stand them.
adventure movies	☐	☐	☐	☐
classic films	☐	☐	☐	☐
comedies	☐	☐	☐	☐
horror films	☐	☐	☐	☐
science-fiction movies	☐	☐	☐	☐
suspense movies	☐	☐	☐	☐

Indiana Jones and the Last Crusade

Dracula

Eyes of Laura Mars

Star Trek III

Heaven Help Us

16

3 GUESS THE STORY

Watch the first two minutes of the video with the sound off.
Answer these questions.

1) Are the young men friends?   2) What are they doing?   3) What's the problem?

 Watch the video

4 GET THE PICTURE

Check (✓) **True** or **False**. Then compare with a partner.

	True	False
1) Pat, Alfredo, and Bill all like movies.	☐	☐
2) Nobody likes science fiction.	☐	☐
3) They can't agree on a movie.	☐	☐
4) They decide to go to a country and western concert.	☐	☐

Pat   Alfredo   Bill

5 MAKING INFERENCES

What do Pat, Bill, and Alfredo like? Write **Y** (yes), or **N** (no). Then compare in groups. (Sometimes they don't say exactly, but try to give your opinion.)

	Pat	Bill	Alfredo
Movies			
science fiction	Y	N	■
suspense thrillers	■	Y	■
classic films	■	■	....
horror films	■	■	....
westerns	■	....	■
Music			
country and western	■	....	■
jazz	■	....	

6 WHAT'S THE PROBLEM?

Pair work Answer these questions.

1) Which person is difficult to please?
2) Do you know anyone like this?

Alfredo   Bill   Pat

 *Follow-up*

7 FINISH THE STORY

Group work What do you think happens in the end?
Finish the story.

8 MAKING PLANS

Group work Plan what to do this evening. Choose
one of these activities. Give your opinions like this:

There's a great .... tonight at ....
Do you really like .... ?
That sounds good. How about you, ... ?
I don't really like ....
Well, what kind of .... do you like?

THE Country Gold Club *presents*

country and western music

THE BLUE RIDGE TRIO

Showtimes:
8:30 p.m. and 11 p.m.
236 North Hill Street
555-8123

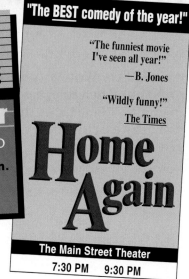

"The BEST comedy of the year!"

"The funniest movie
I've seen all year!"
—B. Jones

"Wildly funny!"
The Times

Home Again

The Main Street Theater
7:30 PM   9:30 PM

The Star Movie Theater

SCIENCE FICTION
Alien Abduction
White Mountains, Arizona

VISITORS FROM SPACE

8:00 p.m. 10:00 p.m.

The Back Door

NEW ORLEANS JAZZ BAND

Shows: 9 p.m. and 11 p.m.
Credit Cards Reservations
(555-6073)

Language close-up

9 WHAT DID THEY SAY?

Watch the video and complete the conversation. Then practice it.

Bill, Alfredo, and Pat are trying to decide how to spend the evening.

Bill: So, . . . what ..*do*.. we ..*do*.. now?

Alfredo: What .... is it?

Bill: .... o'clock.

Pat: Look, ... all like .... Why don't we
             .... a video and .... it at my .... ?

Bill: That's .... a bad .... , Pat.

Alfredo: It's .... with ....

Pat: Well, then, ... on! . . . Now here .... some
             great ....-fiction movies! .... do
             you .... , Bill?

Bill: Uh, I can't .... sci-fi. How .... a good
             .... thriller?

Pat: Uh . . . Alfredo, ... about you? .... do you
             .... of science .... ?

Alfredo: Oh, it's ....

Alfredo   Bill   Pat

10 OBJECT PRONOUNS

A Fill in the blanks with **him**, **her**, **it**, or **them**.

1) A: Do you like horror films?
   B: No, I can't stand ....*them*.... .

2) A: Who's your favorite actress?
   B: Michelle Pfeiffer. I like .... a lot.

3) A: Do you like rap music?
   B: Yes, I like .... a lot.

4) A: What do you think of Robert DeNiro?
   B: I don't like .... at all.

5) A: Do you like westerns?
   B: No, I don't like .... very much.

6) A: What do you think of science fiction?
   B: I like .... a lot.

B *Pair work* Take turns asking and answering the questions above.
Give your own opinions.

11 EXPRESSING LIKES AND DISLIKES

Pair work Take turns giving opinions about movies, actors, and actresses.
Your partner responds with surprise, as in the conversations below.

1) A: I can't stand science fiction!
   B: Really?

2) A: I love Julia Roberts.
   B: Are you kidding?

3) A: I hate old movies.
   B: Is that right?

4) A: I think Tom Cruise is fantastic.
   B: Do you really like Tom Cruise?

What's your favorite kind of music?

Preview

1 VOCABULARY Kinds of music

Class activity In this documentary, some people are going to talk about music. How many kinds of music can you think of? List them.

Watch the video

2 GET THE PICTURE

How many different kinds of music do people talk about? Check (✓) them. Then compare with a partner.

☐ classical   ☐ jazz   ☐ rap
☑ country and western   ☐ new wave   ☐ rhythm and blues (R & B)
☐ folk   ☐ pop   ☐ rock

3 WATCH FOR DETAILS

A What kind(s) of music do these people like? Check (✓) all correct answers. Then compare with a partner.

	1	2	3	4	5	6
country and western	✓	☐	☐	☐	☐	☐
jazz	☐	☐	☐	☐	☐	☐
rock	☐	☐	☐	☐	☐	☐
classical	☐	☐	☐	☐	☐	☐
new wave	☐	☐	☐	☐	☐	☐

B Which people play a musical instrument? Write **S** for saxophone, **G** for guitar, or **P** for piano. Then compare with a partner. (One person doesn't play an instrument.)

saxophone   guitar   piano

1) ....   2) ....   3) ....   4) ....   5) ....

4 THE REPORTER'S QUESTIONS

What interview questions does the reporter ask? Check (✓) them.
Then compare with a partner.

✓ How often do you get to go to nightclubs?	☐ Do you play a musical instrument (yourself)?
☐ What's your favorite kind of music?	☐ What do you think of country and western music?
☐ Do you like rap?	
☐ How often do you listen to live music?	☐ Where's a good place to go dancing?
☐ What's your least favorite kind of music?	☐ How often do you go dancing?
☐ Do you like classical music?	☐ What's your favorite nightclub?

 *Follow-up*

5 CLASS INTERVIEW

A *Class activity* Use the questions in Exercise 4 to interview at least three classmates. Have conversations like this:

A: How often do you go to nightclubs?
B: About twice a week.
A: What's your favorite kind of music?
B: Country.

B Now tell about the people you interviewed. What kinds of music are the most popular? Least popular?

5 A family picnic

1 CULTURE

In the United States and Canada, 97 percent of all people say that family is the most important part of life. But people in the U.S. and Canada move often, and children often leave home at age 18. Many families only see each other on important holidays or at family parties.

- Six percent of all families move every year.
- On an average day, 116,438 people move.
- People often live far away from their parents and grandparents.
- Only 36 percent of families see their relatives once a week.

In the U.S. and Canada, 70 percent of all husbands and wives say they're happy with each other.

In your country, when do children leave home?
Do children live near their parents and grandparents?
When do families see each other?

2 VOCABULARY *Family*

Pair work How are these people related to Jane? Fill in the blanks in her family tree.

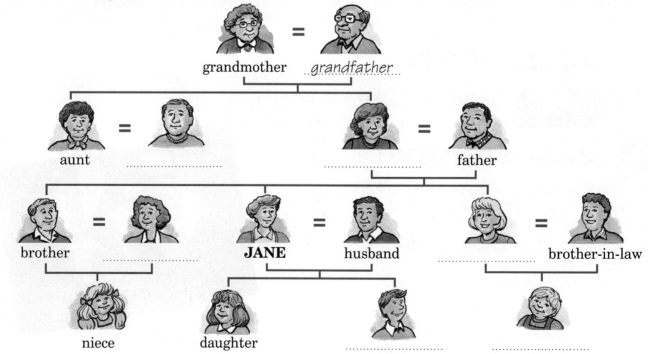

grandmother   *grandfather*

aunt .... father

brother ....   **JANE** husband   .... brother-in-law

niece   daughter   ....

3 GUESS THE STORY

Watch the first minute of the video with the sound off.
The young man takes his friend Betsy to a family picnic.
Who do you think she meets? Look at the photo and list
five more people.

1) *his mother* ....

2) ....

3) ....

4) ....

5) ....

6) ....

 Watch the video

4 GET THE PICTURE

Who's at the picnic? Check (✓) **Yes** or **No**. Then compare with
a partner.

	Yes	No
1) Rick's parents	✓	☐
2) his brother	☐	☐
3) his brother's wife	☐	☐
4) his niece	☐	☐
5) his grandparents	☐	☐
6) his younger sister	☐	☐
7) his older sister	☐	☐
8) his aunt	☐	☐

5 WATCH FOR DETAILS

Check (✓) the correct answer. Then compare with a partner.

1) Rick's grandmother lives in
   ✓ Mexico.
   ☐ New Mexico.

2) Rick has
   ☐ one brother and a sister.
   ☐ one brother and two sisters.

3) Rick's brother Freddy
   ☐ is a doctor.
   ☐ owns a business.

4) Freddy's wife Linda manages
   ☐ a boutique.
   ☐ a bookstore.

5) Angela is
   ☐ three years old.
   ☐ four years old.

6) Rick knows Betsy from
   ☐ work.
   ☐ night school.

6 WHAT'S YOUR OPINION?

Pair work Read the culture box on page 22 again. Is Rick's family like most families in the United States and Canada? How is it the same and how is it different?

 *Follow-up*

7 YOUR FAMILY

A *Pair work* Is your family like Rick's? Tell about your family and find out about your partner's. Ask questions like these:

Are you living with your parents right now?
Are you married?
Do you have any children?
How old are they?
Do you have any brothers and sisters?
Are they still going to school or are they working?

B Draw a simple picture (or show your partner a photo) of your family. Your partner will ask questions about each person.

Is this your sister?
What does she do?
Is she studying English?

8 AN INTERESTING PERSON

A *Pair work* Find out about your partner's most interesting relative or friend. Ask questions like these:

Who's your most interesting relative or friend?
What's his/her name?
What does he/she do?
Where is he/she living at the moment?
How old is he/she?
Is he/she married?

B Now tell another classmate about the person like this:

Yong Su has an interesting cousin.
Her name is Son Hee.
She owns a travel agency.
She's from Seoul.
She's working in New York at the moment.
She's 30 years old.

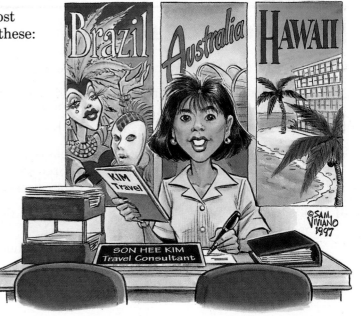

Language close-up

9 WHAT DID THEY SAY?

Watch the video and complete the conversation. Then practice it.

Betsy and Rick are arriving at the picnic.

Betsy: So, how many ....*people*........ are there in your
........*family*........ , Rick?

Rick: A .... , if you count all my ....

Betsy: Do they all .... here in the .... now?

Rick: Oh, ... I have relatives in .... My
grandmother and .... are
there, and my older .... , too.

Betsy: How many .... do you have?

Rick: .... , plus an older .... There's my
.... Freddy over there with his
.... Linda.

Betsy: Oh, really. What do they .... ?

Rick: Freddy .... an import-export business, and
Linda manages .... boutique.

Betsy: Is that their .... ?

Rick: Yeah. Her ....'s Angela.

10 PRESENT CONTINUOUS VS. SIMPLE PRESENT
Asking about relatives

A Complete the conversation using the present continuous or simple present.
Then practice with a partner.

A: Do all of your relatives live in the United States?

B: No, I ....*have*........... (have) relatives in Mexico. My grandparents and
older sister .... (live) there.

A: What does your sister do? Does she have a job?

B: No, she .... (work) right now. She .... (go) to school.

A: Really? What is she studying?

B: She .... (study) English literature. She .... (love) it.

A: What about your grandparents? Are they still working or are they retired?

B: They .... (work)! And they're both 80 years old!

B *Class activity* Now write similar questions of your own. Then go
around the class and interview your classmates about their families.

1) *Do your parents live in ....?* ....

2) ....

3) ....

4) ....

6 I like to stay in shape.

1 CULTURE

In the United States and Canada, most people nowadays think regular exercise is important. They exercise at home, or at a gym or health club. They play sports after school, after work, and on weekends. They also bicycle, walk, swim, or jog. People exercise for different reasons: to lose weight, to stay in shape, or just to relax.

Do you exercise or play sports?
What sports are popular in your country?

In the U.S. and Canada:

Thirty-five percent of people exercise every day.

Eighteen percent of people play team sports regularly.

2 VOCABULARY *Sports and exercise*

A *Pair work* Here are some things people do to stay in shape. Write the words under the pictures.

aerobics   basketball   ✓jogging   soccer   swimming   volleyball

1) jogging......................

2) ....

3) ....

4) ....

5) ....

6) ....

B Put the words in the chart. Can you add two more words?

Individual activities		Team sports	
jogging...............	....	....	....
....	....	....	....

I like to stay in shape.

3 GUESS THE STORY

Watch the first minute of the video with the sound off.
Who do you think likes to exercise more, the woman or the man?

Watch the video

4 GET THE PICTURE

Check (✓) **True** or **False**. Correct the false statements. Then compare
with a partner.

	True	False	
1) Mark is a friend of Anne's.	☐	☐	....
2) Mark really likes to exercise.	☐	☐	....
3) Anne is in better shape than Mark.	☐	☐	....

5 WATCH FOR DETAILS

A How does Mark stay in shape? Check (✓)
the things he *says* he does.

B Which things do you think he *really* does?
Circle them. Then compare with a partner.

☐ He jogs to stay in shape.

☐ He gets up early.

☐ He bicycles.

☐ He does aerobics.

☐ He swims.

☐ He goes to the health club.

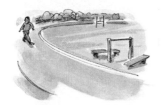

☐ He takes long walks.

☐ He plays tennis.

☐ He plays team sports.

27

6 WHAT'S YOUR OPINION?

Pair work What kind of person is Anne? What kind of person is Mark? Choose at least one word for each person.

Anne	Mark
....	....
....	....
....	....

friendly   intelligent

polite   pushy

 *Follow-up*

7 INTERVIEW

A ***Pair work*** Add three questions to the list about sports and exercise.

1) What kinds of sports do you play?
2) What kinds of exercise do you do?
3) Are you in good shape?

4) ....
5) ....
6) ....

B Take turns asking and answering your questions. Your partner will answer playing the role of Anne or Mark.

8 HOW ABOUT YOU?

A Complete the chart. Then compare with a partner.

Things you sometimes do

I sometimes .... after school. ....

....

....

Things you never do

I never go .... in the morning. ....

....

....

Things you don't usually do

I don't usually .... on the weekend. ....

....

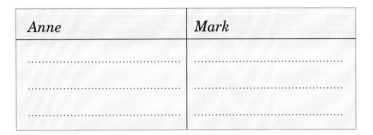

B ***Class activity*** Who in the class likes to exercise? Who doesn't? Make a class chart.

Language close-up

9 WHAT DID THEY SAY?

Watch the video and complete the conversation.
Then practice it.

Anne is jogging in the park when Mark introduces himself.

Mark: Hi there. Nice ...day..., isn't it?
Anne: Oh, yes, very ....
Mark: Do you .... come out here this .... ?
Anne: Usually. I like to stay in ....
Mark: I do, too. I .... get up around .... o'clock.
Anne: Oh, ... ?
Mark: Yeah. I .... start with some .... There's a .... aerobics program on TV at ....
Anne: No .... ! I guess you really do .... to stay in shape.
Mark: Hey, ... days a .... I go straight to my health club after ....

10 ADVERBS OF FREQUENCY

A Put the adverbs in the correct place. Write the sentences.

1) I get up before 5 A.M. (never)
   I never get up before 5 A.M.

2) I don't have a big breakfast. (usually)
   ....

3) I play tennis after work. (sometimes)
   ....

4) I take a long walk on the weekend. (often)
   ....

5) I watch TV. (never)
   ....

6) I jog in the morning. (always)
   ....

B Imagine you are Mark. Change the frequency adverbs in the sentences where necessary. Compare with a partner.

C How often do you do these things? Use the phrases below or ones of your own. Then compare with a partner.

| every evening | very often | about three times a month |
| twice a week | once a year | every day |

1) go to sleep by 10 P.M.
   ....

2) work late
   ....

3) ride a bicycle
   ....

4) do aerobics
   ....

7 How was your trip to San Francisco?

1 CULTURE

More than two million people visit San Francisco every year. San Francisco is famous for its shops, its restaurants, its beautiful old buildings, and its cable cars. San Francisco's Chinatown is an important part of the city. There are more than 80,000 people living in Chinatown. San Francisco is also famous for fog and hills. In fact, the city is built on 43 hills!

Do you know anything else about San Francisco?
Would you like to visit San Francisco?
What cities in North America would you like to visit?

There are more than 3,300 restaurants in San Francisco!

2 VOCABULARY Places in San Francisco

Pair work How much do you know about San Francisco?
Write the names under the pictures.

Fisherman's Wharf   Chinatown   The Japanese Tea Garden
The Golden Gate Bridge   ✓A cable car   Ghirardelli Square

1) *A cable car*

2) ....

3) ....

4) ....

5) ....

6) ....

3 GUESS THE STORY

Watch the video with the sound off. Which of the things
in Exercise 2 do you think the woman and her husband see?
Write a check (✓) next to them.

 *Watch the video*

4 GET THE PICTURE

A Look at your answers to Exercise 3.
Did you guess correctly?

B Correct the mistakes in Phyllis's
travel diary. Then compare with
a partner.

DAY	NOTES
FRIDAY ~~sight-seeing~~ work	*Fisherman's Wharf was my favorite place!*
SATURDAY work	
SUNDAY morning: sight-seeing	

5 WATCH FOR DETAILS

What did Phyllis and her husband do in these places?
Check (✓) the correct answers. Then compare with
a partner.

1) Ghirardelli Square
   - ☐ They bought some clothes.
   - ☐ They bought some postcards.

2) Fisherman's Wharf
   - ☐ They bought some souvenirs.
   - ☐ They had lunch.

3) Golden Gate Park
   - ☐ They visited a tea garden.
   - ☐ They had lunch.

4) Chinatown
   - ☐ They walked for hours.
   - ☐ They visited a temple.

6 *A DAY IN SAN FRANCISCO*

A *Group work* Which things to see in San Francisco seem most interesting to you? Number them from 1 to 6 (1 = the most interesting).

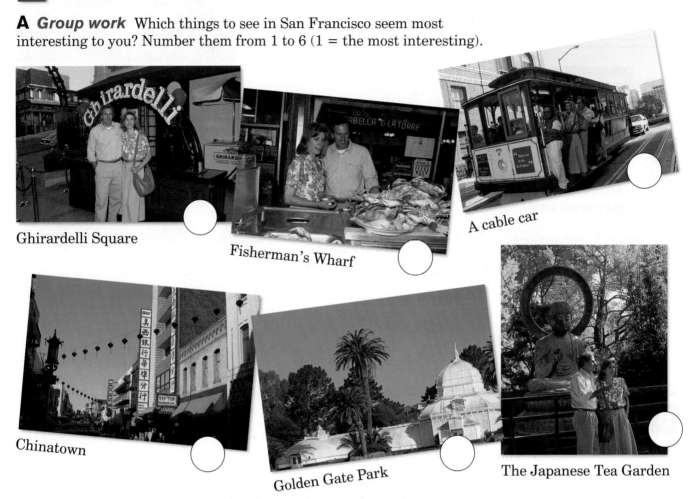

Ghirardelli Square

Fisherman's Wharf

A cable car

Chinatown

Golden Gate Park

The Japanese Tea Garden

B Plan an afternoon in San Francisco. Choose three places to visit or things to do.

7 *WHAT'S YOUR OPINION?*

A *Pair work* What do you like to do when you visit a new city? Number them from 1 to 5. Can you add three things to the list?

.... go sight-seeing   1) ....
.... eat at local restaurants 2) ....
.... buy souvenirs   3) ....
.... take photographs
.... go shopping

B Now compare answers with another pair. Have conversations like this:

A: Do you like to go shopping?
B: No, I don't. I hate to go shopping.

Language close-up

8 WHAT DID THEY SAY?

Watch the video and complete the conversation. Then practice it.

Phyllis and Yoko are on their way to work.

Yoko: Hi, Phyllis.

Phyllis: Hi, Yoko. ...*How*... have you been?

Yoko: Oh, ... How .... you?

Phyllis: Great! Just .... !

Yoko: So, ... was your .... to San Francisco?

Phyllis: Fantastic! We really .... it.

Yoko: Well, that .... surprise me. I love to ....
San Francisco. Uh, so, your .... went with you?

Phyllis: Yes. I .... on Friday, and Bill had business to do in
the .... , too.

Yoko: Oh, that's .... So, what did you do over the .... ?

Phyllis: We went .... together all day Saturday and
Sunday ....

Yoko: Oh, really? .... me about it.

9 PAST TENSE Describing a trip

A Fill in the blanks with the correct past tense forms of the verbs in
parentheses. Then practice the conversations.

1) Yoko: Tell me about your trip to San Francisco.

 Phyllis: Well, we ....*did*.... (do) a lot of interesting things. Naturally,
 we .... (start) Saturday morning with a ride on a cable car.

 Yoko: Naturally! And then?

 Phyllis: Then we .... (go) straight to Ghirardelli Square to do some shopping.

 Yoko: Isn't it wonderful? I .... (go) there the last time I .... (be)
 in San Francisco.

2) Yoko: .... you .... (visit) Alcatraz Island?

 Phyllis: No, we .... (have / not) time.

 Yoko: Oh, what .... you .... (do) then?

 Phyllis: We .... (take) a cab to Golden Gate Park.

 Yoko: Great! .... you .... (see) the Japanese Tea Garden?

 Phyllis: Oh, yes, it .... (be) really beautiful. But, to tell the truth,
 the thing we .... (like) best .... (be) Chinatown.

B *Pair work* Have similar conversations about a real or imaginary trip of
your own. Start like this:

A: I went to . . .
B: Really! Tell me about your trip. . . .

8 Are you sure it's all right?

Preview

1 CULTURE

In the United States and Canada, people often invite friends to their homes for a meal or a party. Here are some simple rules to follow:
- When someone invites you to dinner, do not bring anyone with you. Your host will tell you if you can bring a guest, such as your husband or wife.
- When someone invites you to a party, you can often bring a friend. But always call your host first to ask if it's OK.

PARTY

Date: June 15

Time: 8:00 P.M.

Place: 26 Elm St.
Apt. 2C

Bring a Friend!

In your country, do people often invite friends to their home for dinner?
Is it OK to bring a friend to dinner? To a party?

2 VOCABULARY Places

Pair work Write the numbers of the places on the map. (There is one extra place.)

1) There's a **coffee shop** on the corner of Hennepin and Lagoon.
2) There's a **movie theater** on Hennepin, just before the coffee shop.
3) There's a **drugstore** across the street from the movie theater.
4) There's a **parking lot** on Lagoon, next door to the coffee shop.
5) Your friend's **apartment building** is across the street from the parking lot.

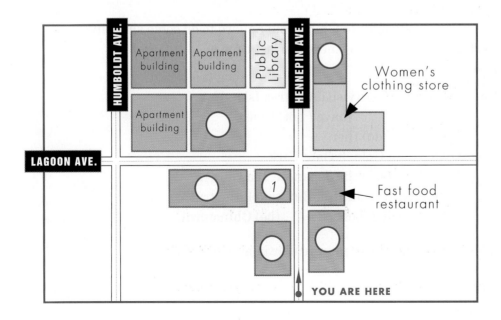

3 GUESS THE STORY

Watch the first minute of the video with the sound off.
These people are going to a party. What do you think
happens? Check (✓) your answer.

☐ They get lost.
☐ They go on the wrong day.
☐ They arrive too late.

 **Watch the video**

4 GET THE PICTURE

A Check (✓) the correct answers. Then compare with a partner.

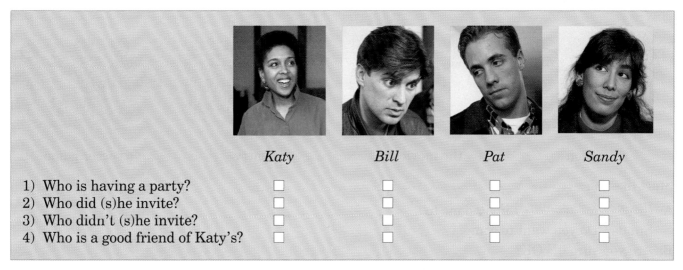

	Katy	Bill	Pat	Sandy
1) Who is having a party?	☐	☐	☐	☐
2) Who did (s)he invite?	☐	☐	☐	☐
3) Who didn't (s)he invite?	☐	☐	☐	☐
4) Who is a good friend of Katy's?	☐	☐	☐	☐

B What mistake do Bill, Pat, and Sandy make? Did you guess
correctly in Exercise 3?

5 WATCH FOR DETAILS

Correct the mistakes below. Then compare with a partner.

          Sandy   *Katy's*
Pat, Bill, and ~~Katy~~ are going to a party at ~~Sandy's~~ apartment. The

party is very formal. Pat doesn't remember the exact address, but he

remembers there's a coffee shop just before you turn. When they arrive,

they don't hear any music. It's a little late. The party was last week.

6 WHAT'S YOUR OPINION?

Pair work Answer these questions.

1) Is it OK for Bill to take
   Sandy and Pat to the party?
   ☐ Yes, it's fine.
   ☐ No. It's not a good idea.
   ☐ I'm not sure.

2) How do you think Katy feels
   when her friends arrive?
   ☐ amused
   ☐ angry
   ☐ surprised
   ☐ other ....

3) How do you think Pat and
   Sandy feel?
   ☐ embarrassed
   ☐ angry
   ☐ amused
   ☐ other ....

Follow-up

7 INVITING

Group work Invite two or three classmates to one of these activities.

the beach

the movies

a party

a soccer game

Start like this:

A: *(Name of classmate)* invited me to .... on
   Sunday. Do you want to come?
B: Are you sure it's OK?
A: Of course it is! .... is a good friend of mine.
C: Well, I don't know. Why don't you ask .... first? . . .

8 ROLE PLAY *A surprise guest*

A *Group work* Work in groups of four. Play the roles
of Katy, Sandy, Bill, and Pat. Knock on Katy's door and
act out the situation three times.

1) The first time, act out the conversation just like
   in the video.
2) The second time, imagine Katy is busy and
   doesn't want company.
3) The third time, make up your own ending.

B Now act out your third conversation for the
class. Who has the best ending?

Language close-up

9 WHAT DID THEY SAY?

Watch the video and complete the conversation. Then practice it.

Pat, Bill, and Sandy are going to Katy's party. Pat is asking for directions.

Pat: OK. Well, we're at the ......*corner*...... of 31st Street. ...*Now*... what?

Bill: Well, I don't remember her .... ,
        but I know she lives .... here.

Pat: Fine. But do I go .... , right, or straight
        .... ?

Bill: .... ahead. . . . I remember there's
        a .... theater just before you ....

Pat: Hey, is .... it?

Bill: No, I .... think so. . . . There was a coffee
        shop .... door and a drugstore ....
        the street.

Sandy: Oh, I don't see a .... Well, there's a Vietnamese
        .... with a bookstore .... to it.

Pat: Yeah, and no .... shop either. Hey, look! There's another
        movie theater up ahead on the ....

Bill: Great! .... a drugstore.

10 LOCATIONS

A Look at the map of Katy's neighborhood. Answer the questions using these prepositions.

across from   near   next to
on the corner of   on

1) Where's the Suburban World Theater?
   It's across from the Vietnamese restaurant.

2) Where's Border's Book Shop?
   ....

3) Where's Figlio's Restaurant?
   ....

4) Where's the Rainbow Cafe?
   ....

5) Where's the clothing store?
   ....

B *Pair work* Now ask similar questions about places near your school.

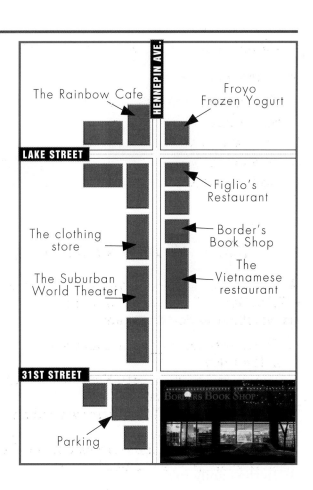

In a suburban home

Preview

1 VOCABULARY Guess the rooms of a house

Pair work Match the words and the photos.

child's bedroom   family room   ✓kitchen
dining room   guest room   living room

1) *kitchen*

2) ....

3) ....

4) ....

5) ....

6) ....

Watch the video

2 GET THE PICTURE

A Look at your answers to Exercise 1. Were they correct?

B What is one thing the Bartlett family does in each room? Complete
the sentences. Then compare with a partner.

1) In the kitchen, they ....
2) In the dining room, they ....
3) In the family room, they ....

3 WATCH FOR DETAILS

Write down all of the things you see in each room. Then combine
answers in groups. Which group has the most things on its list?

1) the kitchen	2) the dining room	3) the living room	4) Matthew's room
a sink			
......	......	......	......
......	......	......	......
......	......	......	......
5) the guest room	6) Daniel's room	7) the large bedroom	8) the family room
......	......	......	......
......	......	......	......
......	......	......	......
......	......	......	......

4 WHAT'S YOUR OPINION?

Pair work Answer these questions.

1) Do you like the Bartletts' home? Name one thing that you
   like. Is there anything you don't like?
2) Is the Bartlett home like homes in your country? How is
   it different?

 **Follow-up**

5 YOUR HOME

Group work Find out about the homes or apartments
your classmates live in. Ask questions like these:

1) Do you live in a city?
2) How big is your home?
3) What are some interesting things in your home?
4) What's your favorite room?

Do you live in a city?

No, I live on a farm.

9 Help is coming.

Preview

1 CULTURE

To protect their homes against crime, people in the United States and Canada:
- Put special locks on their doors.
- Leave lights on when they go out.
- Have a "peephole" (or hole in the door) to see who's outside.
- Buy an alarm that makes noise if someone opens the door or window.
- Buy a dog.

What other ways can you protect your home?
How do people protect their homes in your country?

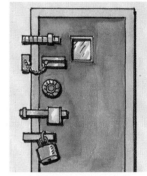

On an average day in the U.S., people spend over $2 million on home security.

2 VOCABULARY *Physical appearance*

A *Pair work* Write the words and phrases in the chart. (One of the words can go in two places.) Can you add two more words or phrases?

✓early forties   late forties   short   blond   elderly
long   curly   tall   bald

Age	Height	Hair
early forties		

B List two ways to describe the man and two to describe the woman.

The man	The woman
late forties	

40

3 GUESS THE STORY

Watch the first minute of the video with the sound off.
Who do you think comes to the couple's house?

 *Watch the video*

4 GET THE PICTURE

What really happens? Check (✓) your answer. Then compare
with a partner.

☐ Strange men come to the door.
☐ Dave's cousin comes to visit.
☐ The prisoners come to the house.
☐ Some friends come to visit.

5 WATCH FOR DETAILS

Put the pictures in order (1 to 6). Then write the correct sentence
under each picture. Compare with a partner.

✓Sarah and Dave are reading.   Sarah is looking at the minivan.
  Dave is calling the police.   The men are getting out of the minivan.
  The men are standing in the driveway.   The men are introducing themselves to Sarah and Dave.

....
....

....
....

....
....

Sarah and Dave are
reading.

....

....

6 *DESCRIBING SOMEONE*

A Circle the correct answers. Then compare with a partner.

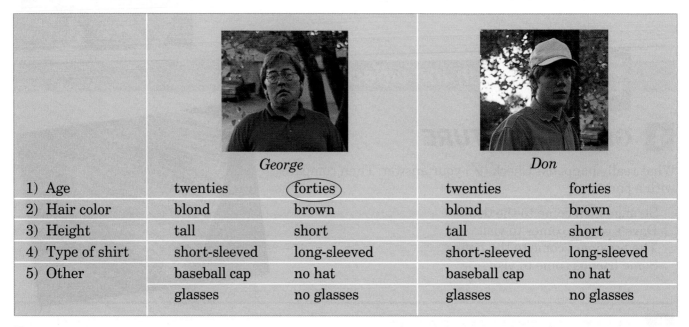

	George		Don	
1) Age	twenties	(forties)	twenties	forties
2) Hair color	blond	brown	blond	brown
3) Height	tall	short	tall	short
4) Type of shirt	short-sleeved	long-sleeved	short-sleeved	long-sleeved
5) Other	baseball cap	no hat	baseball cap	no hat
	glasses	no glasses	glasses	no glasses

B What else can you add about George and Don? Compare your descriptions. Who has the best description?

 *Follow-up*

7 **THE RIGHT DECISION?**

Pair work Sarah and Dave call the police. What is the best thing to do in a situation like this?

☐ Call the police.
☐ Open the door and ask, "Who's there?"
☐ Call a friend or relative.
☐ other ....

8 **WHAT HAPPENS NEXT?**

A *Group work* What do you think happens when the police arrive? Write out the conversation between Sarah, Dave, and the police. Start like this:

Officer: Is there a problem here?
Dave: Well, uh, . . .

B *Class activity* Act out your conversation for the class.

Language close-up

9 WHAT DID THEY SAY?

Watch the video and complete the conversation. Then practice it.

Sarah and Dave are relaxing at home.

Sarah: Would you .....*like*..... another cup of ......*coffee*...... ?
Dave: ...., thanks. I don't .... so.
Sarah: Is there anything .... in the .... ?
Dave: Well, there's something about a .... escape.
Sarah: Oh, really?
Dave: Yeah. A couple of .... escaped from the state
       prison in a .... van.
Sarah: Hmm . . . . we know .... with a minivan?
Dave: A minivan? What .... is it?
Sarah: I .... know. Light .... , maybe,
       or .... I can't .... very well.
Dave: Where is this .... ?
Sarah: It's parked right in .... of the ....
       And there are .... guys in it.

10 MODIFIERS WITH PARTICIPLES AND PREPOSITIONS

A Look at the picture. Match the information in columns A, B, and C.

A	B	C
Sarah	is the young one	holding his hat
Dave	is the heavy one	with glasses
George	is the blonde woman	wearing a green shirt
Don	is the bald man	wearing a blue T-shirt

B *Pair work* What else do you remember about the people in the video? Write at least three more sentences of your own.

1) .... 3) ....

2) ....

11 DESCRIBING SOMEONE

A *Pair work* Take turns asking and answering questions about a classmate. Try to guess who the person is.

A: Is it a tall person with short hair?
B: No, the person is short . . .

B Write five sentences describing your classmates. Two of your sentences should be false. Then read your sentences. Your partner says **True** or **False** and corrects the false sentences.

A: Steve's the tall guy wearing a blue shirt.
B: False. He's wearing a white shirt.

10 Sorry I'm late.

1 CULTURE

In the United States and Canada, people usually like others to be on time, but for some occasions it's OK to be a little late.

For class or a business appointment,	**plan to arrive**	on time or a little early.
When you meet a friend,		on time or 5 to 10 minutes late.
When someone invites you to dinner,		about 10 to 15 minutes late.
For an informal party,		a little late (15 to 30 minutes).

Are people usually on time for appointments in your country?
Is it OK to arrive late when you meet a friend for dinner? When you
  go to an informal party?

2 VOCABULARY *Past tense of verbs*

Pair work Do you know the past tense of these verbs? Complete the chart.

Present	Past	Present	Past
call	*called*	lock	
do		open	
find		pay	
get		remember	
go		send	
leave		start	

3 GUESS THE STORY

Watch the first minute of the video with the sound off.
What do you think happened? Check (✓) all correct answers.

☐ The man arrived very late for dinner.
☐ The woman was angry.
☐ The man didn't have his wallet.
☐ The woman paid for dinner.

44

 *Watch the video*

4 GET THE PICTURE

What really happened? Check (✓) the correct answers. Then compare with a partner.

1) What was the problem with Tom's car?
   - ☐ It didn't start.
   - ☐ He locked his keys in it.
   - ☐ He forgot to buy gasoline.

2) What was the problem with Tom's wallet?
   - ☐ He left it in the car.
   - ☐ He lost it.
   - ☐ He had no money in it.

3) Who paid for dinner?
   - ☐ Tom paid.
   - ☐ Marie paid.
   - ☐ Tom and Marie each paid half.

5 WATCH FOR DETAILS

A Put the pictures in order (1 to 6). Then write the correct sentence under each picture. Compare with a partner.

Tom remembered his wallet was in the house.
Tom tried to call Marie.
Tom called a lock service.

Tom remembered his wallet was in the car.
Tom saw his keys inside the car.
✓Tom left the house and started his car.

Tom left the house and started his car.

B *Pair work* What else happened? Can you add two things?

1) ....

2) ....

6 *WHAT'S YOUR OPINION?*

Pair work Complete the chart. Check (✓) the words that describe Tom and Marie.

	Angry	Upset	Tired	Embarrassed	Understanding	Worried
Tom	☐	☐	☐	☐	☐	☐
Marie	☐	☐	☐	☐	☐	☐

Follow-up

7 *QUESTION GAME*

A Write three more questions about the story. Use the past tense and **how**, **why**, **how much**, **who**, or **where**.

1) *Why did Tom go back to his apartment?* ....
2) *When did Tom lock his keys in the car?* ....
3) ....
4) ....
5) ....

B *Pair work* Answer your partner's questions. If you don't think the answer was in the video, say **It didn't say**.

8 *TELL THE STORY*

Pair work Write out the story using **first**, **after that**, **next**, **then**, and **finally**. Include one mistake. Then read your story to another pair. Can they find the mistake?

First, Tom left his apartment and started ....

....

....

....

....

....

....

....

9 *WHAT DID THEY SAY?*

Watch the video and complete the conversation. Then practice it.

Marie is waiting for Tom in the restaurant when he arrives late.

Marie: Hi. ....*There*...... will be ...*two*... of us. . . . Thank you. . . .

Tom: Marie! I'm really .... How ....
have you been waiting?

Marie: It's .... , Tom. I've only .... here
for a little .... Is everything all .... ?

Tom: Yes, it is .... , but you won't .... what
just happened to ....

Marie: Well, what .... ?

Tom: Well, ... of all, I was a little ....
leaving my .... , and so I was in a
.... Then, just after I .... the car,
I .... I didn't have any ....
with me, so I went .... to get my ....

Marie: Did you .... it?

Tom: Oh, yes! I .... it. That wasn't the ....
The problem .... when I got .... to
my .... , I couldn't .... in.

Marie: Do you mean you .... your keys in the car?

Tom: That's .... So, guess what I did .... that!

Marie: I .... guess.

---

10 *PRESENT PERFECT*

A *Pair work* Write questions using **Have you ever . . . ?** and the correct
forms of the verbs in parentheses. Can you add three questions to the list?

1) *Have you ever locked* .... (lock) your keys in the car?
2) .... (call) a lock service?
3) .... (leave) your wallet in the car?
4) .... (arrive) late for an important dinner?
5) .... (go) to a restaurant without money?
6) .... (wait) a long time for someone in a restaurant?
7) ....
8) ....
9) ....

B *Class activity* Go around the class and interview at least three classmates.
Who answered "yes" to the most questions?

11 Across the Golden Gate Bridge

1 CULTURE

The city of San Francisco is surrounded by water on three sides. To the east, the Oakland Bay Bridge crosses San Francisco Bay to the city of Berkeley, home of the Berkeley campus of the University of California. To the north, visitors can see the famous Golden Gate Bridge. The first stop across this bridge is Sausalito, a beautiful town with shops and restaurants on the water. A short drive away is the redwood forest Muir Woods. It has some of the tallest trees in the world. Less than an hour away by car is the Napa Valley, famous for some of California's best wine.

Do you know any other places near San Francisco?
When you visit a city, do you use the bus or train, or do you rent a car?

2 VOCABULARY Taking a trip

Pair work Match the pictures with the words in the glossary below.

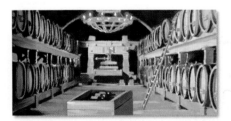

1) _winery_........................

2) ....

3) ....

4) ....

5) ....

6) ....

bay a wide opening of water that is an entrance to the sea
forest an area of land covered with trees
valley an area of land between two hills or mountains

vineyard a piece of land planted with grapes for making wine
waterfront part of a town near a sea or ocean
✓**winery** a factory that makes wine

48

3 GUESS THE STORY

Watch the video with the sound off. Where do you think the couple goes first?

1) Sausalito

2) The Napa Valley

3) Muir Woods

 Watch the video

4 GET THE PICTURE

What places does the car-rental agent talk about? Circle them.
Then compare with a partner.

(The Napa Valley)   Oakland   Alcatraz Island

Sausalito   Muir Woods   The Golden Gate Bridge

5 WATCH FOR DETAILS

Why should the Changs go to the places below? Complete the sentences.
Then compare with a partner.

1) The _wineries_ and .... there are some of the most famous in California.

2) It's a fascinating little .... just across the ....

3) It's right on the .... , and there's a wonderful view of .... across the ....

4) It's a beautiful redwood ....

6 COMPLETE THE STORY

Complete the paragraph below. Choose words from the list. Then compare with a partner.

| Golden Gate | hungry | the Napa Valley | Sausalito | week |
| ✓Honolulu | Muir Woods | rent | waterfront | wineries |

The Changs arrive in San Francisco from ....*Honolulu*............ . They ....
a car at the airport for one .... because they plan to visit friends in
.... The rental agent tells them about the famous ....
there. They decide to drive across the .... Bridge and have lunch in
.... on the way.

Follow-up

7 SAN FRANCISCO

Group work Imagine you have two days in San Francisco. Plan your itinerary.

1) Decide which places you will go to each day.
2) Decide if you need a car.

DAY 1	DAY 2
....	....
....	....
....	....

Ghirardelli Square

Golden Gate Park

Fisherman's Wharf

Muir Woods

Chinatown

Sausalito

8 YOUR CITY

A Group work Now imagine the Changs are visiting your city. Plan their itinerary. Give at least six suggestions like this:

A: First, I think they should drive to . . .
B: Yes, and they should also go to . . .

B Class activity Share your information with the class.

9 *WHAT DID THEY SAY?*

Watch the video and complete the conversation. Then practice it.

The Changs are at the car-rental agency at the airport.

Ken:	Good ....*morning*........ . May I ....*help*..... you?
Mr. Chang:	Yes, we're .... to pick up a ....
Ken:	Do you .... a reservation?
Mr. Chang:	Yes. The .... is Chang.
Ken:	OK, Chang, Chang. Here it is, Mr. Chang. .... in advance. .... here and here. And that's for one .... then?
Mr. Chang:	That's .... One week.
Ken:	Are you .... in San Francisco?
Mrs. Chang:	No, we're .... to visit .... in the Napa Valley.
Ken:	Oh, Napa Valley. That's one of my .... places. The wineries and .... there are some of the most .... in California.

10 SHOULD *AND* SHOULDN'T *Giving advice*

A Complete these sentences with **should** or **shouldn't**. Then compare with a partner

1) When you visit a foreign country, you ......*should*....... learn a few words of the local language.
2) You .... find out about the weather before you travel.
3) You .... carry a lot of cash when you travel.
4) You .... talk to a travel agent about interesting places to visit.
5) You .... be afraid to ask local people questions.

B *Pair work* Give advice for things visitors to your city should or shouldn't do. Write three suggestions in each column.

They should . . .	*They shouldn't . . .*
1)	1) ....
2)	2) ....
3)	3) ....

12 Feeling bad

1 CULTURE

In the United States and Canada, people spend more on health care than in other parts of the world. In drugstores, people buy over-the-counter drugs for colds, coughs, and sore throats. In health-food stores, they buy vitamins and natural foods. Home remedies for common illnesses such as colds and sore throats are also popular.

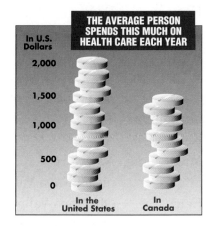

THE AVERAGE PERSON SPENDS THIS MUCH ON HEALTH CARE EACH YEAR

In U.S. Dollars

2,000

1,500

1,000

500

0

In the United States | In Canada

Do you take vitamins or other food supplements?
Do you have health-food stores in your country? What do they sell?

2 VOCABULARY Cold remedies

Pair work Put the remedies in the chart. Can you add two more to each category?

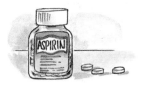

aspirin

chicken soup

cough medicine

garlic juice

ginseng tea

tea with lemon

Home remedies		Over-the-counter drugs	
chicken soup	....	....	....
....	....	....	....
....	....	....	....

3 GUESS THE STORY

Watch the video with the sound off. Answer these questions.

What's the man's problem?
Which remedies in Exercise 2 do you think his co-workers suggest?

 Watch the video

4 GET THE PICTURE

Check (✓) the correct answers. Compare them with a partner.

1) Sandy offers Steve
   - ☐ something she made.
   - ☐ something from the drugstore.
   - ☐ something from a health-food store.

2) Jim offers Steve
   - ☐ something he bought.
   - ☐ something his mother makes for him.
   - ☐ something from a health-food store.

3) Rebecca says Steve should
   - ☐ see the doctor.
   - ☐ take some more medicine.
   - ☐ go out to lunch.

5 WATCH FOR DETAILS

Check (✓) all correct answers. Then compare with a partner.

1) Sandy says her remedy
   - ☐ tastes bad.
   - ☐ contains ginseng.
   - ☐ makes you sleepy.

2) Jim says his remedy
   - ☐ is great for a cold.
   - ☐ makes you sleepy.
   - ☐ has garlic, onions, and carrots in it.

3) Rebecca says her remedy
   - ☐ is the best cure of all.
   - ☐ can be made at home.
   - ☐ mixes with water.

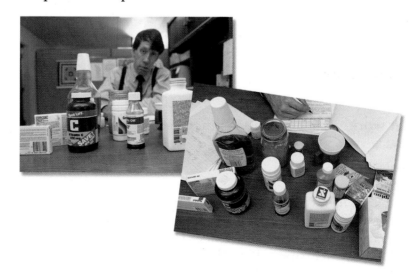

6 WHAT'S YOUR OPINION?

Pair work Answer these questions.

1) Which remedy does Steve like best?
2) Which remedy do you think is best for Steve's cold?
3) Do you think Steve should be at work today?

Follow-up

7 HEALTH PROBLEMS

A *Group work* What do you do for these problems? Can you add two more remedies for each? Compare around the class. Who has the best remedies?

1) a bad cold
It's a good idea to stay in bed and rest. Try some . . . .
....
....

2) a cough
You should drink hot tea.
It's important to . . . .
....
....

3) a headache
Take some aspirin.
It's helpful to . . . .
....
....
....

4) a backache
You should lie on the floor.
Get some . . . .
....
....

B *Pair work* Take turns playing the role of Steve. Your partner will give you advice.

A: How do you feel?
B: Not too good. I've got . . .
A: That's too bad. Listen. I've got the perfect cure . . .

C Do you need advice for a problem of your own? Have a similar conversation, using personal information.

Language close-up

8 WHAT DID THEY SAY?

Watch the video and complete the conversation. Then practice it.

Steve is at work with a bad cold when Sandy comes in.

Sandy: How are those ....*papers*...... coming for this
.........*afternoon*........., Steve?

Steve: .... finished.

Sandy: Do you .... have that .... ?

Steve: Yeah, ... still pretty .... , Sandy.

Sandy: Listen, I've .... just the .... for you. Just a
.... Here.

Steve: What's .... ?

Sandy: It's .... I picked up at the ....-food
store. You just mix it with .... water and .... it.

Steve: But .... is it?

Sandy: I'm not really .... I think it .... ginseng in it or
something .... that. Try it.

Steve: Are you sure it .... ?

Sandy: Of .... it does.

Steve: Well, ... , Sandy. That's really .... Maybe later.

9 REQUESTS AND SUGGESTIONS

A Complete the conversations with **may** or **could** to make
requests and **should**, **try**, or **suggest** to give suggestions.
Then compare and practice with a partner.

1) *At the office*

A: Here's the perfect cold medicine: garlic juice, onions,
and carrots. You .....*should*..... drink a cup every two hours.

B: But I don't like carrots.

A: Well, then I .... an old-fashioned bowl of chicken
soup! And .... to get some rest, too.

2) *At a pharmacy*

A: .... I help you?

B: Yes. .... I have something good for a cold? It's a bad one.

A: Yes. I have these pills. They're a little strong. Just don't drive after
you take them.

B: Hmm . . . I drive to work. .... I have something else?

A: Well, ... these other pills then. They won't make you sleepy.

I HAVE THE PERFECT CURE FOR YOU.

B *Pair work* Act out the conversations. The first time, act them out as is.
The second time, change the problems and the remedies.

Documentary 4
At the Mall of America

1 CULTURE

The Mall of America is the largest shopping and entertainment mall in the United States. It takes up 4.2 million square feet (or 390,000 square meters) of space. In addition to four major department stores, you can find almost 400 other stores, an entertainment park with 50 rides, over 30 restaurants, a movie theater with 14 screens, and numerous live music clubs. Built in 1990, the mall is still very new. The original idea for the mall came from the Triple Five Corporation, a Canadian company that built the largest shopping mall in the world in West Edmonton, Alberta.

Are shopping malls popular in your country?
What do you think are the advantages of shopping at a mall?
  The disadvantages?

 Watch the video

2 GET THE PICTURE

Check (✓) the correct answers. Then compare with a partner.

1) The Mall of America is in
   ☐ Bloomington, Indiana.
   ✔ Bloomington, Minnesota.

2) The mall has
   ☐ hundreds of stores.
   ☐ thousands of stores.

3) There are
   ☐ 14 cinemas.
   ☐ 40 cinemas.

4) There are more than
   ☐ 14 places to eat.
   ☐ 40 places to eat.

5) The name of the amusement park is
   ☐ Camp Winnie.
   ☐ Camp Snoopy.

3 WATCH FOR DETAILS

What did these people do at the mall? Check (✓) all true
answers. Then compare with a partner.

1) ☐ She went to Camp Snoopy.
☐ She bought some shoes.
☐ She ate lunch.

2) ☐ They went on rides.
☐ They looked in stores.
☐ They ate lunch.

3) ☐ They listened to music.
☐ They bought some tapes.
☐ They went to Camp Snoopy.

4 WHAT THE SHOPPERS SAY

How did these people answer the reporter's questions?
Fill in the blanks. Then compare with a partner.

1) What do you think people
should do first?

2) What would you recommend
for visitors from another
country?

3) Can you describe the Mall of
America in one word?

Wear .... shoes.

Come here if there's anything
.... you're
looking for.

....

Follow-up

5 WHAT'S YOUR OPINION?

Pair work Answer these questions.

1) Do you like shopping malls?
2) How would you describe the Mall of America?
3) What places would you like to visit at the mall?

13 At the state fair

1 CULTURE

In rural areas of the United States and Canada, where farming is important, a state or county fair is a popular summer event. At the fair, farmers show their fruits and vegetables, their best animals, and their new equipment. There are competitions such as horseback riding and rodeos. People sell paintings and handmade products such as pottery. There are rides and games for the entire family. And there are always lots of things to eat. For young children, a day at the fair is one of the happiest days of the year.

Do you have fairs in your country? What kind? What can you do and see there?

Where can families go in your country to have fun together?

2 VOCABULARY At a state fair

Pair work Here are some things you can do at a state fair. Write the activities under the pictures.

eat corn on the cob   ride a horse   ride on a roller coaster
eat ice cream   ride on a merry-go-round   ✓win a prize

1) *win a prize* ....

2) ....

3) ....

4) ....

5) ....

6) ....

3 GUESS THE STORY

Who do you think wins the prize? Check (✓) your answer.

☐ Rick   ☐ Betsy   ☐ Nancy

 Watch the video

4 GET THE PICTURE

What did each group of people do? Check (✓) all correct answers.
Then compare with a partner.

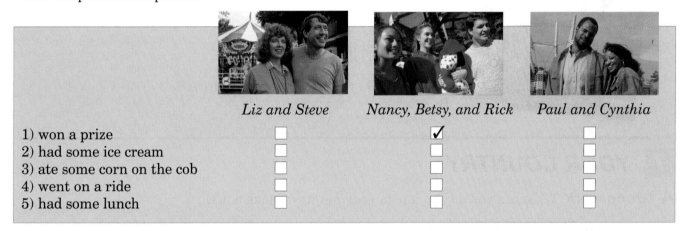

	Liz and Steve	Nancy, Betsy, and Rick	Paul and Cynthia
1) won a prize	☐	✓	☐
2) had some ice cream	☐	☐	☐
3) ate some corn on the cob	☐	☐	☐
4) went on a ride	☐	☐	☐
5) had some lunch	☐	☐	☐

5 WATCH FOR DETAILS

A List the things to do, eat, and see at a state fair. Then combine
answers as a class and complete the chart.

Things to do	Things to eat	Things to see
ride a horse		

B Which of these things have you done? Check (✓) them.
Then compare with a partner.

6 A DAY AT THE FAIR

A *Group work* Plan a day at the state fair in the video. Agree on five things to do and see.

1) ....
2) ....
3) ....
4) ....
5) ....

B *Pair work* Order lunch at the state fair. One student will play the waiter or waitress.

A: May I take your order, please?
B: . . .
A: Would you like anything else?
B: . . .
A: And would you like anything to drink?
B: . . .

7 YOUR COUNTRY

A *Group work* What can you do at a fair in your country? Make a list.

Things to do	*Things to eat*	*Things to see*
....	....	....
....	....	....
....	....	....
....	....	....

B Which things are your favorite? Check (✓) at least three. Then have conversations like this:

A: I like to go on rides.
B: I like to play games and try to win prizes.

C In the United States, corn on the cob is very popular. What foods are popular where you're from?

8 WHAT DID THEY SAY?

Watch the video and complete the conversations. Then practice them.

Some people are enjoying a day at the state fair.

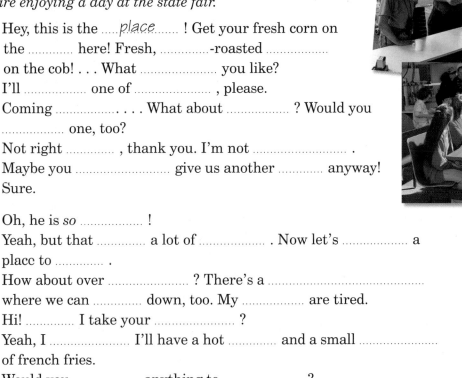

1) Vendor: Hey, this is the ....*place*..... ! Get your fresh corn on
   the .... here! Fresh, ...-roasted ....
   on the cob! . . . What .... you like?

   Steve: I'll .... one of .... , please.

   Vendor: Coming .... What about .... ? Would you
   .... one, too?

   Liz: Not right .... , thank you. I'm not ....

   Steve: Maybe you .... give us another .... anyway!

   Vendor: Sure.

2) Nancy: Oh, he is *so* .... !

   Rick: Yeah, but that .... a lot of .... Now let's .... a
   placc to ....

   Betsy: How about over .... ? There's a ....
   where we can .... down, too. My .... are tired.

   Waitress: Hi! .... I take your .... ?

   Betsy: Yeah, I .... I'll have a hot .... and a small ....
   of french fries.

   Waitress: Would you .... anything to .... ?

   Betsy: I'll have a .... diet cola.

   Waitress: OK. And .... can I .... for you?

   Nancy: I guess .... like the .... plate and a cup of .... , please.

9 WOULD AND WILL Ordering food

A Rewrite these questions using **Would you like . . . ?**
Then compare with a partner.

1) What do you want to eat?
   What would you like to eat?

2) Do you want french fries with that?

   ....

3) Do you want dessert?

   ....

4) Do you want anything to drink?

   ....

B *Pair work* Now answer the questions with **I'll have . . .**

A: What would you like to eat?
B: I'll have . . .

14 Around the World: the game show

1 CULTURE

One of the most popular TV programs in the United States and Canada is the game show. In most game shows, players test their knowledge on different subjects, and the questions are sometimes difficult. But there are also game shows that are games of chance. The winner must be lucky, but doesn't have to be smart. And there are even dating "game shows." The prize isn't money, but a chance to meet someone new!

POPULAR TV

JEOPARDY
A Game of Knowledge
Love Connection
A Dating Game
Wheel of Fortune
A Game of Chance

GAME SHOWS IN THE U.S.

Do you have game shows on TV in your country?
What kinds of game shows are popular?

2 GUESS THE FACTS

Pair work How good is your geography?
Check the correct answers.

1) Which is longer?
   ☐ the Nile River
   ☐ the Amazon River

the Amazon River

the Nile River

2) Which is higher?
   ☐ Mt. McKinley
   ☐ Mt. Kilimanjaro

3) Which country is called the "island continent"?
   ☐ New Zealand
   ☐ Australia

Mt. McKinley

Mt. Kilimanjaro

62

4) What's the largest desert in Asia?
- ☐ the Great Indian desert
- ☐ the Gobi desert

Los Angeles

Mexico City

Angel Falls

5) Which is the largest city in North America?
- ☐ Los Angeles
- ☐ Mexico City

6) Where is Angel Falls, the world's highest waterfall?
- ☐ Brazil
- ☐ Venezuela

Watch the video

3 CHECK THE FACTS

Now correct your answers to Exercise 2. Did you guess the facts correctly? Compare with a partner.

4 WATCH FOR DETAILS

Check (✓) the correct answers. Then compare with a partner.

1) Marlene is from
- ☐ Seattle, Washington.
- ☐ Washington, D.C.

2) Marlene is a
- ☐ computer programmer.
- ☐ computer engineer.

3) Jack is from
- ☐ Cambridge, Massachusetts.
- ☐ Boston, Massachusetts.

4) Jack is a
- ☐ high school teacher.
- ☐ college teacher.

5) Kathy is from
- ☐ Vero Beach, Florida.
- ☐ Miami Beach, Florida.

6) Kathy is an
- ☐ actress.
- ☐ accountant.

5 *WHO WINS THE GAME?*

A What is each person's score at the end of the game? Write the number. Then compare with a partner.

Marlene ....   Jack ....   Kathy ....

B Is the winner happy with the prize? Why or why not?

Follow-up

6 *AROUND THE WORLD*

A *Group work* Write questions for the game "Around the World." Write three questions for each category in the chart. Give one question 25 points, one question 50 points, and one question 75 points. (You can also add categories of your own.)

Deserts and mountains	Oceans and islands
....	....
....	....
....	....
Rivers and waterfalls	Cities and countries
....	....
....	....
....	....

B *Class activity* Now play "Around the World." Half the class is in Group A. The other half is in Group B.

Group A: Choose one student to be the game-show host.

Group B: Take turns choosing a category for 25, 50, or 75 points. Then answer the host's questions. Play for five minutes.

Ask questions like this:

    A: Are you ready?
    B: Yes, I'll try (*name of category*) for 25 points.
    A: OK. (*Asks question.*)
    B: (*Answers question.*)
    A: That's right! **or** Sorry. That's not correct.

Now change roles. Group B chooses a host and Group A answers questions. Play for five more minutes. Which group wins the game?

Language close-up

7 WHAT DID THEY SAY?

Watch the video and complete the conversation. Then practice it.

Marlene, Jack, and Kathy are about to begin playing "Around the World."

Announcer: And now it's ..... *time* .... to play "Around the ..... *World* ..... "
with your host, Johnny Traveler.

Johnny: .... and gentlemen, ... to
"Around the World," the .... show about world
.... And now, let's .... our players.

Announcer: A .... engineer from .... ,
Washington, Marlene Miller! A high ....
teacher from .... , Massachusetts, Jack
Richardson! And from Vero Beach, Florida, an
.... , Kathy Hernandez!

Johnny: .... to "Around the World." And now, let's
.... our game. Our categories are ....
and Mountains, ... and Waterfalls, Oceans and
.... , Cities and .... Marlene, please begin.

8 COMPARISONS WITH ADJECTIVES

A Write questions using the comparative or superlative form of each adjective in parentheses. Then add three questions of your own.

1) city: New York – Tokyo? (cold)
Which city is colder, New York or Tokyo?

2) planet: Earth – Saturn – Mars? (big)
....

3) plane: the Concorde – a 747? (fast)
....

4) building: the Parthenon – the Empire State
Building? (old)
....

5) country: Brazil – Canada – Argentina? (large)
....

6) ....

7) ....

8) ....

New York is colder!

B *Pair work* Take turns asking and answering the questions. Who answered the most questions correctly?

15 May I speak to Cathy?

Preview

1 CULTURE

In the United States and Canada, people like to talk on the telephone. In many places, the cost of a local call is fixed. You can talk for five minutes or two hours for the same price. The telephone is now very convenient because of new technology. Here are some examples:

- *Call waiting* – You can answer a second call when you are on the telephone.
- *Call forwarding* – You can receive telephone calls at a different phone number.
- *Answering machines* – You don't miss calls when you're busy or not at home.
- *Cellular phones* – You can make and receive telephone calls in your car.
- *Two telephone lines on one phone* – Different rings tell you who the call is for.

How much time do you spend on the telephone each day?
What kinds of new technology are common in your country?
  Which do you like best?

2 VOCABULARY *Telephone expressions*

A *Pair work* Match.

....*c*.... 1) Cathy's not here right now.
.... 2) May I speak to Cathy?
.... 3) She's not in just now.
.... 4) Will she be back soon?
.... 5) Could you tell her that Kevin called?
.... 6) Is she coming back soon?
.... 7) Is Cathy home?
.... 8) Could you just tell her to call me?

a) Asking to speak to someone
b) Leaving a message
c) Saying someone is out
d) Asking for information about someone

B Can you add three other telephone expressions?

1) ....

2) ....

3) ....

3 GUESS THE STORY

Watch the first two minutes of the video with the sound off.
What do you think these people are saying? Write one sentence from
Exercise 2 in each balloon.

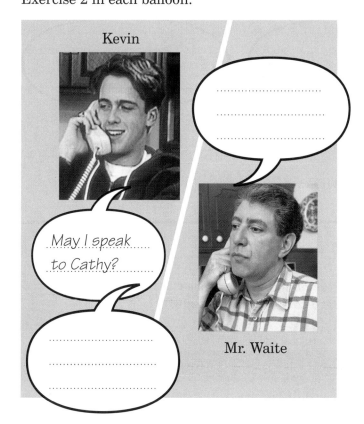

Kevin

May I speak
to Cathy?

Mr. Waite

Mr. Waite

Jenny

Watch the video

4 GET THE PICTURE

A Put the phone calls in order. Number them from 1 to 3. Then compare with a partner.

Kevin

Rachel

Jenny

B Complete the telephone messages for Cathy. Fill in the names of the callers
and check the correct messages. Then compare with a partner.

1) .... called.
   ☐ will call Cathy back
   ☐ wants Cathy to call

2) .... called.
   ☐ will call Cathy back
   ☐ wants Cathy to call

3) .... called.
   ☐ will call Cathy back
   ☐ wants Cathy to call

5 *TELEPHONE ETIQUETTE*

A When you make a phone call, it's polite to give your name. What does each person say when Mr. Waite answers the phone? Fill in the balloons. Then compare with a partner.

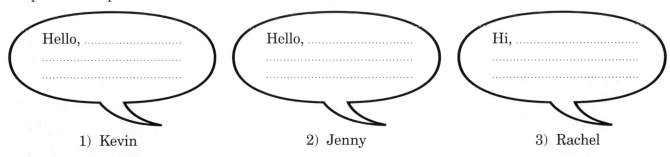

Hello, ...
....
....

1) Kevin

Hello, ...
....
....

2) Jenny

Hi, ...
....
....

3) Rachel

B *Pair work* Who do you think is the most polite? Why?

6 *WHAT'S YOUR OPINION?*

Pair work Look at the culture preview again. Which telephone conveniences do you think Mr. Waite needs? Give each a number from 1 to 5 (1 = most useful).

Follow-up

7 *FINISH THE STORY*

A *Pair work* What do you think Mr. Waite says to his boss? What do you think the urgent call was about? Write a possible telephone conversation.

Start like this:

Mr. Waite: John speaking.
Boss: I'm very sorry to bother you, John. I hope it's not a problem.
Mr. Waite: Oh no, no! Uh, no problem! No problem at all!
Boss: I'm calling because . . .
Mr. Waite: . . .

B *Class activity* Practice your conversations in front of the class. Who has the best conversation?

Language close-up

8 WHAT DID THEY SAY?

Watch the video and complete the conversations. Then practice them.

Cathy's father is home alone when the phone rings.

1) Mr. Waite: Hello?
   Kevin: Hello, ...*may*.. I speak ..*to*.. Cathy?
   Mr. Waite: I'm .... She's not .... just now.
   Kevin: Is she .... back soon?
   Mr. Waite: Uh, ..., I think ....
   Kevin: Well, ... you tell .... that
   Kevin .... and that I'll call .... later?
   Mr. Waite: ...., Kevin.
   Kevin: .... you. Good-bye.
   Mr. Waite: Bye.

2) Mr. Waite: Hello?
   Jenny: ...., Mr. Waite. .... is Jenny. Is
   Cathy .... ?
   Mr. Waite: Oh, hi, Jenny. No, Cathy's .... here
   right ....
   Jenny: .... she be .... soon?
   Mr. Waite: Uh, I'm not .... Would you ....
   to leave a .... ?
   Jenny: Well, ... you just .... her to call ....
   when she .... in?
   Mr. Waite: Sure, ... tell her. .... , Jenny.
   Jenny: Bye, ... Waite.

3) Mr. Waite: Hello?
   Rachel: ...., this is Rachel. .... Cathy home?
   Mr. Waite: Uh, no, she's .... , Rachel. .... you like
   her to .... you .... she comes .... ?
   Rachel: Yes, ... She has my ....
   Mr. Waite: I'll .... her, Rachel. Bye.
   Rachel: Bye.

9 REQUESTS WITH TELL AND ASK

Pair work Practice the conversations in Exercise 8 again.
This time use your own information and make requests with
ask or **tell** like this:

Would you tell Cathy the party is at Kevin's house?
Could you ask Cathy to meet us at Burger Heaven at 2:00?

16 A whole new Marty

1 CULTURE

Self-improvement is an important part of Canadian and American cultures. Many people believe that life will be better for them if they change their appearance in some way. Magazines and newspapers often have advertisements for exercise machines, vitamins, skin and hair products, and courses on self-improvement. Among young people, a good appearance is usually important, and so is the ability to make friends easily.

Is self-improvement an important part of your culture?
Do you want to change anything about yourself?

3 Steps to a Better You

1 Exercise bicycle $119.95

2 Self-help book $19.95

I Love Me

3 Super vitamins $39.95

VITAN

TO ORDER, CALL 800-555-3210

2 VOCABULARY Verb and noun pairs

Pair work Choose a verb from the list to go with each word or phrase.
(Some items have more than one answer.)

buy	cut	gain	✓improve	make
✓change	do	get	lose	meet

1) *change or improve* .... my appearance
2) .... more people
3) .... more friends
4) .... weight
5) .... more exercise

6) .... some new clothes
7) .... my hairstyle
8) .... my hair
9) .... in shape
10) .... confidence

3 GUESS THE STORY

Watch the first minute of the video with the sound off.
Check (✓) the phrases you think describe each person.

	Marty	John
1) looks unhappy	☐	☐
2) is popular with girls	☐	☐
3) dresses well	☐	☐
4) has trouble with a calculus problem	☐	☐

Marty

John

 *Watch the video*

4 GET THE PICTURE

A Check your answers to Exercise 3. Did you guess correctly?

B Check (✓) **True** or **False**. Correct the false statements. Then compare with a partner.

Marty

John

Michelle

		True	*False*	
1)	John asks Marty for help with his schoolwork.	☐	☐	....
2)	Michelle doesn't know Marty.	☐	☐	....
3)	Michelle and John decide to study calculus together.	☐	☐	....
4)	John thinks Marty should be more outgoing.	☐	☐	....
5)	Michelle recognizes Marty in the cafeteria.	☐	☐	....
6)	Marty is too busy to study with Michelle.	☐	☐	....

5 WATCH FOR DETAILS

Check (✓) the things Marty does to improve his appearance.

☐ He lifts weights.

☐ He gets a haircut.

☐ He changes his diet.

☐ He buys new clothes.

☐ He shaves.

☐ He takes vitamins.

71

Follow-up

6 WHAT HAPPENED?

A Write the story in your own words.

1) *John and Marty were in the library.*

2) ....

3) ....

4) ....
....

5) ....
....

6) ....
....

B *Pair work* Now share your description of what happened with a partner. How are your stories different?

7 GOOD ADVICE

What advice would you give to these people? Think of as many things as you can for each person.

1) Maria has trouble meeting boys.
2) Tina has trouble with math.
3) Tony is shy.
4) Karen wants to get in shape.

> He could . . .
> She should . . .
> It's important/helpful/useful/a good idea to . . .

Language close-up

8 WHAT DID THEY SAY?

Watch the video and complete the conversation. Then practice it.

John and Marty are in the library when Michelle comes by.

John: I'm just ....*terrible*.... at calculus. I don't ....
anything in this ....

Marty: I .... what you .... It is a .... course.

John: Did you .... out the answer to this .... ?

Marty: That's in Chapter 11. I .... that .... week. Let's see.

Michelle: Hi, John. I .... you're .... on calculus.

John: Oh, hi, Michelle. Yes, I .... Michelle, you .... Marty,
.... you?

Michelle: Yeah, hi, Marty. Say, John, I've got a .... of
.... about Chapter 12. Do you want to
.... together?

John: Well, uh, actually, I'm .... on Chapter 11, but Marty
.... is working on Chapter 12.

Michelle: Oh, that's OK. Actually, I've .... go to class
.... now. See you ....

John: OK, Michelle. ....

9 DESCRIBING CHANGES

A Complete the sentences with the correct form of each word.
Then compare with a partner.

busy   buy   change   drive
long   paint   start   wear

1) I .... glasses now.

2) I don't .... to work anymore. I take the bus.

3) I haven't cut my hair in four months. It's .... than before.

4) I got a promotion at work recently. I'm much .... now.

5) I .... my bedroom blue last weekend.

6) I .... a new computer course last week.

7) I've .... a dog.

8) I've .... my hairstyle.

B Now write four similar sentences about yourself and read them to your partner.
Who has changed more in the past year?

1) ....   3) ....

2) ....   4) ....

What is American food?

 **Preview**

1 CULTURE

Many people think American food is just hot dogs and pizza. Of course, these things are popular, but even in small towns in the United States, you can find Chinese, Italian, and Mexican restaurants. In many places there are Japanese, Thai, and German restaurants. The United States is a country of immigrants, and there are as many kinds of food as there are people from different backgrounds.

What foods are typical of your country or region?
What is your favorite food?

 Watch the video

2 GET THE PICTURE

In the video, in what kind of restaurant can you find these foods?
Write **CA** for California style, **A** for American, **C** for Chinese,
or **G** for German.

1) bratwurst

2) Caesar salad

3) a hamburger

4) Kung-pao chicken

5) pasta

6) pork Szechwan

3 WATCH FOR DETAILS

Match the people with what they ate. Choose foods
from the list. Then compare with a partner.

Bavarian goulash	Caesar salad	German potato salad	pasta
bratwurst	chicken salad	Kung-pao chicken	pork Szechwan

1) ....

2) ....

3) ....

4) ....

5) ....

6) ....

4 IT'S ALL AMERICAN FOOD

Answer the questions. Then compare with a partner.

1) California-style restaurants are famous for
their interesting use of
   ☐ fresh fish.
   ☐ pasta.
   ☑ fresh fruits and vegetables.

2) The Chinese restaurant has
   ☐ food with live music.
   ☐ a self-service buffet.
   ☐ vegetarian food.

3) In the German restaurant people can
   ☐ listen to music and eat.
   ☐ cook their own food.
   ☐ order a hamburger.

4) Most people in the video think typical
American food is
   ☐ steak.
   ☐ a hamburger and french fries.
   ☐ barbecue.

Follow-up

5 HOW ABOUT YOU?

Group work Answer these questions.

1) What does the reporter say American food is?
   What is American food to you?
2) How often do you eat out in restaurants?

3) What's your favorite kind of restaurant?
4) What do you usually order?
5) What's your favorite American food?

75

Acknowledgments

Illustrators

Adventure House 6 (*top*), 12 (*top*), 16, 18, 26 (*top*), 34 (*all*), 37, 48 (*top*), 52 (*top*), 62, 70

Brian Battles 12 (*bottom*), 14 (*bottom*)

Keith Bendis 2, 8, 10, 26 (*bottom*), 30, 42, 54, 66, 71

Mark Kaufman 48 (*bottom*), 58 (*top*)

Wally Neibart 4, 14 (*top*), 22 (*top*), 27, 36, 52 (*bottom*), 58 (*bottom*), 65

Andrew Toos 6 (*bottom*), 22 (*bottom*), 28, 39, 40, 44, 55, 61

Sam Viviano 24

Photographic Credits

49 (*top left*) © Bill Dean

62 (*clockwise from top left*) © Richard Steedman/The Stock Market; © Claudia Parks/The Stock Market; © Harvey Lloyd/The Stock Market; © Tom Bean/The Stock Market

63 (*top; clockwise from top left*) © Pete Saloutos/The Stock Market; © Nigel Atherton/Tony Stone Worldwide; © Rob Crandall/Stock Boston

All other photographs by Rick Armstrong and John Hruska

Author's Acknowledgments

A great number of people assisted in the development of both the original *Interchange* Video 1 and *New Interchange* Video 1. Particular thanks go to the following:

The **reviewers** for their helpful suggestions:

Valerie A. Benson, Julie Dyson, Dorien Grunbaum, Cynthia Hall Kouré, Mark Kunce, Peter Mallett, Pamela Rogerson-Revell, Chuck Sandy, and Jody Simmons.

The **students** and **teachers** in the following schools and institutes who pilot-tested the Video or the Video Activity Book; their valuable comments and suggestions helped shape the content of the entire program:

Athenée Français, Tokyo, Japan; **Centro Cultural Brasil-Estados Unidos**, Belém, Brazil; **Eurocentres**, Virginia, U.S.A.; **Fairmont State College**, West Virginia, U.S.A.; **Hakodate Daigaku**, Hokkaido, Japan; **Hirosaki Gakuin Daigaku**, Aomori, Japan; **Hiroshima Shudo Daigaku**, Hiroshima, Japan; **Hokkaido Daigaku, Institute of Language and Cultural Studies**, Hokkaido, Japan; **The Institute Meguro**, Tokyo, Japan; **Instituto Brasil-Estados Unidos**, Rio de Janeiro, Brazil; **Instituto Cultural de Idiomas**, Caxias do Sul, Brazil; **Musashino Joshi Daigaku**, Tokyo, Japan; **Nagasaki Gaigo Tanki Daigaku**, Nagasaki, Japan; **New Cida**, Tokyo, Japan; **Parco-ILC English School**, Chiba, Japan; **Pegasus Language Services**, Tokyo, Japan; **Poole Gakuin Tanki Daigaku**, Hyogo, Japan; **Seinan Gakuin Daigaku**, Fukuoka, Japan;

Shukugawa Joshi Tanki Daigaku, Hyogo, Japan; **Tokai Daigaku**, Kanagawa, Japan; **YMCA Business School**, Kanagawa, Japan; and **Yokohama YMCA**, Kanagawa, Japan.

The **editorial** and **production** team on the original or revised classroom video and the accompanying print materials:

Sarah Almy, Suzette André, John Borrelli, Will Capel, Mary Carson, Karen Davy, Andrew Gitzy, Deborah Goldblatt, Deborah Gordon, Stephanie Karras, James Morgan, Kathy Niemczyk, Chuck Sandy, Kathleen Schultz, Ellen Shaw, and Mary Vaughn.

The **editorial** and **production** team on *New Interchange* Level One: Suzette André, Sylvia P. Bloch, John Borrelli, Mary Carson, Natalie Nordby Chen, Karen Davy, Randee Falk, Andrew Gitzy, Pauline Ireland, Penny Laporte, Kathy Niemczyk, Kathleen Schultz, Rosie Stamp, and Mary Vaughn.

And Cambridge University Press **staff** and **advisors**: Carlos Barbisan, Kate Cory-Wright, Riitta da Costa, Peter Davison, Stephen Dawson, Peter Donovan, Cecilia Gómez, Colin Hayes, Thares Keeree, Jinsook Kim, Koen Van Landeghem, Carine Mitchell, Sabina Sahni, Helen Sandiford, Dan Schulte, Ian Sutherland, Chris White, and Ellen Zlotnick.

And a special thanks to the video producer, Master Communications Group.

new interchange

English for international communication

Jack C. Richards

with Jonathan Hull and Susan Proctor

workbook

1

New Interchange Workbook
revision prepared by Jonathan Hull.

CAMBRIDGE
UNIVERSITY PRESS

Contents

Acknowledgments

ILLUSTRATORS

Barbara Griffel 16, 52 (*top*)
Randy Jones 1, 9, 12, 21, 36, 46, 47, 49, 51, 52 (*bottom*), 66, 73, 78, 79, 86, 95
Mark Kaufman 13 (*bottom*), 17
Kevin Spaulding 5, 11, 13 (*top*), 23, 38, 48, 50, 53, 71
Sam Viviano 2, 3, 6, 7, 14, 15, 25, 35, 42, 54, 60, 69, 70, 72, 76, 77, 90, 91, 92

PHOTOGRAPHIC CREDITS

The authors and publishers are grateful for permission to reproduce the following photographs. Every endeavor has been made to contact copyright owners, and apologies are expressed for omissions.

4 (*top left*) George Ancona/International Stock; (*top right*) Superstock; (*bottom left*) David R. Frazier/Photo Researchers; (*bottom right*) Noblestock/International Stock

8 (*clockwise from upper left*) Zigy Kaluzny/Tony Stone Images; Mugshots/The Stock Market; Flip Chalfont/The Image Bank; Adam Smith/FPG; John Riley/Tony Stone Images

10 (*top left*) Frank Herholdt/Tony Stone Images; (*top right*) Phyllis Picardi/International Stock; (*bottom*) Larry Gatz/The Image Bank

18 (*left, center left, and center right*) The Sharper Image 1-800-344-444; (*right*) The Sharp Wizard OZ 5600 electronic organizer

19 (*both*) Photofest

20 (*top left*) Columbia Records/photographer: Stephen Meisel; (*top right*) Virgin Records/photographer: Mark Seliger; (*bottom left*) Scott McKiernan/Gamma Liaison; (*bottom right*) Photofest

23 Virgin Records/photographer: Peter Lindbergh

24 (*top*) Jack Vartoogian; (*bottom*) Photofest

26 (*left*) Donald C. Johnson/The Stock Market; (*right*) Alan Smith/Tony Stone Images

27 (*from top to bottom*) Simone Huber/Tony Stone Images; Anthony Edgeworth/The Stock Market; Bill Aron/Photo Researchers; Dan Bosler/Tony Stone Images; Graham Harris/Tony Stone Images; Ken Fisher/Tony Stone Images

30 (*left*) Bill Losh/FPG; (*right*) Paul Barton/The Stock Market

31 (*top*) Jim Cummins/FPG; (*center*) Alan Becker/Tony Stone Images; (*bottom*) Dave Rosenberg/Tony Stone Images

34 (*top left*) Jean Francois Causse/Tony Stone Images; (*top right*) Paul Elson/The Image Bank; (*bottom*) Dick Dickenson/International Stock

37 Superstock

38 Ted Horrowitz/The Stock Market

40 Benjamin Rondel/The Stock Market

41 (*top*) William E. Townsend/Photo Researchers; (*bottom*) Clem Hager/Photo Researchers

55 Photofest

56 (*clockwise from top left*) Blair Seitz/Photo Researchers; Richard Price/FPG; Thatcher Kalunzy/Tony Stone Images

57 (*upper left*) Doug Armand/Tony Stone Images; (*upper right*) Ken Straiton/The Stock Market; (*center left*) Ned Gillette/The Stock Market; (*center right*) Gary Landsman/The Stock Market; (*bottom left*) Jon Riley/Tony Stone Images; (*bottom right*) Viviane Moos/The Stock Market

59 (*from left to right*) Michael Goldman/FPG; Robert A. Isaacs/Photo Researchers; Hoa-Qui/Gamma Liaison; Frederick McKinney/FPG

61 (*top*) Will & Deni McIntyre/Tony Stone Images; (*bottom*) ZEFA, London/The Stock Market

62 (*left*) Richard Passmore/Tony Stone Images; (*center*) Guy Marche/FPG; (*right*) Superstock

63 Eric Sander/FPG

64 (*left*) Gavin Hellier/Tony Stone Images; (*center*) Jeffrey Sylvester/FPG; (*right*) Alexis Duclos/Gamma Liaison

65 Noboru Komine/Photo Researchers

74 (*top to bottom*) Matthew Klein/Photo Researchers; Peter Johansky/FPG; Roy Morsch/The Stock Market; Karen Leeds/The Stock Market; Alan Bergman/FPG

80 Travelpix/FPG

81 (*left*) Guido Alberto Rossi/The Image Bank; (*center*) Bob Abraham/Pacific Stock; (*right*) A & L Sinibaldi/Tony Stone Images

82 (*top*) Dennis Puleston/Photo Researchers; (*bottom*) Robert W. Hernandez/Photo Researchers

83 (*top to bottom*) Ken Fisher/Tony Stone Images; Telegraph Colour Library/FPG; Wolfgang Kaehler/Gamma Liaison; Karl Weidman/Photo Researchers; Donovan Reese/Tony Stone Images

93 (*left*) L.D. Gordon/The Image bank; (*center*) Ariel Skelley/The Stock Market; (*right*) John Henly/The Stock Market

94 Superstock

1 Please call me Chuck.

1 Write about yourself.

My first name is _____ .

My last name is _____ .

Please call me _____ .

2 Names

A Write **M** for male names and **F** for female names.

1. _M_ Joseph   5. _____ Robert
2. _____ James   6. _____ Susan
3. _____ Catherine   7. _____ William
4. _____ Elizabeth   8. _____ Jennifer

Hello
MY NAME IS:
Joseph

B Match each of these nicknames with a name above.

a. _5_ Bob   c. _____ Jenny   e. _____ Liz   g. _____ Sue
b. _____ Kate   d. _____ Jim   f. _____ Joe   h. _____ Bill

C Match the following.

☐ Michael Charles Kennedy   ☐ Kate
☐ Smith   ☑ Ms. Sarah Rachel Jones

1. a full name with a title
   Ms. Sarah Rachel Jones

2. a nickname
   Kate

3. a full name without a title
   Michael Charles Kennedy

4. a family name
   Smith

3 **Choose the correct responses.**

1. A: Hi, I'm Liz.

   B: _Oh, hi._
   - Oh, hi.
   - What do people call you?

2. A: My name is Jim Holmes.

   B: Nice to meet you. Mr. Holmes
   - Nice to meet you, Mr. Jim.
   - Nice to meet you, Mr. Holmes.

3. A: This is Jenny Parker.

   B: Nice to meet you, Ms Parker
   - Nice to meet you, Ms. Parker.
   - Hello, Ms. Jenny Parker.

4. A: Hello, I'm William Dean. Please call me Bill.

   B: Pleased to meet you, Bill
   - Pleased to meet you, Mr. Dean.
   - Pleased to meet you, Bill.

5. A: Excuse me, what's your name again?

   B: Joe King
   - K-I-N-G.
   - Joe King.

6. A: How do you spell your first name?

   B: C-H-A-R-L-E-N-E
   - I'm Charlene.
   - C-H-A-R-L-E-N-E.

4 **Look at the answers. What are the questions?**

1. Jim: What 's your first name?
   Bob: My first name's Bob.

2. Jim: What 's your last name?
   Bob: My last name's Hayes.

3. Jim: Who is that?
   Bob: That's my wife.

4. Jim: What is her name
   Bob: Her name is Rosa.

5. Jim: Where is she from?
   Bob: She's from Mexico.

6. Jim: Who are they
   Bob: They're my wife's parents.

2

5 **Choose the correct words.**

1. They're my classmates. ___*Their*___ names are Noriko and Kate. (They/Their)

2. We're students. ___Our___ classroom number is 108-C. (Our/We)

3. Excuse me. What's ___your___ last name again? (you/your)

4. That's Mr. Kim. ___he___ is in my class. (He/His)

5. ___My___ name is Elizabeth. Please call me Liz. (I/My)

6. This is Paul's wife. ___her___ name is Jennifer. (His/Her)

7. My parents are on vacation. ___they___ are in South Korea. (We/They)

8. I'm from Venice, Italy. ___It___ is a beautiful city. (It/It's)
   ___Italy___

6 **Complete this conversation with am, are, or is.**

Lisa: Who ___are___ the men over there, Amy?

Amy: Oh, they ___are___ on the volleyball team. Let me introduce you.
   Hi, Surachai, this ___is___ Lisa Neil.

Surachai: Pleased to meet you, Lisa.

Lisa: Nice to meet you, too, Surachai. Where ___are___ you from?

Surachai: I ___am___ from Thailand.

Amy: And this ___is___ Mario. He ___is___ from Brazil.

Lisa: Hi, Mario.

Pablo: And my name ___is___ Pablo. I ___am___ from Colombia.

Homework

7 *Hello and welcome!*

A Can you remember the names of two students in your class? Where are they from?

Name	Where from?
1. *Ana Laura Pichardo*	*Chihuahua*
2. *Erika Reynoso*	*Delicias*

B Read about four students, and complete the chart below.

INTERNATIONAL 🌐 LANGUAGE 🌐 SCHOOL

Every month, we introduce new students to the school. This month, we want to introduce four new students to you. Please say "hello" when you see them in school.

Mario is in English 101. He is from Cali, Colombia. His first language is Spanish, and he also speaks a little French. He wants to be on the school volleyball team. He says he doesn't play very well, but he wants to learn!

Su Yin is in English 102. She is from Taiwan. She says she can write and read English pretty well, but she needs a lot of practice speaking English. Her first language is Mandarin Chinese. In her free time, she wants to play volleyball on the school team.

Eileen is in Mario's class. She is from Mozambique, in southern Africa. She speaks Swahili and Portuguese. She is studying English and engineering. She wants to be an engineer. She says she does not play any sports, but she wants to make a lot of new friends in her class.

Finally, meet Ahmed. He is in English 103. He says he can speak a lot of English, but his writing is very bad! Ahmed is from Luxor in Egypt, and his first language is Arabic. He is a baseball player, and he wants to be on the school baseball team.

Name	Where from?	Languages	Sports?
1. *Mario*	*he is from Cali Colombia*	*Spanish, French*	*Volleyball*
2. *Eileen*	*Mozambique, Africa*	*Swahili and Portugues*	*Any*
3. *Su Yin*	*Taiwan*	*Mandarin Chinese and English*	*Volleyball*
4. *Ahmed*	*Luxor Egypt*	*Arabic*	*baseball*

8   *Choose the correct sentences to complete this conversation.*

> ☑ And what are you studying?
> ☐ No, she's not. She's my sister!
> ☑ Hi, Sarah. I'm Rich. How are you?
> ☑ Oh, really? Is Susan Miller in your class?
> ☑ No, I'm not. I'm on vacation. Are you a student?

Sarah: Hello, I'm Sarah.

Rich: *Hi, Sarah. I'm Rich. How are you?*

Sarah: Pretty good, thanks. Are you a student here?

Rich: No, I'm not. I'm on vacation. Are you a student

Sarah: Yes, I am.

Rich: And what are you studying?

Sarah: I'm studying Spanish.

Rich: Oh, really? Is Susan Miller in your class?

Sarah: Yes, she is. Is she your friend?

Rich: No, she's not. She's my sister!

---

9   *Complete the answers to the questions. Use contractions where possible.*

> **Grammar note: Contractions**
>
> **Do not use contractions for short answers with Yes:**
>   A: Are you from Argentina?   A: Is he from Greece?
>   B: Yes, I am. (*not* Yes, I'm.)   B: Yes, he is. (*not* Yes, he's.)

Alex: Hello. _____ I'm _____ Alex Lam.

And this is my sister Amy.

Tina: Hi. _____ I'm _____ Tina Fernandez.

Amy: Are you from South America, Tina?

Tina: Yes, I am . I'm from Argentina.

Where are you and your sister from, Alex?

Alex: We're from Taiwan.

Tina: Are you from Taipei?

Alex: No, I'm not . I'm from Tainan.

Say, are you in English 101?

Tina: No, I'm not . I'm in English 102.

10 **Look at the answers. What are the questions?**

1. A: _Are you on vacation here?_
   B: No, I'm not on vacation. I'm a student here.

2. A: _Where Are you from Spain?_
   B: No, we're not from Spain. We're from Mexico.

3. A: _Are they on the same baseball team?_
   B: No, they're not on the same baseball team. They're on the same volleyball team.

4. A: _Are they in your class?_ // _Are Kim and Mika in your class_
   B: Yes, Kim and Mika are in my class.

5. A: _It's like your class?_ // _It's nice your class?_
   B: Yes, it's a nice class.

6. A: _Is Mr. Brown your teacher?_ _Is your teacher Mr B_
   B: No, my teacher isn't Mr. Brown. I'm in Ms. West's class.

11 **Look at the statements. Which statements say "hello"?
Which ones say "good-bye"?**

Homework

	Saying "hello"	Saying "good-bye"
1. How are you?	✓	☐
2. See you later.	☐	✓
3. Take care.	☐	✓
4. How's everything?	✓	☐
5. Good evening.	✓	☐
6. Good night.	☐	✓

12 **Answer these questions about yourself. Use contractions where possible.**

Homework

1. Where are you from? _I am from Delicias_

2. Are you on vacation? _I am not, I am student_

3. Are you a student at a university? _Yes I am_

4. Are you studying English? _Yes, I am_

2 How do you spend your day?

1 Match the words in columns A and B. Write the names of the jobs.

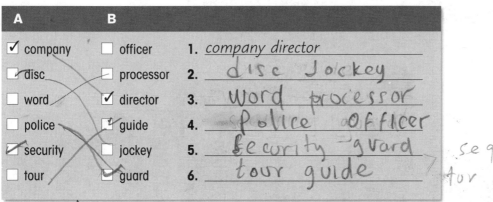

A	B	
☑ company	☐ officer	**1.** _company director_
☐ disc	☐ processor	**2.** disc Jockey
☐ word	☑ director	**3.** word processor
☐ police	☐ guide	**4.** police officer
☑ security	☐ jockey	**5.** security guard
☐ tour	☑ guard	**6.** tour guide

I

sequrity gard
tour gaid

2 Write the sentences. Use **He** or **She**.

1. I'm a security guard. I work in a department store. I guard the store at night.

   He's a security guard. He works in a
   department store. He guards the store at night.

2. I work in a travel agency and take people on tours. I'm a tour guide.

   eyency

   She works in a travel agency and
   takes people on tours. she's
   a tour guide

3. I work in an office. I'm a word processor. I like computers a lot.

   complurer

   He Workin an office. He's a word
   He Likes computer a Lot

4. I'm a disc jockey. I work in a nightclub. I play music.

   naigtclub

   She's a disc Jockey. I work in a
   nightclub. She play music

3 *Write a or an in the correct places.*

> ### Grammar note: *Articles* a *and* an
>
> **Use** *a* **+ singular noun before a consonant sound.**
> **Use** *an* **+ singular noun before a vowel sound.**
>
> He is **a c**arpenter.   He is **an a**rchitect.
> He is **a g**ood carpenter.   He is **an e**xpensive architect.
>
> **Do not use** *a* **or** *an* **+ plural nouns:**
> They are carpenter**s**.   They are expensive architect**s**.

1. He's *a* carpenter. He works for *a* construction company. He builds schools and hospitals.

2. She works for *a* travel company and arranges tours. She's *a* travel agent.

3. He has *an* interesting job. He's *a* teacher. He works in *a* high school.

4. She's *an* architect. She works for *a* large company. She builds houses. It's great job.

5. She works with computers in *an* office. She's *a* word processor. She's also part-time student. She takes English class in the evening.

4 **Complete this conversation with the correct words.**

Tom: What ___does___ your husband ___do___ exactly?
  (do/does)   (do/does)

Liz: He ___works___ for a department store. He's a store manager.
  (work/works)

Tom: How ___does___ he ___like___ it?
  (do/does)   (like/likes)

Liz: It's an interesting job. He ___likes___ it very much.
  (like/likes)

  But he ___works___ long hours. And what ___do___ you ___do___ ?
  (work/works)   (do/does)   (do/does)

Tom: I'm a student. I ___study___ architecture.
  (study/studies)

Liz: Oh, really? Where ___do___ you ___go___ to school?
  (do/does)   (go/goes)

Tom: I ___go___ to Lincoln University. My wife, Jenny, ___goes___ there, too.
  (go/goes)   (go/goes)

Liz: Really? And what ___does___ she ___study___ ?
  (do/does)   (study/studies)

Tom: She ___studies___ hotel management.
  (study/studies)

Liz: That sounds interesting.

5 **Complete the questions in this conversation.**

Mark: Where _do you work?_

Victor: I work for American Express.

Mark: And what ___do you do___ there?

Victor: I'm in management.

Mark: How ___do you like your job?___

Victor: It's a great job. And what ___do you do?___

Mark: I'm a salesperson.

Victor: Really? What ___do you do exactly?___

Mark: I sell computers. Do you want to buy one?

9

Homework

6 Read these two interviews, and answer the questions.

Today, *Job Talk* interviews two people with interesting jobs.

Job Talk: Felix, where do you work?

Felix: I work at home, and I work in Europe a lot.

Job Talk: Really? Well, what do you do at home?

Felix: I'm a chef. I practice cooking new things, and then I write cookbooks.

Job Talk: That sounds interesting. And what do you do in Europe?

Felix: I make TV programs about Chinese cooking.

Job Talk: You have an interesting life, Felix.

Felix: Yes, but it's hard work!

Job Talk: How do you like your job, Julia?

Julia: I love it, but I work long hours.

Job Talk: Do you work late?

Julia: Yes, I work until eight or nine o'clock in the evening. But I take three or four hours for lunch.

Job Talk: Really! But what do you do exactly?

Julia: I stay in all the best new hotels and . . .

Job Talk: Are you a hotel manager?

Julia: No, I'm an electrician! I do the electrical work in new hotels.

1. What does Felix do?   He _____

2. What does he do in Europe?   _____

3. When does Julia finish work?   She _____

4. What does she do?   _____

7 Meet Pat. Write questions about Pat using What, Where, *and* How.

1. *How does he spend his day?*
2. Where does he to work?
3. What does he does there?
4. How does he Like your Job?

MERCY HOSPITAL

Patrick Kennedy

Registered Nurse/Night Shift

8 *How does Pat spend his weekends? Complete this paragraph with the words from the list.*

☐ around ☑ at ☐ before ☐ early ☑ in ☐ late ☑ on ☐ until

Everyone knows Pat at the hospital. Pat is a part-time night nurse. He cares for patients at night. _____On_____ Saturdays and Sundays, Pat sleeps most of the day and wakes up a little _____before_____ nine _____in_____ the evening, usually at 8:45 or 8:50. He has breakfast very late, _____at_____ 9:30 or 10:00 P.M.! He watches television _____until_____ eleven o'clock, and then starts work _____around_____ midnight. _____early_____ in the morning, usually around 5 A.M., he leaves work, has a little snack, goes home, goes to bed, and sleeps _____late_____. It's a hard schedule, but he loves his work.

9 *Use these words to complete the crossword puzzle.*

☑ answers   ☑ sells   ☑ types
☐ does   ☑ serves ☑ works
☑ gets   ☑ starts ☑ writes
☑ goes   ☑ takes

Across

1 Lauren _____ work at 5:00 P.M.
4 Brandon _____ in a restaurant.
5 Ellen _____ up early in the morning.
7 The Elephant Restaurant _____ good Thai food.
9 Rodney _____ to bed after midnight.
10 Andrea is a receptionist. She _____ the phone and greets people.

Down

2 Linda is a tour guide. She _____ people on tours.
3 She _____ 100 words a minute on her new computer.
4 Julia _____ about five letters a week.
6 My father works in a bookstore. He _____ books and magazines.
8 What _____ your sister do?

11

Homework

10 ***These sentences usually have the same meaning.***

He's an aerobics teacher. = He teaches aerobics.

Choose the sentences in the box that have the same meaning as the sentences below.

> ☐ He goes to the university.
> ☐ She serves food in a restaurant.
> ☐ She stays up late.
> ☐ What does he do?
> ☑ He's an aerobics teacher.
> ☐ He works part time.

1. He teaches aerobics.

   He's an aerobics teacher.

2. Where does he work?

   _____

3. She's a waitress.

   _____

4. He's a student.

   _____

5. She goes to bed at midnight.

   _____

6. He works four hours every day.

   _____

---

11 ***Fill in the missing words or phrases from these job advertisements.***

1. ☐ at night
   ☐ part time
   ☐ weekends
   ☑ nurses

2. ☐ Interesting
   ☐ Spanish
   ☐ tours

3. ☐ manager
   ☐ long hours
   ☐ restaurant
   ☐ until

New York Hospital needs
__*nurses*__ .

Work during the day or
_____ ,

weekdays or
_____ ,

full time or
_____ .

Call 278-1191.

_____
job for language student.

Mornings only. Take people
on _____ .

Need good English and
_____ .

Call 989-3239.

No need to work
_____ !

Only work from 6:00
_____ 11:00

four evenings a week. Our
_____

serves great food! Work as our
_____ .

Call 735-6845.

12

3 How much is it?

1 Choose the correct sentences to complete this conversation.

- ☐ Which one?
- ☑ Which ones?
- ☐ Oh, Sam. Thank you very much.
- ☐ Well, I like it, but it's expensive.
- ☐ Yes. But I don't really like light blue!

Sam: Look at those pants, Rebecca.

Rebecca: *Which ones?* _____

Sam: The light blue ones over there. They're nice.

Rebecca: _____

Sam: Hmm. Well, what about that sweater? It's perfect for you.

Rebecca: _____

Sam: This red one.

Rebecca: _____

Sam: Hey, let me buy it for you. It's a present!

Rebecca: _____

2 Complete these conversations with How much is/are . . . ? and this, that, these, or those.

1. A: *How much is this* _____ backpack?
   B: It's $31.99.

2. A: _____ bracelets?
   B: They're $29.

3. A: _____ shoes?
   B: They're $64.

4. A: _____ dog?
   B: That's my dog, and he's not for sale!

3 Write the plurals of these words.

Spelling note: Plural nouns

Most words:		Words ending in *-ss, -sh, -ch*, and *-x*:	
cap	cap**s**	glass	glass**es**
shoe	shoe**s**	watch	watch**es**

Words ending in *-fe*:		Words ending in consonant + *-y*:	
knife	kni**ves**	country	countr**ies**

1. backpack   *backpacks*
2. bookshelf   _____
3. dress   _____
4. company   _____
5. glove   _____
6. hairbrush   _____

7. necklace   _____
8. ring   _____
9. scarf   _____
10. sweater   _____
11. tie   _____
12. dish   _____

4 What do you think of these prices? Write a response.

That's cheap.	That's not bad.	That's reasonable.	That's pretty expensive!

1. $90 for a tie

   That's pretty expensive!

2. $10 for two scarves

   _____

3. $500 for a dress

   _____

4. $40 for gloves

   _____

5. $2,000 for a computer

   _____

6. $5 for two hairbrushes

   _____

5 *Choose the correct words to complete these conversations.*

1. Clerk: Good afternoon.

   Luis: Oh, hi. How much is _____*this*_____ watch?
   (this/these)

   Clerk: It's $195.

   Luis: And how much is that _____ ?
   (one/ones)

   Clerk: _____ $255.
   (It's/They're)

   Luis: Oh, really? Well, thanks, anyway.

2. Kim: Excuse me. How much are _____ jeans?
   (that/those)

   Clerk: _____ only $59.
   (It's/They're)

   Kim: And how much is _____ sweater?
   (this/these)

   Clerk: Which _____ ? They're all different.
   (one/ones)

   Kim: I like this green _____ .
   (one/ones)

   Clerk: _____ $34.
   (It's/They're)

   Kim: Well, that's not bad.

3. Sonia: I like _____ sunglasses over there.
   (that/those)

   Clerk: Which _____ ?
   (one/ones)

   Sonia: The small brown _____ .
   (one/ones)

   Clerk: _____ $199.
   (It's/They're)

   Sonia: Oh, they're expensive!

6 **What do you make out of these materials? Complete the chart.**
Use words from the list. (You will use words more than once.)

| boots | pants | bracelet | ring | gloves | shirt | jacket | necklace |

Cotton	Gold	Leather	Silk	Plastic	Wool
pants					

---

7 **Make comparisons using the words given. Add than if necessary.**

cotton gloves

1. A: These cotton gloves are nice.

   B: Yes, but the leather ones are _____*nicer*_____ . (nice)

   A: They're also *the most expensive* . (expensive)

leather gloves

silk jackets

2. A: Those silk jackets look __*more attractive than*__
   the wool ones. (attractive)

   B: Yes, but the wool ones are _____*warmer*_____ . (warm)

wool jackets

purple shirt

3. A: This purple shirt is an interesting color!

   B: Yes, but the color is __*prettier than*__
   the design. (pretty)

   A: The design isn't bad.

   B: I think the design on that red shirt is __*better than*__
   the design on this purple one. (good)

red shirt

$650 $1000

4. A: Hey, look at this gold ring! It's nice.

   And it's __*cheaper than*__ that silver ring. (cheap)

   B: But it's __*smaller than*__ the silver one. (small)

   A: Well, yeah. The silver one is __*bigger than*__ the gold one. (big)
   But look at the price tag. One thousand dollars is a lot of money
   for a ring!

8 *Complete the chart. Use words from the list.*

☐ bracelet   ☐ necklace   ☐ compact disc player
☐ computer   ☐ dress   ☐ sweater
☐ earrings   ☐ ring   ☐ television
☑ cap   ☐ athletic shoes ☐ laptop computer

Clothing	Electronics	Jewelry
cap	computer	bracelet
dress	compact disc player	earrings
athletic shoes	television	necklace
sweater	laptop computer	ring

9 *Answer these questions. Give your own information.*

1 small earrings   **2** wool cap   **3** high-top shoes   **4** laptop computer   **5** 19-inch television

large earrings   leather cap   tennis shoes   desktop computer   25-inch television

1. Which ones do you prefer, the small earrings or the large earrings?
   I prefer the small ones.
2. Which cap do you like more, the wool one or the leather one?
   I like the leather one
3. Which ones do you like more, the high-tops or the tennis shoes?
   I like more the tennis ones
4. Which one do you prefer, the laptop computer or the desktop computer?
   I prefer the laptop one
5. Which television do you like better, the 19-inch one or the 25-inch one?
   I like the 25 inch one

17

10 *Great gadgets!*

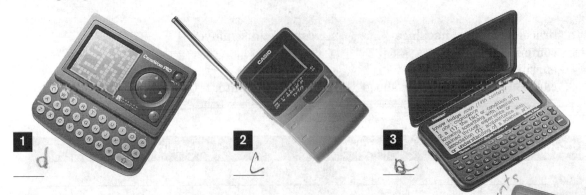

1 _d_   **2** _c_   **3** _a_   **4** _b_

A Match the ads and the pictures.

a. Find the correct spelling and pronunciation of more than 80,000 words with this electronic dictionary! Made of strong plastic. Comes in two colors, dark gray or light blue. $104.50. *four hundred four. dollars and fifty cents*

b. Use the electronic address book for the names and addresses of all your friends. Takes up to 400 names, addresses, and phone numbers. Plastic case included. Regular model $59.95. Desktop model available for $64.95. *four hundred) fifty Nine dolars and naintyfive*

c. Watch your favorite baseball game at work or at school! This TV fits in your pocket, only 6" × 1" (15 cm × 2 cm). Gives an excellent picture. Yours for only $299.50.

d. Problems with a crossword puzzle? Try this crossword puzzle solver! Simply key in the letters you know and a "?" for the ones you don't know. In seconds, the gadget fills the blanks. Has a database of 130,000 words. Great value at only $49.95.

B Check (✔) True or False.

tru

	True	False
1. The electronic dictionary comes in many colors.	✔	☐
2. The desktop model of the electronic address book is more expensive than the regular model.	✔	☐
3. The pocket television is about $300. *tri Jaund*	✔	☐
4. The crossword puzzle solver can find the answers.	✔	☐

C Which one is your favorite? Number the items from 1 (you like it the most) to 4 (you like it the least).

_2_ electronic dictionary   _4_ pocket television

_1_ electronic address book   _3_ crossword puzzle solver

4 Do you like jazz?

1 *Check (✓) the boxes to complete the survey about music and movies.*

1 How often do you listen to these types of music?

	Often	Sometimes	Not often
pop	☐	☐	☐
classical	☐	☐	☐
gospel *relig☐ios▢*	☐	☐
rock	☐	☐	☐
jazz	☐	☐	☐

2 How often do you watch these types of movies?

	Often	Sometimes	Not often
science fiction	☐	☐	☐
horror films	☐	☐	☐
thrillers	☐	☐	☐
westerns	☐	☐	☐
comedies	☐	☐	☐

2 *What do you think of these kinds of entertainment? Answer the questions with the expressions and pronouns in the box.*

Yes, I do.	Object pronouns
I love	him
I like . . . a lot.	her
No, I don't.	it
I don't like . . . very much.	them
I can't stand	

Tom Cruise

Demi Moore

1. Do you like jazz?
   Yes, I do. I like it a lot.

2. Do you like Tom Cruise?
   Yes, I do. I like him a lot

3. Do you like rap?
   No, I don't. I don't like it very much

4. Do you like Demi Moore?
   No, I don't. I don't like her very much

5. Do you like TV game shows?
   No, I don't. I don't like them very much

6. Do you like soap operas?

3 *Choose the correct job for each picture.*

☐ an actor   ☑ a rock group   ☑ a pop singer   ☐ a TV talk show host

1. Mariah Carey is _____
   a pop singer

2. The Rolling Stones are _____
   a rock group

3. Oprah Winfrey is _____
   a TV talk show host

4. Bruce Willis is _____
   an actor

4 *Complete these conversations.*

Garth Brooks

1. Ed: _____*Do*_____ you _____*like*_____ country music, Sarah?

   Sarah: Yes, I _____*do*_____ it a lot. I'm a real fan of Garth Brooks.

   Ed: Oh, _____*is*_____ he play the guitar?

   Sarah: Yes, he _____*is play*_____ . He's my favorite musician.

2. Anne: _____*what*_____ kind of music _____*like*_____ ?

   your parents _____ , Jason?

   Jason: They _____ classical music.

   Anne: Who _____ they _____ ? Mozart?

   Jason: No, they _____ like him very much. They prefer Beethoven.

3. Scott: Teresa, _____ you _____ Mariah Carey?

   Teresa: No, I _____ . I can't stand her. I like Celine Dion.

   Scott: I don't know her. What kind of music _____ she sing?

   Teresa: She _____ pop songs. She's really great!

5 *Complete these questions and write answers.*

1. *What kinds* of movies do you like? _____

2. _____ is your favorite movie? _____

3. _____ of TV shows do you like? _____

4. _____ is your favorite TV actor or actress? _____

5. _____ is your favorite song? _____

6. _____ is your favorite rock group? _____

6 *What do you think? Answer these questions.*

funny

scary

1. Which films are funnier, horror films or comedies?
   Comedies are funnier than horror films.

2. Which movies are more interesting, thrillers or science fiction films?

   _____

3. Which films are scarier, horror films or thrillers?

   _____

4. Which films are more exciting, comedies or thrillers?

   _____

7 *Collocation*

A Which nouns often go with which verbs? Complete the chart.
Use each word only once.

play	listen to	watch
the piano	_____	_____
_____	_____	_____
_____	_____	_____

☑ the piano   ☐ the guitar
☐ videos   ☐ a film
☐ jazz   ☐ the trumpet
☐ TV   ☐ CDs
☐ music

B Write a sentence with each verb.

1. _____

2. _____

3. _____

8 *Movie guide*

A Read the movie guide. Choose a title from the box for each review.

☐ A Question of $1 Million   ☐ Then and Now   ☐ The Best Man Wins

1.
_____

A crazy scientist makes a time machine and travels back in time 1,000 years. She learns some interesting things about life in the past. She has a problem with her time machine and almost doesn't come back to the present. But everything is OK in the end. A great movie.

2.
_____

In this movie, Rosie Stamp works for an electronics company. As usual, she is very funny. One night, someone takes a million dollars from the company. The police think Rosie Stamp took the money. But it's all a big mistake. The film will make you laugh a lot!

3.
_____

In this classic movie, Terence Neal is the good guy and Alex White is the bad guy. They are cowboys, and they are in love with the same woman. For most of the movie, it looks like the bad guy will marry her. It looks like she prefers him. But, of course, the good guy marries her in the end.

B What kinds of movies are they? Check (✓) the answers.

1. ☐ horror film   2. ☐ classic   3. ☐ western
   ☐ science fiction   ☐ thriller   ☐ comedy
   ☐ travel film   ☐ comedy   ☐ science fiction

9 *Choose the correct responses.*

1. A: Would you like to see a movie this weekend?

   B: *That sounds great!*
   - That sounds great!
   - I don't agree.

2. A: Do you like gospel music?

   B: _____
   - I can't stand it.
   - I can't stand them.

3. A: There's a baseball game tonight.

   B: _____
   - Thanks. I'd love to.
   - Great. Let's go.

4. A: What do you think of Tina Turner?

   B: _____
   - How about you?
   - I'm not a real fan of hers.

Tina Turner

10 *Yes or no?*

A Jake invites friends to a movie. Do people accept the invitation or not? Check (✓) Yes or No for each response.

Accept?	Yes	No
1. I'd love to, but I have to work until midnight.	☐	✓
2. I'd love to. What time does it start?	☐	☐
3. Thanks. I'd really like to. What time do you want to meet?	☐	☐
4. Thanks, but I'm not a real fan of his.	☐	☐
5. That sounds great.	☐	☐

There's a Tom Cruise movie at the Central Theater tonight. Would you like to see it?

B Respond to these invitations.

1. I have tickets to a rap concert on Saturday. Would you like to go?

   _____

2. There's a soccer game tonight. Would you like to go with me?

   _____

11 **Choose the correct phrases to complete these conversations.**

1. Robin: _Do you like_____ gospel music, Kate?
   (Do you like/Would you like)

   Kate: Yes, I do. _____ it a lot.
   (I like/I'd like)

   Robin: There's a concert on Friday. _____
   (Do you like/Would you like)

   to go with me?

   Kate: Yes, _____ . Thanks.
   (I love to/I'd love to)

2. Carlos: _____ to go to a French film at 11:00 tonight?
   (Do you like/Would you like)

   Phil: _____ , but I have to study tonight.
   (I like to/I'd like to)

   Carlos: Well, _____ Brazilian films?
   (do you like/would you like)

   Phil: Yes, I _____ . I love them!
   (do/would)

   Carlos: There's a great Brazilian movie on TV tomorrow.

   _____ to watch it with me?
   (Do you like/Would you like)

   Phil: _____ . Thanks.
   (I like to/I'd love to)

12 **Rewrite these sentences. Find another way to say each
sentence using the words given.**

1. Do you like jazz?

   _What do you think of jazz?_____ (think of)

2. Richard doesn't like classical music.

   _____ (can't stand)

3. I think horror films are great!

   _____ (love)

4. She doesn't like country music.

   _____ (be a fan of)

5. Do you want to go to a baseball game?

   _____ (would like)

5 Tell me about your family.

1 **Complete the chart. Use words from the list.**

- ☑ aunt
- ☑ brother
- ☐ daughter
- ☐ father
- ☐ husband
- ☐ mother
- ☐ nephew
- ☐ niece
- ☐ sister
- ☐ son
- ☐ uncle
- ☐ wife

Male	Female
brother ♂	aunt ♀

2 **Complete this conversation. Use the present continuous of the verbs given.**

Joel: You look tired, Don. ___Are you studying___ (study)
late at night these days?

Don: No, I'm not. My brother and sister _____ (stay)
with me right now. We go to bed after midnight every night.

Joel: Really? What _____ (do) this
summer? _____ (take) classes, too?

Don: No, they aren't. My brother is on vacation now, but he
_____ (look) for a part-time job here.

Joel: What about your sister? _____
(work)?

Don: Yes, she is. She has a part-time job at the university.
What about you, Joel? Are you in school this summer?

Joel: Yes, I am. I _____ (study)
two languages.

Don: Oh, _____ (take) French and
Spanish again?

Joel: Well, I'm taking Spanish again,
but I _____ (start) Japanese.

Don: Really? That's exciting!

25

3 *Rewrite these sentences. Find another way to say each sentence using the words given.*

1. Joseph is Maria's uncle.
   Maria is Joseph's niece. _____ (niece)

2. Liz is married to Peter.
   Peter is _____ (husband)

3. I'm single.
   _____ (married)

4. We have two children.
   _____ (son and daughter)

5. My wife's father is a painter.
   _____ (father-in-law)

6. Michael does not have a job right now.
   _____ (look for)

4 *Choose the correct sentences to complete this conversation.*

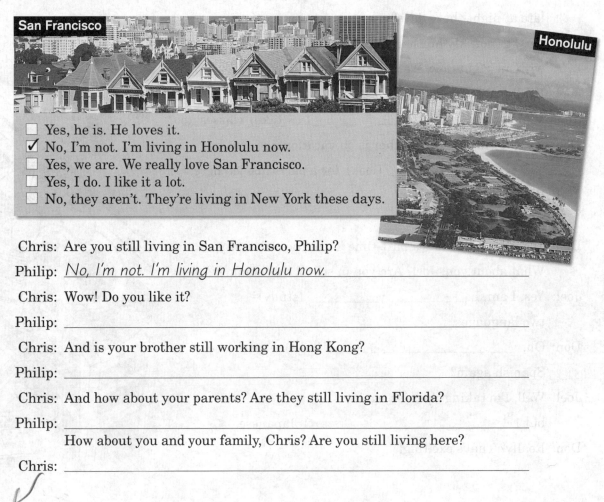

San Francisco

Honolulu

- ☐ Yes, he is. He loves it.
- ☑ No, I'm not. I'm living in Honolulu now.
- ☐ Yes, we are. We really love San Francisco.
- ☐ Yes, I do. I like it a lot.
- ☐ No, they aren't. They're living in New York these days.

Chris: Are you still living in San Francisco, Philip?

Philip: *No, I'm not. I'm living in Honolulu now.* _____

Chris: Wow! Do you like it?

Philip: _____

Chris: And is your brother still working in Hong Kong?

Philip: _____

Chris: And how about your parents? Are they still living in Florida?

Philip: _____
         How about you and your family, Chris? Are you still living here?

Chris: _____

5 **Complete these sentences. Use the simple present or the present continuous of the verbs given.**

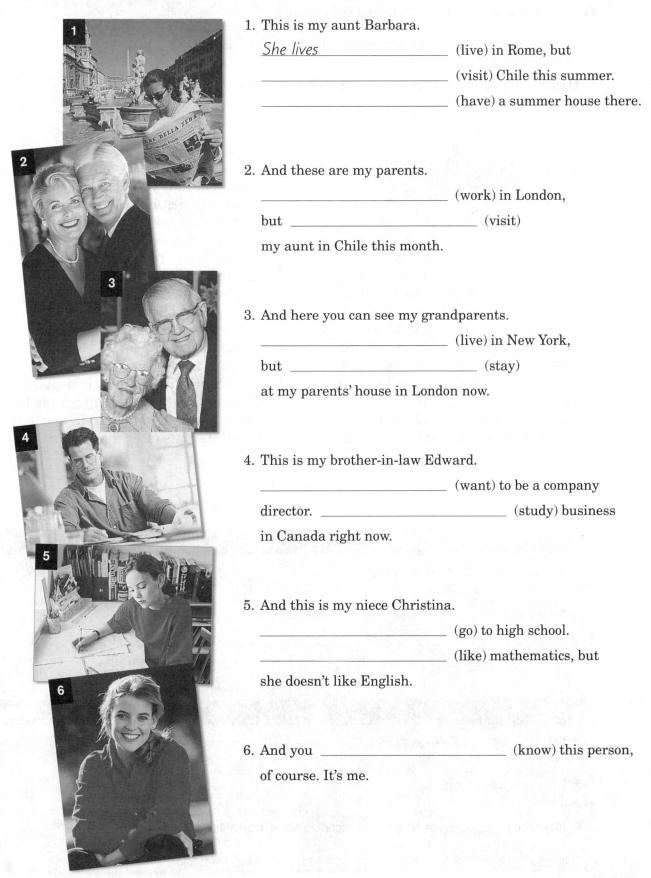

1. This is my aunt Barbara.

   She lives _____ (live) in Rome, but

   _____ (visit) Chile this summer.

   _____ (have) a summer house there.

2. And these are my parents.

   _____ (work) in London,

   but _____ (visit)

   my aunt in Chile this month.

3. And here you can see my grandparents.

   _____ (live) in New York,

   but _____ (stay)

   at my parents' house in London now.

4. This is my brother-in-law Edward.

   _____ (want) to be a company

   director. _____ (study) business

   in Canada right now.

5. And this is my niece Christina.

   _____ (go) to high school.

   _____ (like) mathematics, but

   she doesn't like English.

6. And you _____ (know) this person,

   of course. It's me.

6 Home or away?

A Answer these questions. Then read the passage.

1. At what age do most young people leave their parents' home in your country? _____

2. Do some young people live with their parents after they get married? _____

Leaving Home

Young people leave their parents' homes at different ages in different parts of the world.

In the United States, a lot of college students do not live at home. Many choose to go to college in different cities – away from their parents. At college, they live in university housing. After college, most people prefer to live in their own homes. They often live alone, but some people rent apartments with others.

These people are *roommates*. By the age of 22, few young people in the United States live with their parents.

Families stay together longer in many Asian countries and cities. In Hong Kong, for example, nearly all university students live with their parents. Rents in the city are very expensive, and few students have the money to pay for their own apartments.

Very few young people live alone or become roommates in a shared apartment. Many young people in Hong Kong continue to live with their parents after they marry.

B Check (✓) True or False. For statements that are false, write the true information.

In the United States	True	False
1. Very few students live in university housing.	☐	☐
2. Some young adults share apartments with roommates.	☐	☐
3. Nearly all young adults live with their parents.	☐	☐

In Hong Kong	True	False
4. Not many students live with their parents.	☐	☑
5. Few young people live alone.	☑	☐
6. Most young married couples have enough money to live in their own apartments.	☐	☑

28

7 *Arrange the determiners from the most to the least.*

☐ a lot of	☐ no	1. *all*	6. _Some_
☐ most	☐ few ᶠˡᵘ	2. _nearly all_	7. _not many_
☐ a few	☐ not many	3. _most (mous)_	8. _a few_
☐ nearly all	☐ many	4. _many_	9. _few_
☑ all (all)	☐ some (som)	5. _a lot few_	10. _no one_

8 *Rewrite these sentences using the determiners given.*

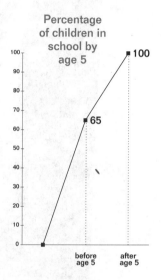

Percentage of children in school by age 5

1. Sixty-five percent of children start school before the age of five. A hundred percent of children go to school after the age of five.
   ☐ all   ☑ many

   Many children start school before the age of five.
   _____
   _____

2. Ninety-five percent of young people get a job after they finish high school. Only twenty percent go to college.
   ☐ nearly all   ☐ a few
   _____
   _____
   _____

What they do after finishing school

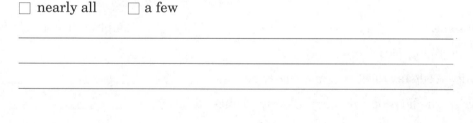
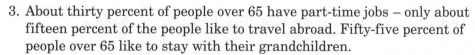

3. About thirty percent of people over 65 have part-time jobs – only about fifteen percent of the people like to travel abroad. Fifty-five percent of people over 65 like to stay with their grandchildren.
   ☐ many   ☐ not many   ☐ few
   _____
   _____
   _____

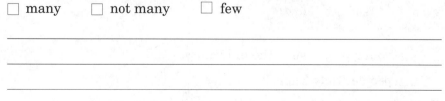

Activities of those over age 65

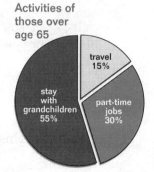

travel 15%

stay with grandchildren 55%

part-time jobs 30%

Homework

9 **Choose the correct words or phrases to complete this paragraph.**

In my country, some _____ *couples* _____ (couples/cousins/relatives)

get married fairly young. Not many marriages _____

(break up/get divorced/stay together), and nearly all _____

(divorced/married/single) people remarry. Elderly couples often _____

(divorce again/move away/live at home) and take care of their grandchildren.

10 **Complete these sentences about your country. Use the words in the box.**

all	most	a lot of	some	few

1. I think _____ young people go to the university.

2. I think _____ people study English.

3. I'm not sure, but I think _____ married couples have more
   than five children.

4. I think _____ elderly people have part-time jobs.

30   *Homework*

6 How often do you exercise?

1

Complete the chart. Use words from the list.
(Some of the words can be both individual sports and exercise.)

basketball	baseball	aerobics
yoga	jogging	bicycling
swimming	football	tennis

Team sport

Team sports	Individual sports	Exercise
basketball	yoga	aerobics
baseball	swimming	yoga
fotball	jogging	bicycling
swimming	bicycling	
tennis	tennis	

Individual sport

Exercise

2

Arrange these words to make sentences.

1. go   never   I   almost   bicycling
   I almost never go bicycling.

2. hardly   they   tennis   play   ever
   they hardly ever play tennis. I am R

3. go   do   often   jogging   how   you
   How often do you go jogging ?

4. often   mornings   do   on   we   yoga   Sunday
   We often do yoga on sunday mornings

5. ever   Charlie   do   does   aerobics
   Does Charlie ever do aerobics ?

6. do   on   you   what   usually   Saturdays   do
   What do you do usually on Saturday?

31

3 *Write questions for these statements.*
Use **How often do you . . . ? Do you ever . . . ?** *and* **What do you usually . . . ?**

1. A: *Do you ever exercise?*

    B: Yes, I often exercise on weekends.

2. A: _____

    B: Well, I usually do karate on Saturdays and yoga on Sundays.

3. A: _____

    B: No, I never go to the gym after work.

4. A: _____

    B: I don't exercise very often at all.

5. A: _____

    B: Yes, I sometimes play sports on weekends – usually baseball.

6. A: _____

    B: I usually play tennis in my free time.

4 *Keeping fit?*

A Check (✓) how often you do each of the things in the chart.

	Every day	Once or twice a week	Sometimes	Not very often	Never
do aerobics	☐	☐	☐	☐	☐
do karate	☐	☐	☐	☐	☐
go jogging	☐	☐	☐	☐	☐
go swimming	☐	☐	☐	☐	☐
exercise	☐	☐	☐	☐	☐
play basketball	☐	☐	☐	☐	☐

B Write about yourself using the information in the chart.
For example:

1. *I don't do aerobics very often.* _____

2. _____

3. _____

4. _____

5. _____

6. _____

5 *Complete this conversation.*
Write the correct prepositions in the correct places.

Susan: What time do you go jogging ᴵⁿ the morning, Jerry? (around/in/on)

Jerry: I always go jogging ____ seven o'clock. (at/for/on)

How about you, Susan?

Susan: I usually go jogging ____ noon. (around/in/with)

I jog ____ about an hour. (at/for/until)

Jerry: And do you also play sports ____ your free time? (at/in/until)

Susan: Not very often. I usually go out ____ my classmates in my free time. (around/for/with)

What about you?

Jerry: I go to the gym ____ Mondays and Wednesdays. (at/on/until)

And sometimes I go bicycling ____ weekends. (for/in/on)

Susan: Wow! You really like to stay in shape.

6 *Complete the crossword puzzle.*

Across

4 Pierre never ____ . He's a real couch potato.

6 How often do you ____ yoga?

7 I like to stay in ____ . I play sports every day.

8 Jeff does weight ____ every evening. He lifts weights of 40 kilos.

10 Diana goes ____ for three miles twice a week.

Down

1 Andrew always watches TV in his ____ time.

2 Kate has a regular ____ program.

3 I do ____ at the gym three times a week. The teacher plays great music!

5 Paul is on the ____ team at his high school.

7 Marie never goes ____ when the water is cold.

9 Amy ____ bicycling twice a month.

7 Choose your activity.

A Read these ads.

Do you enjoy the outdoors? Do you need exercise? Do you like walking and meeting people?

Join the Hiking Club!
Call 745-1191.

We go on a different hike every weekend. Sometimes we go on a two-day hike and camp overnight!

Adult Education Program at Monroe High School.
Mondays to Fridays 6:00 9:00 P.M.

For more information, call 535-6845.

Fall classes: photography; computers for business; typing and word processing; Chinese cooking; Spanish, Portuguese, and Arabic language classes.

Come to the YWCA or YMCA! Look at our new activities!
Aerobics, racquetball, softball, yoga!
For anyone from 9 to 90! Singles, couples, and families welcome.
Friday night, teen disco! Saturday night, seniors night!
Phone us at 235-7439.

B Where can you do these activities? Check (✓) the answers.

	Hiking Club	Adult Education Program	YWCA/ YMCA
Play indoor sports	☐	☐	☐
Do outdoor activities	☐	☐	☐
Take evening classes	☐	☐	☐
Go dancing	☐	☐	☐
Learn to cook	☐	☐	☐
Meet new people	☐	☐	☐

8 *Choose the correct responses.*

1. A: How often do you go swimming, Linda?

   B: *Once a week.*
   - I guess I'm OK.
   - Once a week.
   - About an hour.

2. A: How long do you spend in the swimming pool?

   B: _____
   - About 45 minutes.
   - About average.
   - About three miles.

3. A: And how well do you swim?

   B: _____
   - I'm not very well.
   - I almost never do.
   - I'm about average.

4. A: How good are you at other sports?

   B: _____
   - Not too good, actually.
   - I sometimes play twice a week.
   - Pretty well, I guess.

5. A: How much time do you spend working out?

   B: _____
   - Not very often.
   - Around an hour a day.
   - About three miles twice a week.

9 *Look at the answers. Write questions using* **how.**

1. A: *How much time do you spend exercising* _____ ?

   B: I don't spend much time at all. In fact, I don't ever exercise.
   But I watch a lot of sports on TV.

2. A: _____ for a walk?

   B: Almost every day. I really enjoy it.

3. A: _____ ?

   B: I spend about an hour jogging.

4. A: _____ at racquetball?

   B: I'm pretty good at it. I'm on the school team.

5. A: _____ ?

   B: Basketball? Pretty well, I guess. I like it a lot.

10 **Rewrite these sentences. Find another way to say each sentence, using the words given.**

1. I don't watch TV very much.

   I seldom watch TV. _____ (seldom)

2. Tom exercises twice a month.

   _____ (not very often)

3. Philip tries to keep fit.

   _____ (stay in shape)

4. Jill often exercises at the gym.

   _____ (work out)

5. How long do you spend at the gym?

   _____ (time)

6. How good are you at tennis?

   _____ (play)

11 **What do you think about sports? Answer these questions.**

1. Do you like to exercise for a short time or a long time?

   _____

2. Do you prefer exercising in the morning or in the evening?

   _____

3. Which do you like better, walking or jogging?

   _____

4. Which do you like better, team sports or individual sports?

   _____

5. How good are you at games like basketball or tennis?

   _____

6. Do you prefer fitness freaks or couch potatoes?

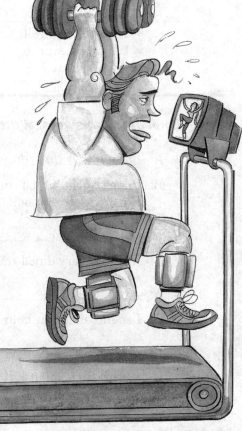

I only exercise for a short time.

7 We had a great time!

1 Past tense

A Write the past tense of these regular verbs.

1. cook ___cooked___
2. enjoy ___enjoyed___
3. invite ___invite d___

4. love ___Loved___
5. study ___studied___
6. try ___tried___

7. visit ___visited___
8. wash ___washed___
9. watch ___watched___

B Write the simple form of these irregular past tense verbs.

1. ___buy___ bought
2. ___give___ gave
3. ___meet___ met
4. ___see___ saw

5. ___sleep___ slept
6. ___spend___ spent
7. ___take___ took
8. ___go___ went

C Use two of the verbs above and write sentences about the past.

We went to a rock concert last night.

2. 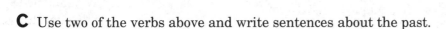 ___We bought Pizza yesterday___
3. ___We saw a movis last night___

2 Use the cues to answer these questions.

1. Where did you go this weekend?

   I went to a party. _____ (to a party)

2. Who did you meet at the party?

   ___I met someone very interesting___ (someone very interesting)

3. What time did you and Eva get home?

   ___We got a little after 1:00___ (a little after 1:00)

4. How did you and Bob like the art exhibition?

   ___We liked a lot the art exhibition___ (a lot)

5. What did you buy?

   ___I bought the new Madonna C.D.___ (the new Madonna CD)

6. Where did Jeff and Joyce go on vacation?

   ___they went to the country___ (to the country)

37

3 *What do you like to do alone? What do you like to do with other people?*
Complete the chart with activities from the list.
Then add one more activity to each list.

Things I like to do alone	Things I like to do with other people	
– read the newspaper – watch TV – see a movie	go shopping do housework exercise have a picnic go to a sport event watch TV	read the newspaper go shopping do housework exercise have a picnic go to a sports event cook dinner take a vacation watch TV see a movie

4 **Complete the questions in this conversation.**

A: How *did you spend your weekend?*

B: I spent the weekend with Joe and Kathy.

A: What did you do on saturday

B: Well, on Saturday, we went shopping.

A: And did you do anything special in the evening?

B: No, nothing special.

A: Where did you go on Sunday?

B: We went to the amusement park.

A: How did you like

B: We had a great time. In fact, we stayed there all day.

A: Really? What time did you get home

B: We got home very late, around midnight.

5   *Answer these questions with negative statements. Then add a positive statement using the information below.*

Grammar note: Past tense negative statements

I **didn't cook** dinner last night.   We **didn't have** a good time.

☑ have a boring time   ☐ finish our homework on Saturday   ☐ go out with friends
☐ watch it on TV   ☐ work all day until six o'clock   ☐ take the bus

1. A: We loved the party. Did you and Jane enjoy it?

   B: *No, we didn't enjoy it. We had a boring time.*

2. A: I stayed home from work yesterday. Did you take the day off, too?

   B: _____

3. A: I slept in all weekend. Did you spend the weekend at home?

   B: _____

4. A: I studied all weekend. Did you and John have a lot of homework, too?

   B: _____

5. A: Carl drove me to work this morning. Did you drive to work?

   B: _____

6. A: Kathy went to the baseball game last night. Did you and Bob go to the game?

   B: _____

---

6   *Read about Andy's week. Match the sentences that have the same meaning.*

A	B
1. He was broke last week. *f*	a. He had people over.
2. He didn't work on Friday. *d*	b. He had a good time.
3. He worked around the house. *e*	c. He didn't do laundry.
4. He didn't wash the clothes. *c*	d. He took a day off.
5. He invited friends for dinner. *a*	e. He did housework.
6. He enjoyed the party. *b*	✓ f. He spent all this money.

7 **Did we take the same trip?**

A Do you ever take summer vacations? What kind of vacations do you like to take: relaxing? educational? exciting?

B Read these reports about Thailand.

A temple in Bangkok, Thailand

William's report

We went to Thailand for our summer vacation last year. It was our first trip to Asia. We loved it. We spent a week in Bangkok and did something different every day. We went to the floating market very early one morning. We didn't buy anything there, we just looked. Another day, we went to Wat Phra Keo, the famous Temple of the Emerald Buddha. It was really interesting. Then we saw two more temples nearby. We also went on a river trip somewhere outside Bangkok. The best thing about the trip was the food. The next time we have friends over for dinner, I'm going to cook Thai food.

Sue's report

Last summer, we spent our vacation in Thailand. We were very excited – it was our first trip there. We spent two days in Bangkok. Of course, we got a river bus to the floating market. We bought some delicious fruit there. The next day we went to a very interesting temple called the Temple of the Emerald Buddha. We didn't have time to visit any other temples. However, we went to two historic cities – Ayuthaya and Sukhothai. Both have really interesting ruins. Everything was great. It's impossible to say what was the best thing about the trip.

C Who did these things on their trip? Check (✓) the answers.

	William	Sue
1. visited Thailand for the first time	✓	✓
2. stayed for two days in Bangkok	☐	☐
3. visited the floating market	☐	☐
4. bought food in Bangkok	☐	☐
5. saw some historic ruins	☐	☐
6. took a trip on the river	☐	☐
7. loved the food the most	☐	☐
8. enjoyed everything	☐	☐

8 *Complete this conversation with* **was, wasn't, were,** *or* **weren't.**

A: How ___was___ your vacation in Peru, Julia?

B: It ___was___ great. I really enjoyed it.

A: How long ___were___ you there?

B: We ___were___ there for two weeks.

A: ___Were___ you in Lima all the time?

B: No, we ___weren't___ . We ___were___ in the mountains
for a few days.

A: And how ___was___ the weather? ___Was___ it good?

B: No, it ___wasn't___ good at all. The city ___was___
very hot, and the mountains ___were___ really cold!

9 *Choose the correct questions to complete this conversation.*

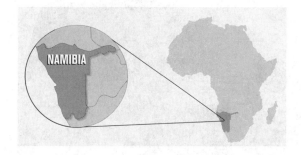

Namibian meerkats

☐ And how did you like it?
☐ How long were you in South Africa?
☑ How was your vacation in Africa?
☐ And how long were you in Namibia?
☐ How was the weather?

A: *How was your vacation in Africa?*

B: It was a great trip. I really enjoyed South Africa and Namibia.

A: ___How long were you in south Africa___

B: For ten days.

A: ___And how long were you in Namibia___

B: I was in Namibia for about five days.

A: Wow, that's a long time. ___how was the weather___

B: It was hot and sunny the whole time.

A: ___and how did you like it___

B: Oh, it was wonderful. And the wildlife was terrific –
we saw some meerkats!

41

10 *Choose the correct words or phrases.*

1. The neighbors had a ___noisy___ party till 3:00 A.M.
   We complained about it.   (noisy/fun/birthday)

2. We didn't see very much in the mountains. The weather was
   ___foggy___.   (cool/rainy/foggy)

3. We went on a ___tour___ of the ruins.   (tour/trip/vacation)

4. I worked very hard in Switzerland. I was there
   ___on business___ .   (on business/in my car/on vacation)

11 *My kind of vacation*

A What do you like to do on vacation? Rank the
activities below from 1 (you like it the most)
to 6 (you like it the least).

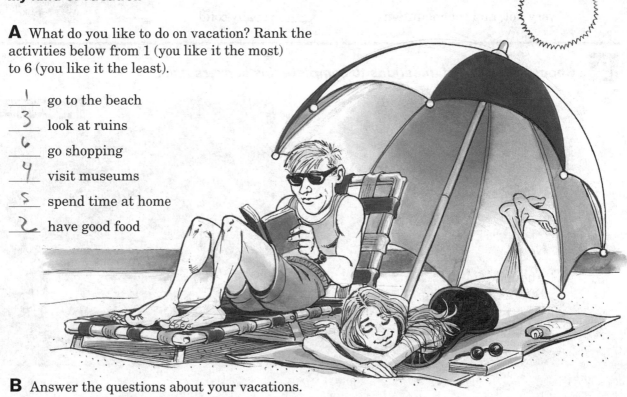

___1___ go to the beach

___3___ look at ruins

___6___ go shopping

___4___ visit museums

___5___ spend time at home

___2___ have good food

B Answer the questions about your vacations.

1. How often do you go on vacation?

_____

2. How long do you spend on vacation?

_____

3. Who do you usually go with?

_____

4. Where do you usually go?

_____

5. What do you usually do on vacation?

_____

8 How do you like the neighborhood?

1 *Places*

A Match the words in columns A and B. Write the names of the places.

A	B	
☑ barber	☐ agency	1. *barber shop*
☐ dance	☐ phone	2. _____
☐ gas	☑ shop	3. _____
☐ grocery	☐ station	4. _____
☐ movie	☐ center	5. _____
☐ pay	☐ store	6. _____
☐ post	☐ theater	7. _____
☐ shopping	☐ club	8. _____
☐ travel	☐ office	9. _____

B Write questions with "Is there a . . . ?" or "Are there any . . . ?" and the names of places from part A.

1. A: I need a haircut. _____ *Is there a barber shop* _____ near here?

   B: Yes, there's one on Elm Street.

2. A: We want to go dancing. _____ near here?

   B: No, there aren't, but there are some on Main Street.

3. A: I want to send this letter. _____ around here?

   B: Yes, there's one next to the laundromat.

4. A: I need to make a phone call. _____
   around here?

   B: Yes, there are some across from the library.

5. A: I need some gas. _____ on this street?

   B: No, there aren't, but there are a couple on Second Avenue.

6. A: We need to make a reservation for a trip.
   _____ near here?

   B: Yes, there's one near the Sheraton Hotel.

Homework   43

Homework

2 Look at these two street maps. There are ten differences between them. Find the other eight. Write about them as in the examples.

> **Grammar note: There are; some *and* any**
>
> | Positive statement | Negative statement |
> |---|---|
> | There **are some** pay phones near the bank. | There **aren't any** pay phones near the bank. |

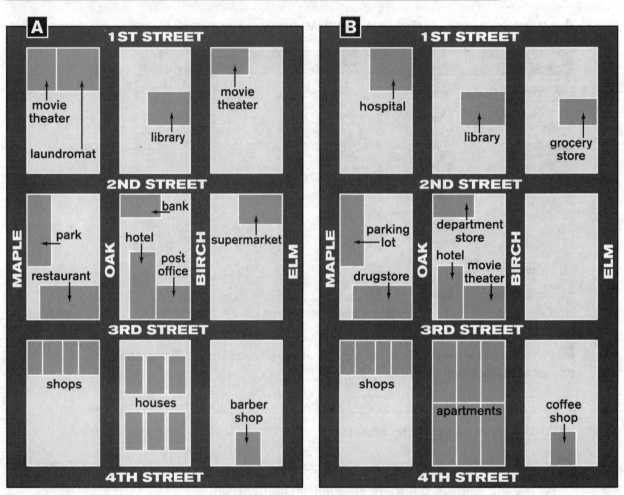

1. <u>*There are some movie theaters on 1st Street in A, but there aren't any in B.*</u>
2. <u>*There's a park on the corner of 2nd Street and Maple in A, but there isn't one in B. There's a parking lot.*</u>
3. _____
4. _____
5. _____
6. _____
7. _____
8. _____
9. _____
10. _____

3 **Answer these questions. Use the map and the expressions in the box.**

☐ in front of	☐ between	☑ near
☐ next to	☐ on the corner of	☐ opposite

Homework

1. Where's the nearest bank?

   There's one near the grocery store.

2. Is there a post office near here?

   _____

   _____

3. I'm looking for a drugstore.

   _____

   _____

4. Is there a laundromat in this neighborhood?

   _____

   _____

5. Is there a department store on Birch Street?

   _____

   _____

6. Are there any pay phones around here?

   _____

   _____

ELM STREET

grocery store ← | hotel

bank | movie theater

MAPLE STREET

1ST AVENUE | 2ND AVENUE | 3RD AVENUE

drugstore | gas station

library | A B C

BIRCH STREET

laundromat | D

YMCA → | post office

OAK STREET

LEGEND
A = travel agency
B = department store
C = gym
D = pay phones

---

4 **Answer these questions about your city or neighborhood. Use the expressions in the box and your own information.**

Yes, there is. There's one on	Yes, there are. There are some on . . . .
No, there isn't.	No, there aren't.

1. Are there any good restaurants around school?

   _____

2. Is there a police station near school?

   _____

3. Are there any good clothing stores in your neighborhood?

   _____

5 *The grass is always greener.*

A Read the interviews.

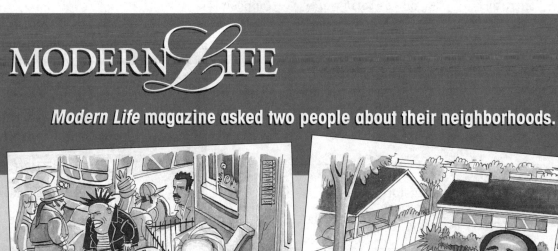

MODERN *L*IFE

Modern Life magazine asked two people about their neighborhoods.

Interview with Diana Towne

Interview with Victor Bord

My neighborhood is very convenient – it's near the shopping center and the bus station. It's also safe. But those are the only good things about living downtown. It's very noisy – the streets are always full of people! The traffic is terrible, and parking is a big problem! I can never park on my own street. I'd like to live in the suburbs.

We live in the suburbs, and it's just too quiet! There aren't many shops, and there are certainly no clubs or theaters. There are a lot of parks, good schools, and very little crime; but nothing ever really happens here. I would really love to live downtown.

B How do the people feel about their neighborhoods? Complete the chart.

	Advantages	Disadvantages
Downtown	*near the shopping center*	
Suburbs		

6 **Complete the chart. Use words from the list.**

| ☑ building | ☑ bank | ☑ pollution | ☑ hospital | ☐ noise | ☐ gas |
| ☑ crime | ☑ traffic | ☑ people | ☑ theater | ☐ school | ☐ water |

Countable nouns		Uncountable nouns	
building	_hospital_	_crime_	_noise_
bank	_theater_	_traffic_	_gas_
people	_school_	_Pollution_	_water_

7 **Write questions about each item using "How much . . . ?" or "How many . . . ?"**
Then look at the picture, and write answers to the questions.
Use the expressions in the box.

| ☑ a lot | ☐ a couple | ☐ a few | ☐ only a little | ☐ not any | ☑ a lot |

1. (noise) _How much noise is there?_ _There's a lot._
2. (buses) _How many buses are there_ _there's a lot_
3. (traffic) _How much traffic Is there_ _there's a lot_
4. (banks) _How many banks are there_ _there are a couple_
5. (people) _How much people are there_ _there's a couple / few_
6. (crime) _How much crime is there_ _there is only a little_

8 *Choose the correct words or phrases to complete this conversation.*

Luis: Are there ____*any*____ (any/one/none) dance clubs around here, Alex?

Alex: Sure. There are ____*one*____ (any/one/a lot).

There's a great club ____*across from*____ (across from/between/on)

the National Bank, but it's expensive.

Luis: Well, are there ____*any*____ (any/none/one) others?

Alex: Yeah, there are ____*few*____ (a few/a little/one).

There's a nice ____*one (one)*____ (any/one/some) near here.

It's called Sounds of Brazil.

Luis: That's perfect! Where is it exactly?

Alex: It's on Third Avenue, ____*between*____ (between/on/on the corner of)

the Royal Theater and May's Restaurant.

Luis: So let's go.

9 *Choose the correct words or phrases.*

1. I'm going to the stationery store to get some ____*food*____.
   (birthday cards/coffee/food)

2. We're taking a long drive. We need to go to the _____.
   (laundromat/gas station/travel agency)

3. I live on the 8th floor of my _____.
   (apartment building/neighborhood/theater)

4. Our apartment is in the center of the city. We live _____.
   (downtown/in the neighborhood/in the suburbs)

9 What does he look like?

1 *Write the opposites. Use the words in the box.*

☑ light   ☑ straight   ☐ young   ☐ short   ☐ tall

(*karly*) (*streit*)
1. curly / *straight* = *Liso*   4. long / *short*

2. dark / *light*   5. short / *tall*

3. elderly / *young*

2 **Collocations**

A Match the words in columns A and B to make descriptions.
Write the descriptions.

A	B	
☑ dark	☑ aged	1. *dark brown*
☑ fairly	☑ brown	2. *middle aged*
☑ good	☑ height	3. *good looking*
☑ medium	☑ long	4. *medium height*
☐ middle	☑ looking	5. *fairly long*

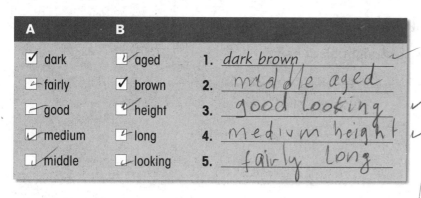

B Answer the questions using the descriptions from part A.

1. A: What does he look like?

   B: *He's good-looking.*

2. A: How long is his hair?

   B: *It's fairly long*

3. A: What color is his hair?

   B: *dark brown*

4. A: How old is he?

   B: *he's dark brown*

5. A: How tall is he?

   B: *he's medium height*

3 **Complete the conversation with questions.**

Jim: *What does she look like?*

Steve: She's quite pretty, with straight black hair.

Jim: And How long is her hair?

Steve: It's medium length.

Jim: How tall is she?

Steve: She's fairly tall.

Jim: And How old is she

Steve: She's in her early twenties.

Jim: Does she wear glases?

Steve: Sometimes. I think she's wearing them now.

Jim: OK. I think I see her over there.

4 **Describe yourself. How old are you? What do you look like?**
What are you wearing today?

5 *Circle two things in each description that do not match the picture.*
Then correct the information.

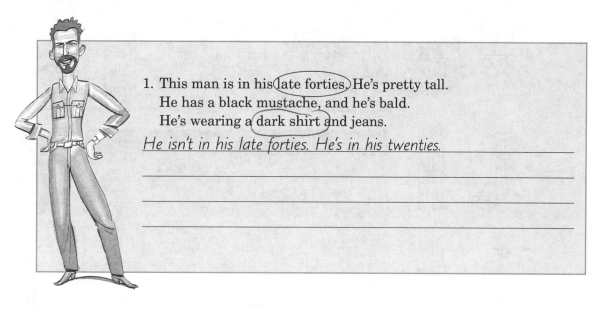

1. This man is in his (late forties.) He's pretty tall.
   He has a black mustache, and he's bald.
   He's wearing a (dark shirt) and jeans.
   He isn't in his late forties. He's in his twenties.
   _____
   _____
   _____

2. This woman is about 25. She's very pretty.
   She's medium height. Her hair is long and blond.
   She's wearing a black sweater and (tennis shoes.)
   She's (standing next to) her motorcycle.
   _____
   _____
   _____
   _____

3. This woman is in her early twenties.
   She's pretty serious-looking. She has (glasses)
   and (straight blond hair.) She's fairly tall, and
   she's wearing a good-looking skirt and blouse.
   _____
   _____
   _____
   _____

6 *Which clothing items are more formal? Which are more informal or casual? Use words from the list. Complete the chart.*

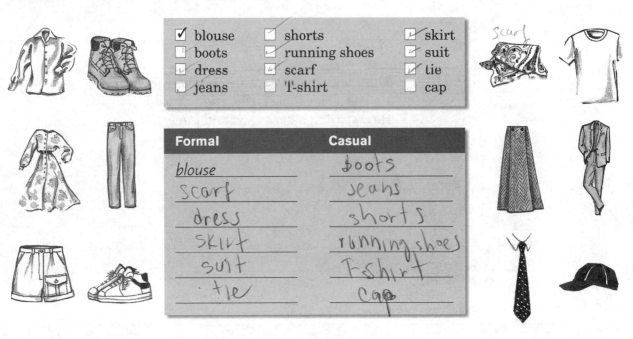

☑ blouse	☑ shorts	☑ skirt
☐ boots	☑ running shoes	☑ suit
☐ dress	☑ scarf	☑ tie
☐ jeans	☐ T-shirt	☐ cap

Formal	Casual
blouse	boots
scarf	jeans
dress	shorts
skirt	running shoes
suit	T-shirt
tie	cap

7 *Write a sentence about each person. Use the words in the box and participles.*

Mandy

Edward and Kate

William

Giorgio

Alice

☑ man	☐ carry a jacket
☐ woman	☑ wear sunglasses
☐ one	☑ stand next to Alice
☐ ones	☐ talk to the man
☐ tall woman	☑ wear a suit and tie

1. *William is the man wearing a suit and tie.*
2. Edward and Kate are ones wear sunglasses
3. Mandy is the woman carrying a jacket
4. Giorgio is the one stand next to Alice
5. tall woman talk to the man

8 *Answer the questions. Use the words given.*

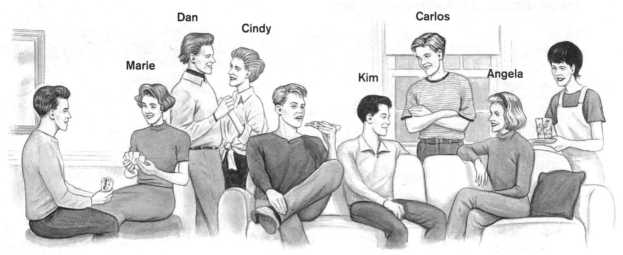

1. A: Which one is Marie?

   B: *She's the one in the gray dress.* _____ (gray dress)

2. A: Which one is Carlos?

   B: he's the one standing near the couch (couch)

3. A: Which ones are Dan and Cindy?

   B: they're the ones next to Marie (Marie) /

4. A: Which one is Angela?

   B: she's the one sitting in the couch (couch)

5. A: Who's Kim?

   B: he's the man between (short black hair)

9 *Rewrite these sentences and questions.*
Find another way to say them using the words given.

1. A: Who's Mika?

   Which one's Mika? _____ (Which)

   B: She's the one in the black dress.

   She's the one wearing the black dress. _____ (wearing)

2. A: Which ones are the teachers?

   who are the teachers (Who)

   B: They're the ones on the couch.

   they are ones sitting on the couch (sitting)

3. A: Which one is Larry?

   Who's Larry ? (Who)

   B: He's the guy wearing the coat.

   He's the one in the coat (in)

53

10 *Complete this description. Use the present continuous or the participle of the verbs in the box.*

☑ ask ☐ carry ☑ look ☑ stand ☑ talk ☑ wait ☑ walk ☑ wear

Yeah, it's really quiet.
Nothing ever really happens here . . . .
I *'m looking* out my window . . . . Let's see . . . .
There's a good-looking middle-aged woman _walking_
her dog, and a young guy _talking_ on the phone. Two people
standing next to him. Hey! The one _wearing_ a
baseball hat is my classmate! Some people _waiting_ at the
bus stop. A serious-looking woman _asking_ for directions.
And hey, here comes a really cute woman _carrying_ a
backpack. Wait a minute! I know her. That's my
old girlfriend. I have to go now! Bye.

11 *Choose the correct responses.*

1. A: Where's Jan?
   B: *She couldn't make it.*
      - I'd like to meet her.
      - She couldn't make it.

2. A: Who's Sam?
   B: _the handsome guy near the door_
      - I'm afraid I missed him.
      - The handsome guy near the door.

3. A: Is she the one on the couch?
   B: _that's right_
      - That's right.
      - Let's see.

4. A: How tall is she?
   B: _Fairly long_
      - Fairly long.
      - Pretty short.

10 Have you ever ridden a camel?

1 *Match the verb forms in columns A and B.*

A	B
1. be _d_	a. gone
2. call _e_	b. done ~~dan~~
3. do _b_	c. seen
4. eat _j_	✓ d. been
5. go _a_	e. called
6. have _h_	f. jogged
7. jog _f_	g. made
8. make _g_	h. had
9. see _c_	i. tried
10. try _i_	j. eaten

2 *Complete the questions in these conversations.*
Use the present perfect of the verbs in Exercise 1.

Keanu Reeves

1. A: _Have you seen_ the new Keanu Reeves movie?

   B: Yes, it's very good.

2. A: _Have you gone_ running lately?

   B: Yes, she usually runs in the morning and evening.

3. A: _Have you eaten_ at the new Brazilian restaurant?

   B: Yes, we've already eaten there. It's excellent, but very expensive.

4. A: How many times _Have you gone_

   shopping at the mall this month?

   B: Actually, I haven't gone at all. Let's go today! I hear

   there's a new music store there.

5. A: How many international phone calls

   Have you made this week?

   B: Only one – on my father's birthday.

3 Already *and* yet

A Check (✓) the things you've done. Put an ✗ next to the things you haven't done.

1. ✗ gone in-line skating
2. ✗ stayed up all night
3. ____ been to a jazz club
4. ____ had a part-time job
5. ____ tried skiing
6. ____ gotten married
7. ____ made friends in class
8. ____ seen a rock concert

getting married

skiing

in-line skating

B Look at the things you checked and marked ✗ in part A. Write sentences about them. Use *already* and *yet*.

> **Grammar note: Already *and* yet**
>
> *Already* **is used in positive statements with the present perfect.**
>   I've **already** gone in-line skating.
> *Yet* **is used in negative statements with the present perfect.**
>   I haven't gone in-line skating **yet.**

1. _____
2. _____
3. _____
4. _____
5. _____
6. _____
7. _____
8. _____

4 *Look at the pictures. How often have you done these things?*
Write sentences using the expressions in the box.

Homework

I've often	I've . . . once or twice.
I've . . . three or four times.	I haven't . . . lately.
I've . . . several times.	I've never . . . .

ride a roller coaster

1. I've never rode a roller coaster

go to a nightclub

4. I haven't went to a night club lately

go bungee jumping

2. I've never gone (went) bungee jumping

call home

5. I've called home several times

see an opera

3. I've saw an opera once or twice

play tennis

6. I've played tennis three or four times

5 Horror stories!

A Have you ever had a terrible day? What happened? What went wrong?

B Read these stories.

Homework

1 NO WAY UP!

Have you ever been in a cable car? Well, I have. Last February, I went on a ski trip to Switzerland. What a trip! The first morning, I got into a cable car. I wanted to go to the top of the mountain and ski down. The cable car started up the mountain. I looked down, and it was so beautiful. Then there was a terrible noise. Suddenly the car stopped. It didn't move, and there was quiet everywhere.

It was cold, and it began to get dark and snow. I was alone for one hour, two hours. I thought, "They've forgotten me!" At last the car started back down the mountain. It went very fast. "Sorry," a man said when I climbed out of the car. "We've never had this problem before. Please, try again tomorrow." "He's joking," I thought. "I've had enough of cable cars for a lifetime."

2 NO WAY OUT!

I have always wanted to go fishing. Last summer, I went on a trip to Taiwan. On the last day of my vacation, I went fishing on a beautiful lake. Unfortunately, I didn't catch any fish, and I got bored. I decided to go swimming. When I stood up, my wallet fell out of my pocket and into the water. It had all my money, my passport, my plane tickets – everything. I jumped into the lake to look for it, but I didn't find anything.

The next morning, I wasn't able to leave the hotel. I had no money to pay the bill and no plane ticket or passport to go home. So what did I do? I called my boss and asked for some money. I have never had such a terrible experience.

C In which story or stories did the writer(s) do these things?
Write *1, 2,* or *1 and 2.*

___1___ stayed in the mountains

_____ lost a wallet

_____ enjoyed the view

_____ got no exercise

_____ spent time on a boat

_____ waited for help

_____ went swimming

_____ had a terrible day

6 *Look at the answers. Write questions using* **Have you ever . . . ?**

flamenco dancing

sumo wrestlers

oysters

wall climbing

1. A: *Have you ever watched flamenco dancing?*
   B: Yes, I have. I watched flamenco dancing last summer in Spain.
2. A: Have you ever seen a sumo wrestling match?
   B: Actually, I saw a sumo wrestling match last month on TV. It was terrific.
3. A: Have you ever been camping?
   B: No, I haven't. I've never been camping.
4. A: Have you ever eaten oysters?
   B: Yes, I have. I ate oysters last year in France.
5. A: Have you ever gone wall climbing?
   B: Yes, I went wall climbing on Friday night.
6. A: Have you ever ridden motorcycle
   B: Yes, I have. My brother once let me ride his motorcycle.
7. A: Have you ever been to India
   B: No, I've never been to India.
8. A: Have you ever have a bad dream
   B: Yes, I had a bad dream just last night.

---

7 *Write your own answers to the questions in Exercise 6.*
Use expressions like the ones from the list.

Yes, I have. I . . . yesterday. I . . . on Monday. I . . . last year. I . . . in August.	No, I haven't. I've never . . . .

1. NO, i haven't. I've never
2. _____
3. _____
4. _____
5. _____
6. _____
7. _____
8. _____

8 *Complete the conversation. Use the past tense or the present perfect of the words given.*

A: ___Have___ you ever ___lost___ (lose) anything valuable?

B: Yes, I ___Lost___ (lose) my watch last month.

A: ___Have___ you ___found___ (find) it yet?

B: No. Actually, I 've___ already ___bought___ (buy) a new one. Look!

A: Oh, that's nice. Where ___Do___ you ___buy___ (buy) it?

B: I ___got___ (get) it at the street market last weekend. What about you? ___Have___ you ever ___Lost___ (lose) anything valuable?

A: Well, I ___Left___ (leave) my address book in a pay phone a couple of months ago.

B: How annoying! Maybe that's why you ___not called___ (not call) me for a while.

A: That's right. I can't even remember my own phone number! But you ___not called___ (not call) me in a long time. What's your excuse?

B: I told you. I ___Lost___ (lose) my watch, so I ___not had___ (not have) the time!

A: Very funny!

I haven't had the time.

9 *Choose the correct responses.*

1. A: Has she called her family lately?
   B: *No, she hasn't.*
   - How many times?
   - No, she hasn't.

2. A: Are you having a good time?
   B: ___Really good___
   - In a long time.
   - Really good.

3. A: How many times has he seen the show?
   B: ___twice___
   - Twice.
   - Already.

4. A: What about a tour of the city?
   B: ___Sure. I hear it's great___
   - I've never, have you?
   - Sure. I hear it's great.

11 It's a very exciting city!

1 Choose the correct words to complete the sentences.

1. Prices are very high in New York City. Everything is

   pretty _____ *expensive* _____ there.

   (cheap/expensive/stressful)

2. My hometown is not an exciting place. The nightlife

   there is pretty _____ nice _____ .

   (boring/nice/interesting)

3. Rome is a beautiful old city. There are not many

   _____ modern _____ buildings.   (big/modern/small)

4. Some parts of this city are fairly dangerous. They're not

   very _____ safe _____ late at night.

   (hot/interesting/safe)

5. Athens is a very quiet city in the winter. The streets are

   never _____ at that time of the year.

   (clean/crowded/relaxing)

New York City

Rome, Italy

2 Choose the correct questions to complete this conversation.

☑ What's the weather like?
☑ Is it big?
☐ Is the nightlife exciting?
☑ What's your hometown like?

A: _____ What's you home town like? _____

B: My hometown? Oh, it's a pretty nice place.

A: _____ Is it big? _____

B: No, it's fairly small, and it has a lot of beautiful buildings.

A: _____ what's the weather like? _____

B: The winter is ^{humedo} wet and too cold. It's very nice in the summer, though.

A: _____ Is the nightlife exciting? _____

B: No! It's really boring after six o'clock in the evening.

3 **Choose the correct conjunctions and rewrite the sentences.**

> **Language note: and, but, however, *and* though**
>
> **Use *and* for additional information.**
> It's an exciting city, **and** the weather is great.
>
> **Use *but, however,* and *though* for contrasting information.**
> It's very safe in the day, **but** it's pretty dangerous at night.
> It is a fairly large city. It's not too interesting, **however.**
> The summers are hot. The evenings are fairly cold, **though.**

Paris, France

Prague, the Czech Republic

A hometown in the U.S.

1. Paris is a very busy place. The streets are always crowded.   (and/but)

   Paris is a very busy place, and the streets are always crowded.

2. Prague is a very nice place. The winters are terribly cold.   (and/though)

   Prague is a very nice place. The
   winters are terribly cold, though

3. Sydney is a relaxing city. It has a wonderful harbor.   (and/however)

   Sydney is a relaxing city and it has a
   wonderful harbor

4. My hometown is a great place for a vacation. It's not too good for shopping.
   (and/but)

   My hometown is a great place for vacation,
   but it's not good for shopping

5. Our hometown is fairly ugly and dirty. It has some beautiful old houses.
   (and/however)

   Our hometown is fairly ugly and dirty.
   It has some beatiful old houses, however

4 Check (✓) if these sentences need a or an. Then write a or an in the correct places.

> **Grammar note: a and an**
>
> Use *a* or *an* with (adverb +) adjective + singular noun.
> It has **a fairly new park.**
> It's **an old city.**
>
> Don't use *a* or *an* with (adverb +) adjective.
> It's not **very old.**
> It's **dirty.**

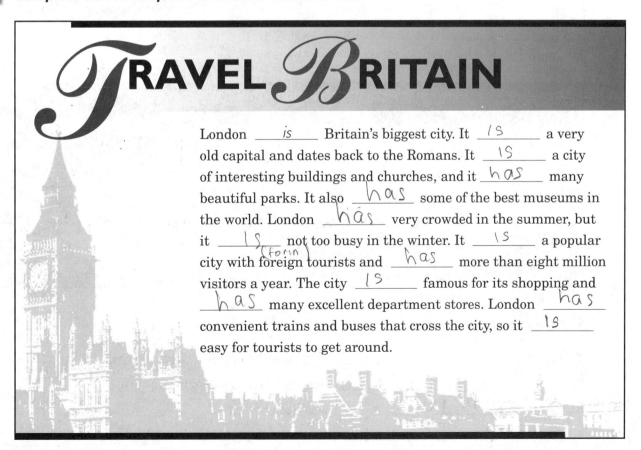

Denver International Airport

1. ✓ Denver has *a* very modern airport.
   adverb adjec sing. noun
   barato
2. ☐ Restaurants are very cheap in Mexico.
3. ✓ Copenhagen is *a* clean city.
4. ☐ The buildings in Paris are really beautiful.
5. ☐ Apartments are very expensive in Hong Kong.
6. ✓ Amsterdam is *a* fairly crowded city in the summer.
7. ☐ Toronto has good museums.
8. ✓ Rio is *an* exciting place to visit.

---

5 Complete this description of London with **is** or **has.**

TRAVEL BRITAIN

London ___is___ Britain's biggest city. It ___is___ a very
old capital and dates back to the Romans. It ___is___ a city
of interesting buildings and churches, and it ___has___ many
beautiful parks. It also ___has___ some of the best museums in
the world. London ___has___ very crowded in the summer, but
it ___is___ not too busy in the winter. It ___is___ a popular
city with foreign tourists and ___has___ more than eight million
visitors a year. The city ___is___ famous for its shopping and
___has___ many excellent department stores. London ___has___
convenient trains and buses that cross the city, so it ___is___
easy for tourists to get around.

Homework 16 Junio - 2004

6 *From city to city*

A Read about these cities.

Budapest

For many centuries, Budapest was two cities, with Buda on the west side of the river Danube and Pest on the east side. Budapest became one city in 1872, and it has been the capital city of Hungary for about eighty years.

The population of Budapest is about three million, and the city is a very popular place for tourists. Visitors like to take boat rides along the Danube. Budapest is also known for its exciting nightlife. The best time to visit is the summer since Budapest is very cold in the winter.

Los Angeles

Los Angeles was founded in 1781. With 3.5 million people, it is now the biggest city in California and the second largest city in the United States. It is famous for its modern freeways, its movie stars, and its smog. When the city is really smoggy, you can't see the nearby mountains. The weather is usually dry and warm. Visitors like to go to the film studios and to drive along Hollywood Boulevard. There are some good beaches near the city, and Los Angeles is also close to Disneyland.

Taipei

Since the founding of Taipei in the eighteenth century, the city has grown to a population of 2.3 million and has become the cultural, industrial, and administrative center of the island of Taiwan. Taipei is an exciting city, but the weather is humid and not always pleasant.

It's also a very busy city, and the streets are always full of people. There is an excellent museum that many tourists visit. Taipei is a fairly expensive city, but not more expensive than some neighboring cities such as Hong Kong and Tokyo. So more and more tourists go to Taipei to shop.

B Complete the chart.

City	Date founded	Population	Weather	Tourist attractions
Budapest	1872	3 million	winter very cold	to take boat rides along the Danube
Los Angeles	1781	3.5	dry and warm	the film studios Hollywood Boulevard
Taipei		2.3	humid	museum

C Complete the sentences.

barata

1. *Taipei* _____ is cheaper than other cities nearby.
2. ___Los Angeles___ has good beaches nearby.
3. ___Buda Pest___ was once two cities.
4. ___Taipei___ were both founded in the eighteenth century.

7   *Complete the sentences. Use words from the list.*

☐ shouldn't miss	☑ can take
☑ should see	☑ shouldn't stay
☑ should travel	☑ shouldn't walk

1. You *should see* _____ the new zoo.
   It's very interesting.
2. You __*shouldn't stay*__ near the
   airport. It's too noisy.
3. You __*shouldn't miss*__ the museum.
   It has some new exhibits.
4. You __*can take*__ ~~bas~~ a bus tour
   of the city if you like.
5. You __*shouldn't walk*__ alone at ~~chuldn't~~
   night. It's too dangerous.
6. You __*should travel*__ by taxi if
   you're out late. (~~schuldn't~~)

---

8   *Complete this conversation with* **should** *or* **shouldn't** *and* **I** *or* **you.**

A: I'm taking my vacation in Indonesia.
   What _____*should I*_____ do there?
B: ___*shouldn't*___ miss Jogjakarta,
   the old capital city. There are a lot of
   beautiful old buildings. For example,
   ____*should*____ see the
   temple of Borobudur.
A: Sounds great. Bali is very popular, too.
   ____*should you*____ go there?
B: Yes, __*I should*__ .
   It's very interesting.
A: ____*should you*____ take a lot of
   money with me?
B: No, ____*I shouldn't*____ . Indonesia
   is not an expensive country.
A: So when ____*should you*____
   go there?
B: Well, it's always hot and humid,
   so it really doesn't matter.

Jogjakarta, Indonesia

9 *Ask questions about a place you want to visit.*
Use can, should, or shouldn't. Ask about:

1. the time to visit

   What time of year should you visit?

2. things to see and do there

   _____

3. things people shouldn't do

   _____

4. special foods

   _____

5. things to buy

   _____

6. other interesting things

   _____

10 *Rewrite these sentences. Find another way to say each sentence using the words given.*

1. It's a stressful city.

   It isn't a relaxing city. _____ (not relaxing)

2. The streets are always full of people.

   the streets are alway crowded of people (crowded)

3. It's not a very beautiful city.

   It's a fairly ugly _____ (fairly ugly)

4. When should we visit the city?

   What _____ (a good time)

5. You really should see the flea markets.

   _____ (not miss)

6. What can we do there?

   _____ (should)

12 It really works!

1 Any suggestions?

A Check (✓) the best advice for each health problem. *salud* *(Ja\z)*

1. a backache *atmohadilla*
- ✓ use a heating pad
- ☐ get some exercise
- ☐ take some vitamin C

2. a headache
- ☐ take some vitamin C
- ✓ take some aspirin *(advais)*
- ☐ take some good advice *(consejo)*

3. a bad cold
- ☐ see a dentist
- ✓ go to bed and rest
- ☐ take some good advice

4. an insect bite
- ✓ put anti-itch cream on it
- ☐ take some aspirin
- ☐ drink lots of liquids

5. the hiccups
- ✓ drink lots of hot water
- ☐ take some cold medicine
- ☐ chop up some garlic

B Write a question about each problem in part A. Then write answers using the words from the list. Use the ideas in part A or your own suggestions in your answers.

It's important	It's helpful . . . .
It's a good idea	It's useful . . . . *util*

1. A: _What should you do for a backache?_
   B: _It's helpful to use a heating pad._

2. A: _What should you do for a headache_
   B: _It's a good idea take some aspirin_

3. A: _What should you do for a bad cold_
   B: _It's important go to bed and rest_

4. A: _what should yo do for an insect bite_
   B: _It's useful put anti-itch cream it is?_

5. A: _____
   B: _____

2 *Rewrite these sentences. Find another way to give advice using*
It's a good idea . . . , It's helpful . . . , or It's important . . . .

Language note: Negative infinitive complements

Problem	Advice	Negative infinitive advice
For the flu,	don't exercise a lot.	For the flu, it's a good idea **not to exercise** a lot.

---

1. For a bad cough, don't smoke.

   For a bad cough, it's important not to smoke.

2. For a sore throat, don't talk too much.

   For a sore throat, it's important not to talk too much

3. For a burn, don't put ice on it.

   For a burn, it's helpful to put ice on it

4. For insomnia, don't drink coffee at night.

   For insomnia, it's important not to drink coffee at night

5. For a fever, don't get out of bed.

   For a fever, it's helpful not to get out of bed

---

3 *Check (✓) three health problems you have had this year. Write what you*
did for each one. Use the remedies below or your own remedies.

Health problems

☐ a backache
☑ a headache
☐ a toothache
☑ a cold
☐ a sore throat
☐ the hiccups
☑ a sunburn
☑ stress

Some remedies

take some aspirin   get some medicine from the drugstore
use some lotion   put some ointment on it
take some cough drops   see my doctor/dentist
go to bed   do nothing

Example: *Yesterday, I had a bad headache so I took some aspirin.*

1. _____

2. _____

3. _____

4 *Getting to sleep*

A How many hours do you sleep each night? Do you ever have difficulty getting to sleep? What do you do? Read the article.

Sleep

ost people need seven to eight hours of sleep a night. Some people need less than this, and some people need more.

According to sleep expert Dr. Robert Schachter, many people have difficulty sleeping, but they do not know why. Most people know it is important not to drink coffee or tea before they go to bed –

both beverages have caffeine. Caffeine keeps people awake. However, not everybody knows that some medicines, such as cold tablets, also have caffeine in them. Stress can cause insomnia, too. Busy people with stressful jobs may not be able to sleep at night.

Dr. Schachter suggests, "You shouldn't use your bedroom as a TV room or an exercise room. You should use it for sleeping only. It's a good idea to have a regular sleeping schedule. Get up and go to bed at the same time every day. It's also important not to eat before bedtime. Eating may keep you awake."

And if all this doesn't work, try counting sheep!

B Check (✓) True or False.

	True	False
1. Everyone needs eight hours of sleep a night.	☐	☐
2. Caffeine helps you fall asleep.	☐	☐
3. Cold tablets can keep you awake.	☐	☐
4. Busy people may have trouble falling asleep.	☐	☐
5. It is a good idea to have a TV near your bed.	☐	☐
6. You should have regular sleeping hours.	☐	☐
7. You shouldn't eat just before you go to bed.	☐	☐
8. Counting sheep may help.	☐	☐

5 *What do you suggest?*

A Complete the word map with medicines from the list.

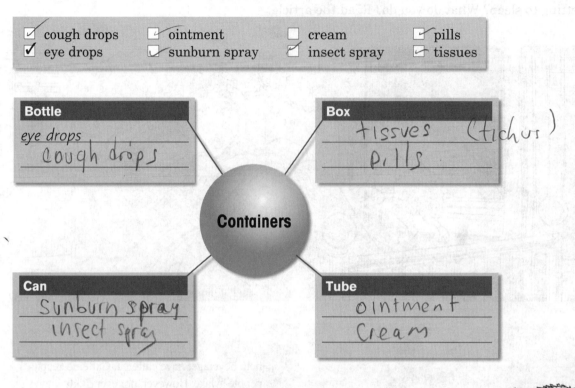

☑ cough drops   ☑ ointment   ☐ cream   ☑ pills
☑ eye drops   ☑ sunburn spray   ☑ insect spray   ☑ tissues

Bottle
eye drops
cough drops

Box
tissues   (tichus)
pills

Containers

Can
sunburn spray
insect spray

Tube
ointment
cream

consejo

B What should these people buy? Give advice. Use the containers and medicine from part A.

1. Joe has very tired eyes.
   He should buy a bottle of eye drops.

2. Mary has a bad cold.
   She should buy a bottle of cough drop

3. Andrew and Carlos have a lot of insect bites.
   Andrew and Carlos should by a can of insect spray

4. David has dry skin.
   David should buy a tube of cream

6 **Check (✓) the correct sentences to make conversations.**

I'm here to help

1. Pharmacist: ☑ Can I help you?
   ☐ Should I help you?

   Customer: ☑ Yes. Can I have a package of bandages?
   ☐ Yes. I suggest a package of bandages.

   Pharmacist: Here you are.

   Customer: ☐ And what do you need for a sunburn?
   ☑ And what do you have for a sunburn?

   Pharmacist: ☐ Do you suggest this lotion?
   ☑ I suggest this lotion.

   Customer: Thanks.

2. Pharmacist: Hi. Can I help you?

   Customer: ☐ Yes. Can I suggest something for sore muscles?
   ☑ Yes. Could I have something for sore muscles?

   Pharmacist: ☑ Sure. Try this ointment.
   ☐ Sure. Could I try this ointment?

   Customer: ☐ Thanks. And what should you get for the flu?
   ☑ Thanks. And what do you suggest for the flu?

   Pharmacist: ☐ Can I have some of these tablets? They really work.
   ☑ Try some of these tablets. They really work.

   Customer: ☐ OK, thanks. I'll take them. And you should get a box of tissues.
   ☑ OK, thanks. I'll take them. And could I have a box of tissues?

   Pharmacist: Sure. Here you are.

7 **Complete this conversation with the correct words.**

A: Wow, you don't look very good! Do you feel OK?

B: No, I think I'm getting a cold. What should I do _for_ it?
<u>(for/to/with)</u>

A: You should stay _in_ home and go _to_ bed.
    (at/in/of)   (in/of/to)

B: You're probably right. I've got a really bad cough, too.

A: Try drinking some hot tea _with_ honey. It really helps.
    (for/of/with)

B: Anything else?

A: Yeah, I suggest you get a big box _of_ tissues!
    (at/in/of)

8 **Give suggestions for these problems. Use words from the box.**

| I suggest . . . . | You should . . . . | Try . . . . |

1. I have a very sore throat.
   Try some hot tea.

2. I think I'm getting a cold.
   you should stay in home and go to bed

3. I have a backache. And don't tell me to go to bed!
   I suggest to use a heating pad

4. I have a terrible stomachache.
   try

13 May I take your order, please?

1 *Show that you agree. Write sentences with the words given.*

I don't want fast food tonight.

1. *I don't either.* _____ (either)
   Neither do I

I really like healthy foods.

2. _____ So do I _____ (so)
   I do, too

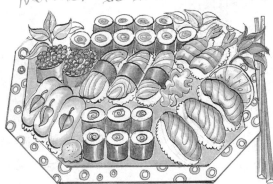

I'm in the mood for Japanese food.

3. _____ I do, too _____ (too)
   So do I

I don't like spicy food.

4. _____ neither do I _____ (neither)

I don't like bland food very much.

5. _____ I don't either _____ (either)

I think Italian food is delicious.

6. _____ I do, too _____ (too)

73

2 What do you think?

A Look at the pictures. Write sentences about the food.
Use the expressions in the box.

Tomorrow

Useful expressions
I like . . . a lot.   I don't like . . . very much.
I love . . . .   I'm not crazy about . . . .
I'm crazy about . . . .   It's a bit too . . . .
I can't stand . . . .

1. *It's a bit too greasy.*

2. I like healthy a lot

3. I don't like salty very much

4. _____

5. _____

6. _____

B List your two favorite kinds of food.

_____

_____

3 *Which restaurant?*

A What kinds of restaurants do you like?
Do you prefer a quiet place or a noisy place?

B Read these restaurant reviews.

★★★★

Trattoria Romana is an excellent Italian restaurant. It has a quiet and relaxing atmosphere, and the service is very good. It's always crowded, so make a reservation early. The menu is not very big. There are only four entrees on the menu, but everything is fresh. The chicken with pasta is wonderful. Desserts are their specialty – rich and delicious! It's a little expensive but very good. You'll spend about $25 per person.

★★

Last Saturday, I was the only customer at ***Dynasty***, a new diner on 57th Street. It's not a good place to go. The waiters are slow and unfriendly. The atmosphere is boring, and so is the menu. It specializes in American food – mostly steak and potatoes; but my steak was raw, and the fries were greasy. It isn't cheap, either. It cost me $22. If you go to Dynasty, you certainly won't need a reservation. My advice, however, is "Don't Go."

★★★

Beirut Cafe is a great new Lebanese restaurant. The specialty is *meze* – lots of different small dishes, some with meat or fish, others with vegetables. The atmosphere is lively, and the service is very friendly. There's live Lebanese music and dancing on weekends. Beirut Cafe is surprisingly inexpensive – about $18 a person, but you need to make a reservation.

C Complete the chart.

	Trattoria Romana	Dynasty	Beirut Cafe
Food	*Italian*		
Atmosphere	*quiet and relaxing*		
Specialties			
Service			
Price/person			
Reservation	☐ yes ☐ no	☐ yes ☐ no	☐ yes ☐ no

4 **Create a menu. Use words from the box.**

☑ beef	☐ clam	☑ milk	☐ onion	☑ salmon
☑ cake	☑ coffee	☑ mixed	☐ pasta	☑ sandwich
☐ chicken	☑ ice	☐ noodle	☑ pie	☑ tea

Kate's Diner

★ Main Dishes ★
(includes salad and choice of potatoes)

grilled _salmon_

(roast) roast _beef_

turkey _Sandwich_

★ Soups ★

chicken _noodle_ soup

French _onion_ soup

clam chowder

★ Salads ★

chicken salad

_____ salad

mixed greens

★ Desserts ★

chocolate _cake_

apple _pie_

ice cream

★ Beverages ★

tea   _coffee_   _milk_

5 **Use one or more words to complete this conversation between a waiter and a customer.**

Waiter: May I take your order?

Customer: _Yes, I'll have_ the roast beef with mashed potatoes.

Waiter: What kind of dressing _Italian would you like_ on your salad – French, Italian or vinaigrette?

Customer: French, _Please_ .

Waiter: And would you like _any thing_ to drink?

Customer: Yes, _I will_ have iced coffee.

Waiter: Anything else?

Customer: No, _thank you._ .

that will be all

6   *Choose the correct responses.*

1. A: Would you like fries or cole slaw?

   B: *I'll have the cole slaw, please.*
- I guess I will, thanks.
- I'll have the cole slaw, please.
- Yes, please.

2. A: What kind of soda would you like?

   B: _____
- I'll have a cola.
- I'd like a hot dog, please.
- A small order, please.

3. A: Would you like anything to drink?

   B: _____
- No, thanks.
- Yes, a hamburger, please.
- I'll have chocolate cake, please.

4. A: What flavor ice cream would you like?

   B: _____
- Baked, please.
- Vanilla, please.
- Ice cream, please.

5. A: Would you like anything else?

   B: _____
- Yes, thank you very much.
- Not at all, thanks.
- That will be all, thanks.

7 Complete the conversation. Use the words and expressions in the box.

☐ am	☑ neither	☐ will	☐ can't stand them
☐ can	☐ so	☐ would	☐ favorite kind of food
☐ do	☐ too	☐ like it a lot	

Sherry: I feel tired tonight. I really don't want to cook.

Whitney: _____Neither_____ do I. Say, do you like Thai food?

Sherry: It's delicious. I _____ .

Whitney: I do, _____ . It's my _____ .
Let's call Chiang Mai restaurant for home delivery.

Sherry: Great idea! Their food is always good. I eat there a lot.

Whitney: _____ do I. Well, what _____ you like tonight?

Sherry: I'm in the mood for some soup.

Whitney: So _____ I. And I think I _____ have spicy chicken and
special Thai rice.

Sherry: OK, let's order. Oh, wait a minute, I don't have any money.

Whitney: Neither _____ I. What should we do?

Sherry: Well, let's look in the refrigerator. Hmm. Do you like boiled eggs?

Whitney: I _____ .

Sherry: Actually, neither _____ I.

8 Choose the correct words.

1. In a restaurant, the waiter or waitress takes your _____order_____ .   (menu/order/service)

2. Baked potatoes are less _____ than french fries.   (greasy/healthy/spicy)

3. Many people like _____ on their salad.   (dessert/dressing/soda)

4. Some people rarely cook with spices. They prefer _____ food.   (bland/hot/rich)

5. Vanilla is a popular ice cream _____ .   (drink/flavor/meal)

14 The biggest and the best!

Geography

A Circle the correct word.

1. This is an area of land between two rows of mountains
   or cliffs, usually with a river running through.
   a. canyon   b. plain   c. waterfall

2. This is a large area of land that has lots of trees on it.
   a. cliff   b. forest   c. valley

3. This is an area of land that is always wet.
   a. canyon   b. plain   c. swamp

4. This is an area of water with land all around it.
   a. lake   b. ocean   c. swamp

5. This is a mountain with a hole at the top. Smoke and
   lava sometimes come from the hole, and it can be dangerous.
   a. hill   b. plateau   c. volcano

6. This is a dry, sandy place. It doesn't rain much here,
   and there aren't many plants.
   a. desert   b. sea   c. volcano

B Complete the names. Use words from the box.

☑ Canyon	☐ Falls	☐ Ocean	☐ Lake
☐ Desert	☐ Mount	☐ River	☐ Sea

1. Grand _Canyon_

2. Amazon _____

3. _____ Superior

4. _____ Fuji

5. Mediterranean _____

6. Niagara _____

7. Pacific _____

8. Sahara _____

2 *Write the comparative and superlative of the words given.*

Spelling note: Comparatives and superlatives			
	Adjective	**Comparative**	**Superlative**
Add **-er** or **-est** to most words:	long	long**er**	the long**est**
Add **-r** or **-st** to words ending in **-e**:	large	larg**er**	the larg**est**
Drop **y** and add **-ier** or **-iest**:	dry	dr**ier**	the dr**iest**
Double the final consonant and add **-er** or **-est**:	big	bigg**er**	the bigg**est**

1. busy   *busier*   *the busiest*   6. noisy   noiser   noisest
2. cool   cooler   the coolest   7. old   older   oldest
3. friendly   friendler   the friendlest   8. safe   safer   safest
4. heavy   heavier   heaviest   9. small   smaller   smallest
5. nice   nicer   nicest   10. wet   wetter   wettest

3 *Complete this conversation.*
Use the superlative of the words given.

The Grand Canal

Ian: So where did you go for your vacation, Val?

Val: Italy.

Ian: How exciting! Did you have a good time?

Val: It was terrific! I think Italy is

 the most exciting (exciting)

country in Europe.

Ian: Well, it certainly has some of

 the most famous (famous)

cities in the world – Rome, Milan, Venice.

Val: Yeah. I had the bettest (good) time in Venice.

It's the most beatiful (beautiful) city I've ever seen.

Of course, it's also one of the most popular (popular)

tourist attractions. It was the most crowded (crowded)

city I visited this summer, and there weren't even any cars!

Ian: I've always wanted to visit Venice. What's it like in the winter?

Val: Actually, that's the worst (bad) time to visit.

Venice is one of coldest and foggest (cold and foggy)

places in Italy in the winter.

4 **Did you know? Complete these sentences. Use the comparative or the superlative of the words given.**

The Suez Canal, Egypt

Mount Waialeale, USA

Death Valley, USA

1. Canada and Russia are _____*the largest*_____ (large) countries in the world.

2. Russia is _____*larger than*_____ (large) Canada.

3. _____the highest_____ (high) waterfall in the world is in Venezuela.

4. The Suez Canal joins the Mediterranean and Red seas. It is 190 kilometers (118 miles) long. It is _____longer than_____ (long) the Panama Canal.

5. The Atacama Desert in Chile is _____the driest_____ (dry) place in the world.

6. Mount Waialeale in Hawaii gets 1,170 centimeters (460 inches) of rain a year. It is _____the wetest_____ (wet) place on earth!

7. _____the hotest_____ (hot) capital city in the world is Muscat, in Oman.

8. The continent of Antarctica is _____ (cold) any other place in the world.

9. The Himalayas are some of _____ (dangerous) mountains to climb.

10. Badwater, in California's Death Valley, is _____ (low) point in North America.

11. Mont Blanc in the French Alps is _____ (high) the Matterhorn in the Swiss Alps.

12. The Pacific Ocean is _____ (deep) the Atlantic Ocean. In some places the Pacific Ocean is 11,033 meters (36,198 feet) deep.

5 *The coldest and the windiest!*

A Where is the coldest place you've ever been?

B Read about Antarctica.

ANTARCTICA is the most southern continent in the world. It is like nowhere else on earth. It is much larger than Europe, and nearly twice the size of Australia. It is an icy plateau with the South Pole at its center. Antarctica is the coldest and windiest place in the world, even colder and windier than the North Pole. In the summer, the sun shines for twenty-four hours a day, but in the winter it's completely dark for about three months. Very few plants grow there, but there is some wildlife, including whales, seals, and penguins.

When Captain James Cook sailed around the continent in the 1770s, he found no one living there. Today, a few scientists work in Antarctica, but they only spend fairly short periods there. Many scientists in Antarctica are studying the ozone layer. The ozone layer is getting thinner and thinner worldwide. The biggest "hole" is over Antarctica, where the weather is getting warmer. Scientists think that this cold and lonely place can teach us a lot about the earth and how to keep it safe.

C Check (✓) True or False.

	True	False
1. Europe is bigger than Antarctica.	☐	☐
2. The North Pole is the coldest and windiest place in the world.	☐	☐
3. In Antarctica, it never gets dark in the summer.	☐	☐
4. There are a lot of animals and birds in Antarctica.	☐	☐
5. Captain Cook found a few scientists living in Antarctica.	☐	☐
6. The weather in Antarctica is getting colder and colder.	☐	☐

6 *Geography quiz*

Use the words in the box. Write questions about the pictures.
Then circle the correct answers.

| ☐ How big | ☐ How deep | ☑ How long |
| ☑ How cold | ☑ How far | ☑ How high |

Angel Falls (Venezuela)

1. *How high is Angel Falls?*
   a. It's 979 meters (3,212 feet) tall.
   b. It's 979 meters high. ⟵ circled

Australia to New Zealand

Australia

New Zealand

2. How far is New Zealand from Australia
   a. It's about 2,000 kilometers (1,200 miles).
   b. It's about 2,000 square kilometers.

the Amazon River

3. How long is the Amazon River
   a. It's 6,437 kilometers (4,000 miles) long.
   b. It's 6,437 kilometers high.

4. How cold is the Antartica
   a. It gets up to −88.3 degrees Celsius
      (−126.9 degrees Fahrenheit).
   b. It gets down to −88.3 degrees Celsius.

Antarctica

the Amazon Rain Forest

5. How big is the Amazon Rain forest
   a. It's 6 million square kilometers (2½ million square miles).
   b. It's 6 million kilometers long.

6. How deep is the Grand Canyon
   a. It's about 1.6 kilometers (1 mile) big.
   b. It's about 1.6 kilometers deep.

the Grand Canyon

7 Write the opposites.

Across

2 biggest
6 bad
7 shorter
8 worse
9 worst
10 near
11 lowest
13 driest
14 hot
15 shortest

Down

1 hotter
3 smaller
4 least crowded (2 words)
5 coldest
9 smallest
10 not famous
11 cold
12 best

15 I'm going to see a musical.

1 *Which nouns often go with which verbs? Complete the chart. Use each word only once.*

☑ an amusement park   ☑ a ballgame on TV   ☑ a museum   ☑ a rock concert
☑ a beach party   ☑ a barbecue   ☑ a play   ☑ a video

have	see	visit	watch
a beach party	a play	a museum	a video
a barbecue	a rock concert	an amusement park	a ballgame on TV

2 *Read Anna's diary, and write about her plans. Use the present continuous.*

July

Sunday	Monday	Tuesday	Wednesday	Thursday	Friday	Saturday
6	**7**	**8**	**9**	**10**	**11**	**12**
morning – visit Forest Green Historic Park	work overtime to finish the report	7:00 P.M. see a play with Tony	night – watch the hockey game with Kate & Sam	12:00 noon have a barbecue	stay home and watch the late show on TV	afternoon – go to an arts festival

1. *On Sunday morning, Anna is visiting Forest Green Historic Park.*
2. On monday Anna is working overtime to finish the report
3. On tuesday at 7:00 P.M Anna is seeing a play with Tony
4. On Wednesday tonight Anna is watching the hockey game with Kate & Sam
5. On thursday at 12:00 noon Anna is haveing a barbecue
6. On friday Anna is staying home and
7.

3 Complete this conversation. Use **be going to** and the verbs given.

Marta: What ___are___ you ___going to do___ this weekend, Mark? (do)

Mark: I ___am going to go___ to an art gallery on Saturday. (go)

Marta: That sounds interesting.

Mark: Yeah. There's a new exhibit at the Modern. And how about you, Marta?

Marta: Well, Brian and I ___are going to see___ a ballgame in the afternoon. (see)

Mark: And what ___are___ you ___going to do___ in the evening? (do)

Marta: Brian ___is going to visit___ his mother in the hospital. (visit)
But I ___am___ not ___doing___ anything really. (do)

Mark: Well, I ___am going to have___ some friends over for a barbecue. Would you like to come? (have)

Marta: Thanks. I'd love to.

4 Choose the correct responses.

1. A: Would you like to go to a movie on Sunday?

   B: _Oh, I'm sorry. I can't._
   - Oh, I'm sorry. I can't.
   - Nothing special.
   - No. I wouldn't.

2. A: Do you want to visit the street fair with us tomorrow?

   B: ___Sure, I'd love to___
   - Yes, I'm going to.
   - Can we go to a late show?
   - Sure, I'd love to.

3. A: We're having friends over for dinner tonight. Would you like to come?

   B: ___I'm working late tonight. I'm sorry___
   - How about this evening?
   - I'm working late tonight. I'm sorry.
   - Yes, it would.

4. A: How about dinner at the Mexican restaurant tonight?

   B: ___No, I'm not doing anything___
   - No, I'm not doing anything.
   - Sorry, I'm going away next week.
   - Great! But it's my turn to pay.

5 *Write invitations to this week's events in Princeville.*

Exciting things to do this week in **Princeville** All events scheduled to begin at 8:00 P.M.

Wednesday	Thursday	Friday	Saturday
Rock concert The Cranberries	**Amusement park** Lots to do for everyone!	**Play** *Funny Money*	**Museum** Exhibition of modern art

1. *Are you doing anything on Wednesday evening? Do you want to see a rock concert?*

   or *I'm going to see the Cranberries on Wednesday. Would you like to come?*

2. Are you doing anything on Friday? Do you want to see a play

3. _____

   _____

4. _____

   _____

6 *Write about how often you do these leisure activities.*
Use the expressions in the box.

I often . . . . I . . . almost every weekend. I sometimes . . . in the summer. I . . . three or four times a year. I never . . . .

1. *I never go to rock concerts.* _____

2. _____

3. _____

4. _____

5. _____

6. _____

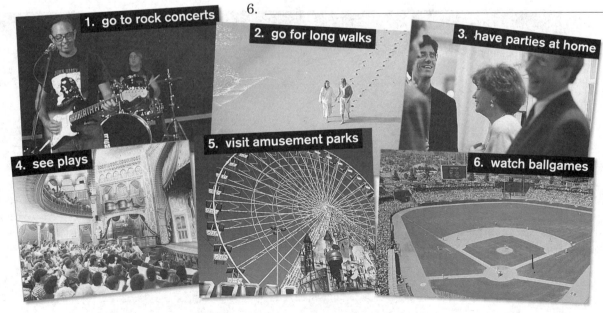

1. go to rock concerts
2. go for long walks
3. have parties at home
4. see plays
5. visit amusement parks
6. watch ballgames

7 Beyond the telephone

A Why do you use the telephone? List some reasons.

_____

_____

B Read the passage. Are the reasons different from the ones in your list?

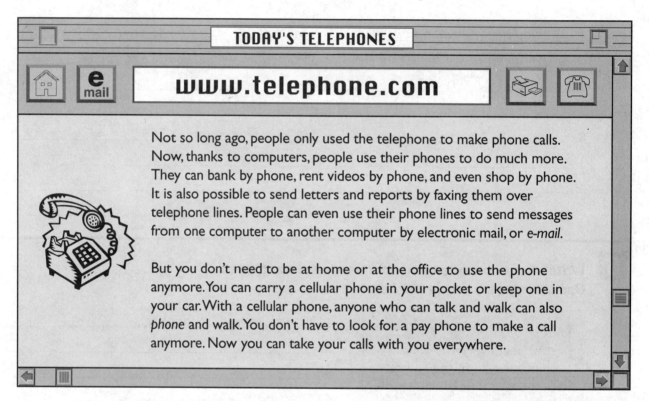

TODAY'S TELEPHONES

www.telephone.com

Not so long ago, people only used the telephone to make phone calls. Now, thanks to computers, people use their phones to do much more. They can bank by phone, rent videos by phone, and even shop by phone. It is also possible to send letters and reports by faxing them over telephone lines. People can even use their phone lines to send messages from one computer to another computer by electronic mail, or *e-mail*.

But you don't need to be at home or at the office to use the phone anymore. You can carry a cellular phone in your pocket or keep one in your car. With a cellular phone, anyone who can talk and walk can also *phone* and walk. You don't have to look for a pay phone to make a call anymore. Now you can take your calls with you everywhere.

C Check (✓) True or False. For statements that are false, write the true information.

	True	False
1. You can pay for things by phone.	☐	☐
2. Fax machines do not use telephone lines.	☐	☐
3. You need a computer and a telephone line to send e-mail.	☐	☐
4. You can use a cellular phone at home or at work.	☐	☐
5. You need a car to make a call on a cellular phone.	☐	☐

8 *Read these messages. What did the caller say?*
Write the messages another way using **tell** *or* **ask.**

| For:
Message: | Ms. Tam
The meeting is at 10:30 tomorrow morning.
Bring the last fax from New York. |

1. *Please tell Ms. Tam that the meeting is at 10:30 tomorrow morning. . . .*
   _____

| For:
Message: | Mr. Alvarez
We need the report by noon. Call Ms. James as soon as possible. |

2. Please tell Mr. Alvarez that we need the
   report by noon

| For:
Message: | Dr. James
The new fax machine is ready. Pick it up this afternoon. |

3. Please tell Dr. James that the new fax machine
   is ready

---

9 *Look at the message slips. Ask someone to give these messages.*

Grammar note: Negative infinitives
Request · **Message**
Don't call him today. · Please ask Jan **not to call** him today.
Don't go home yet. · Could you tell him **not to go** home yet?

Michael –
Don't meet me at the airport
until midnight. The plane is
going to be late.

1. _____
   _____

Lucy –
We're meeting at Dino's house before
the concert. Don't forget the tickets.

2. _____
   _____

Christopher –
The beach party starts at noon.
Don't be late!

3. _____
   _____

10 **Choose the correct words.**

Secretary: Hello. Grant and Lee.

Ms. Curtis: <u>*May I*</u> speak to Ms. Grace Schmidt, please?
(May I/Would you)

Secretary: I'm <u>sorry</u> . She's not in. <u>Can I take</u>
(busy/sorry) (Can I leave/Can I take)

a message?

Ms. Curtis: Yes, please. This is Ms. Curtis. <u>Would</u> you
(Would/Please)

<u>tell her that</u> I'm staying at the Plaza Hotel?
(tell her that/ask her to)

The number is 735-9001, Room 605. <u>Could</u>
(Please/Could)

you <u>tell her to call me</u> ?
(tell her to call me/tell her to call her)

Secretary: OK, Ms. Curtis. I'll <u>giv</u> the message.
(give her/tell her)

Ms. Curtis: Thank you very much. Good-bye.

11 **Match the questions with the correct responses.**

☐ Yes, please. Could you tell him Ros called?   ☐ Let me see if he's in.
☐ That's OK. I'll call back.   ☐ My name's Graham. Graham Lock.
☐ Yes. My number is 669-3241.   ☑ Yes, that would be great. Thanks.

1. Would you like to come to a party?
   Yes, that would be great. Thanks.

2. Could I ask her to call you back?
   _____

3. Who's calling?
   _____

4. Can I take a message?
   _____

5. Could I speak to Paul, please?
   _____

6. I'm sorry. She's busy at the moment.
   _____

16 A change for the better!

1 Choose the correct responses.

1. A: Say, you really look different.

   B: *Well, my hair is a little longer now.*
   - I moved into a new house.
   - I'm more outgoing now.
   - Well, my hair is a little longer now.

2. A: I haven't seen you for ages.

   B: _i know. How have you been?_
   - I know. How have you been?
   - Well, I quit smoking.
   - My new job is more stressful.

3. A: You know, I have three kids now.

   B: _that's terrific_
   - Well, I've grown a mustache.
   - That's terrific!
   - Say, you've really changed your hair.

4. A: How are you?

   B: _Well, actually, I have contact lenses now_
   - I do more aerobics these days.
   - Well, actually, I have contact lenses now.
   - I'm doing really well.

2 Complete the sentences. Use information in the box and the present perfect.

☑ move to a new apartment ☑ start going to the gym
☑ spend a lot of money on clothes ☐ stop eating out in restaurants

1. Judy *'s moved to a new apartment* .
   Her old one was too small.
2. Kim and Anna _start going to the gym_ .
   Now they cook dinner at home every evening. It's much cheaper.
3. Alex _stop eating out in restaurants_ .
   He looks healthier, and he has more energy.
4. Jerry _spend a lot of money on clothes_
   He needs to dress up for his new job.

3 Describe how these people have changed.
Use the present or the past tense.

1. *Shawn lost a lot of weight.*

2. Susan don't smoke anymore

3. Elena quit contact lenses now

4 Rewrite these sentences. Find another way to say each
sentence using the words given.

1. Alice quit eating rich food.
   Alice eats healthier foods now. (healthier)

2. James lost a lot of weight.
   _____ (heavier)

3. Mary goes to a new school now.
   _____ (change)

4. Tess isn't married anymore.
   _____ (divorce)

5. I've grown my hair.
   _____ (longer)

6. We don't smoke anymore.
   _____ (quit)

5 | Life changes

A *Have you ever . . .*

☐ lost a job
☐ had money problems
☐ had trouble making friends
☐ worked in a foreign country

B Read the passages on the left. Then read the passages on the right. Match the people's lives two years ago with their lives today. Underline at least two changes in each person's life.

Aki

Luis and his wife

Rosie

Two years ago	Now
1. Aki Two years ago, I was a student, and I thought life was really good. I got up late. I spent the day talking to friends, and then I studied all night. I wore jeans and sweatshirts and had long hair and a mustache. I felt free. _____	**a.** Now my life has changed. I got married! My wife and I often have friends over for dinner. We're taking evening classes. It's great!
2. Luis I moved to a new town two years ago. My job was interesting, but I was single, and I didn't have any friends. People at work were friendly but not very outgoing. We never did anything after work. _____	**b.** Now I work as a computer programmer for an international company. I've moved to Seoul and have started to learn Korean. Korean food is great, and I've gained several kilos. I feel much happier and healthier.
3. Rosie My life seemed to come to an end two years ago. I lost my job. Then I lost weight, and looked terrible. Money became a problem. I was very sad. I needed some good luck. _____	**c.** Now I actually look forward to getting up early in the morning and going to work. Of course, I dress up now, and my hair is shorter. But I don't really mind. At least my evenings are free!

6 **Complete the sentences. Use words in the box.**

☐ broke	☑ graduation	☐ loan	☐ retire	☐ successful	☐ responsible

1. After _____*graduation*_____ , I plan to look for a job.

2. Marie lost her job. Now she's _____ , and she can't pay her rent.

3. Now that I'm going to college, I want to be more _____ about doing my classwork.

4. Lucy wants to pay off her student _____ before she buys a car.

5. Philip plans to _____ at an early age. He's almost 55 now.

6. I'd like to be _____ in my first job. Then I can get a better job and a raise.

7 **Complete this conversation. Use the words given.**

Melissa: What _____*do you plan to do*_____ (plan, do) this summer, Leo?

Leo: I _____ (want, get) a summer job.

I _____ (like, save) money for a vacation.

Melissa: Really? Where _____ (like, go) ?

Leo: Well, I _____ (love, travel) to

Latin America. What about you, Melissa?

Melissa: I _____ (not go, get) a job right away.

I _____ (want, go) to Spain and Portugal.

Leo: Sounds great, but how _____ (go, pay)

for it?

Melissa: I _____ (hope, borrow)

some money from my brother. I have a good excuse. I

_____ (plan, take) courses

in Spanish and Portuguese.

Leo: Oh, I'm tired of studying!

Melissa: So am I. But I also _____ (hope, take)

people on tours to Latin America. Why don't you come on my first tour?

8

Imagine you have these problems. Write three sentences about changing these situations. Use words in the box.

1. I'm not interested in my job these days. I spend three hours driving to and from work every day, and I don't make enough money! I can't find a new job, though, because of my poor computer skills.

   | I hope to . . . .   I want to . . . .   I plan to . . . . |

   _____

   _____

   _____

2. I've become less careful about my health lately. I've stopped jogging because I'm bored with it. I've started smoking because I have terrible problems at work. And I'm always tired because I can't sleep at night.

   | I'm going to . . . .   I'd like to . . . .   I'd love to . . . . |

   _____

   _____

   _____

3. I just moved to a new town, and I don't know anyone. People at work are friendly but not very outgoing – I never do anything after work. I haven't had a date in about four months. And I live outside of town, so I don't have many neighbors.

   | I'm going to . . . .   I want to . . . .   I plan to . . . . |

   _____

   _____

   _____

9 **Choose the correct words to complete each sentence. Use the correct form of the word or add any words necessary.**

1. William would like _____to retire_____
   early – around 50.   (retire / marry / divorce)

2. Heather's salary is much _____ before.
   She had to take a pay cut.   (low / short / high)

3. I dress up for my new job, and I'm always on time now. I'm _____
   these days.   (different / outgoing / responsible)

4. After graduation, Jack plans _____ for an
   international company.   (retire / work / move)

5. This job is _____ my last job.
   (responsible / stressful / expensive)

6. Mel hopes _____ to a small town.
   (move / live / change)

10 **Advise people how to make changes in their lives. Use expressions like the ones in the box.**

> You should . . . .
> You shouldn't . . . .
> Why don't you . . . ?

1. I've gained a lot of weight this year.
   You should be more careful about your diet.
   or _Why don't you spend more time at the gym?_

2. My hair is longer, but it doesn't look good.
   _____

3. I've gotten tired of wearing the same old clothes.
   _____

4. I want to start a successful business.
   _____

5. I'm often bored on weekends.
   _____

6. The food I cook always tastes bland.
   _____

7. I hope to retire early.
   _____

8. I've finished *New Interchange Book 1,* but I still want to improve my English!
   _____

Combine lo mejor

New Interchange Full Contact es el programa más completo que le da todas las herramientas que necesita para un aprendizaje efectivo. El éxito se obtiene mediante el contacto constante con el idioma. Esta página, y la tabla en la siguiente, contienen sugerencias para el auto estudio y optimización de algunas de las habilidades específicas. En las últimas dos páginas encontrará una **Guía para el uso del CD-ROM** de *New Interchange*, y las instrucciones para su instalación.

FLUIDEZ Para poder utilizar el lenguaje con fluidez es importante un buen conocimiento tanto de vocabulario como de gramática. Esto solo se logra mediante la práctica sistemática. Para un trabajo de auto estudio en estas areas recomendamos las series *Grammar in Use* (*Basic Grammar in Use* y *Grammar in Use Intermediate*) y **Vocabulary in Use** (*Basic Vocabulary in Use* y *Vocabulary in Use Intermediate*). Los niveles *Basic* de estas series cubren perfectamente *New Interchange 1 y 2*. Los niveles *Intermediate* cubren *New Interchange 3*, y *Passages 1 y 2*.

LECTURA Y ESCRITURA La lectura es una manera muy agradable y entretenida para adquirir más vocabulario y un mejor manejo del lenguaje. *Cambridge University Press* desarrolló una serie llamada **Cambridge English Readers** que está integrada por una colección de lecturas graduadas que incluyen un audio cassette para dar vida a las historias. Estas lecturas cubren una gran variedad de géneros, desde suspenso a romance. Existen varios títulos para cada nivel de *New Interchange*, a partir del nivel 1.

INGLÉS PARA NEGOCIOS *New Interchange* es un curso para la comunicación internacional con un enfoque funcional. Para aquellos alumnos que requieren el Inglés para negocios existe una variedad de materiales especializados. Los **New Interchange Business Companion** 1 y 2 son compatibles unidad por unidad con *New Interchange* 1 y 2. Contienen un glosario en español. **Telephoning in English** (*Essential & Intermediate*) le ayudan a desarrollar su habilidad de comunicación por teléfono. Su **CD-ROM** es de gran ayuda para la práctica funcional para niveles de *New Interchange 3* y *Passages 1 y 2*. **Business Vocabulary in Use** es ideal para acompañar a los niveles *New Interchange 3* y *Passages 1 y 2* si quiere expandir su vocabulario con relación a temas como el Trabajo, Gente y Organizaciones, Mercadotecnia, Economía y Finanzas, y Producción entre muchos otros.

SELECCIONAR UN DICCIONARIO Una herramienta que sugerimos para acompañar su aprendizaje es el diccionario. Recomendamos el uso de diccionarios monolingües para un mejor resultado, aunque para los niveles básicos un diccionario bilingüe es más adecuado. Como diccionario bilingüe el **Cambridge Klett Pocket Dictionary** es el más adecuado para los niveles *New Interchange Intro, 1 y 2*. El **Cambridge Klett Compact** (con **CD-ROM**) es la versión más completa, compatible con todos los niveles. El Cambridge Learner's Dictionary (con CD ROM) es el diccionario monolingüe que sugerimos a partir de *New Interchange 2 y 3*. Su lenguaje sencillo lo hace muy accesible para los alumnos de estos niveles. Para estudiantes más avanzados sugerimos nuestros diccionarios **Cambridge Dictionary of American English** y el **Cambridge Advanced Learner's Dictionary**, ambos con **CD-ROM**.

EXÁMENES En la página siguiente encontrará la tabla "Combining the Best" que muestra cómo los niveles de *New Interchange* corresponden con los diferentes exámenes de la Universidad de Cambridge, o el puntaje aproximado de TOEFL.® *Cambridge University Press* ofrece los materiales de preparación más actualizados para dichos exámenes.

Combining the best — Self-study guide

The following table provides suggestions for students of *New Interchange* and *Passages* who are interested in additional study of specific skills. The table correlates skills books published by Cambridge University Press to each of the six levels of the *New Interchange / Passages* series.

	New Interchange				*Passages*	
	Intro	Level 1	Level 2	Level 3	Level 1	Level 2
Grammar						
Basic Grammar in Use	✔	✔	✔			
Grammar in Use				✔	✔	✔
Vocabulary						
Basic Vocabulary in Use	✔	✔	✔			
Vocabulary In Use Intermediate			✔	✔	✔	
Vocabulary in Use Upper Intermediate					✔	✔
Business						
New Interchange Business Companion		✔	✔			
Business Vocabulary in Use				✔	✔	✔
Essential Telephoning in English		✔	✔			
Telephoning in English				✔	✔	
Telephoning in English CD-ROM				✔	✔	
Reading						
Cambridge English Readers		5 titles	7 titles	9 titles	9 titles	7 titles
Dictionaries						
Bilingual						
Cambridge Klett Pocket Dictionary	✔	✔	✔			
Cambridge Klett Compact Dictionary	✔	✔	✔	✔	✔	✔
Monolingual						
Cambridge Learner's Dictionary			✔	✔		
Cambridge Advanced Learner's Dictionary					✔	✔
Cambridge Dictionary of American English					✔	✔

Exams Reference						
Cambridge Exams			KET	PET		FCE
TOEFL® scores — Institutional		250	350	450	500	550
TOEFL® scores — Official (CBT)		25	63	133	173	213

Guía para el uso de los CD-ROMs de New Interchange

El CD-ROM de *New Interchange* contiene dieciséis unidades por nivel, paralelas a las unidades del libro del alumno. En cada unidad del CD-ROM encontrará de ocho a diez actividades. Es conveniente ver las unidades en orden. Cada unidad le dará aproximadamente dos horas de trabajo. Para un uso óptimo recomendamos trabajar en sesiones no mayores a 30 minutos. Si requiere mejorar su inglés oral, le sugerimos que use el CD-ROM en compañía de otra persona que esté tomando el curso.

INSTALACION Inserte el disco en la unidad de CD-ROM. El programa se ejecutará automáticamente. Si no se ejecuta de manera automática, haga doble clic en el icono de "Mi PC" y luego en el icono de la unidad de CD-ROM.

NOTA IMPORTANTE Para poder ver el video es necesario instalar la versión QuickTime 2 de 32 bits. Dicha versión viene incluida en el CD-ROM y puede instalarse junto con versiones posteriores de QuickTime.

INSTRUCCIONES Haga clic en el botón que dice [Instructions] localizado en el lado inferior izquierdo de la pantalla para escuchar las instrucciones. Al hacer clic de nuevo, podrá escuchar y leer las instrucciones de manera simultánea.

RESUMEN Y OBJETIVOS LINGÜÍSTICOS La primera pantalla de cada unidad contiene el resumen de la secuencia del video y los objetivos lingüísticos. Haga clic en el botón que dice [Next] para pasar a la siguiente pantalla.

LISTA DE ACTIVIDADES La segunda pantalla muestra las actividades incluidas en cada unidad. Al pasar el puntero por encima de cada actividad en la lista, aparecerán las instrucciones en el lado derecho de la pantalla.

PARA VER EL VIDEO [Get the picture] [Edit the video]: Haga clic en el botón (▶). Para hacer pausa haga clic en el botón marcado (II).

ACTIVIDADES DE LLENADO DE ESPACIOS
Elija la palabra o frase de la lista correspondiente y arrastre la respuesta correcta hacia el espacio. En ocasiones tendrá que teclear la palabra o frase que se requiere. Coloque el puntero sobre el espacio y haga clic para que pueda empezar a escribir la palabra o frase que corresponda. Teclee *Aceptar* ⏎ al terminar.

SUGERENCIA Si al pasar el puntero por la pantalla éste se transforma en un icono en forma de mano, significa que al hacer clic podrá contestar, escuchar o hacer funcionar ese botón.

COMPRENSIÓN AUDITIVA Haga clic sobre la imagen de la persona, el signo de interrogación, o el icono de escuchar en su caso. Escuche y conteste haciendo clic sobre la respuesta correcta.

ACTIVIDADES INTERACTIVAS En las actividades en las que puede grabar su voz, el icono de grabar [Record] estará presente. Para grabar su voz, asegúrese de que el micrófono esté conectado a la computadora. Si desea, puede comparar su respuesta con un modelo haciendo clic en [Compare]. Esto le permitirá mejorar su pronunciación.

TRANSCRIPCIÓN [Video script]: Puede leer la transcripción y ver el video simultáneamente. Para imprimir la trascripción haga clic en el botón [Print]. En el glosario [Glossary] encontrará la explicación del vocabulario nuevo incluido en la transcripción.

ACLARAR DUDAS Utilice pluma y papel para tomar notas mientras usa el CD-ROM. Puede haber dudas que quiera aclarar con su profesor/a.

EVALUACIONES [T1 - 4]: Para corroborar su avance utilice las evaluaciones que vienen incluidas después de cada cuatro unidades.

NOTA El nivel 1 consta de un CD-ROM en tanto que los niveles *Intro* y *2* están divididos en dos CD-ROMs por nivel.

About New Interchange CD-ROMs

Written and developed by Charles Shields
with Jack C. Richards

Created by Ibis Multimedia

© Cambridge University Press

For full support and answers to frequently asked questions, visit www.cambridge.org/elt/interchange.

LICENSE AGREEMENT

Terms and conditions of use:

SYSTEM REQUIREMENTS

Windows system

486/66MHz or higher processor, Windows 95, 8MB RAM, SVGA with 640x480 display, 256 colors, sound card and speakers, double-speed CD-ROM drive, microphone (for speaking activities), 32-bit QuickTime 2 for Windows (supplied on CD-ROM)

Note that 32-bit QuickTime 2 for Windows (and not a later version) needs to be installed to run the video sequences. The software is included on the CD-ROM and can be installed alongside later versions of QuickTime. To install QuickTime 2, locate the QuickTime folder on the CD-ROM by using the "Explore" function and follow instructions.